J. A. (James Aitken) Wylie

Rome and civil liberty

or the Papal aggression in its relations to the sovereignty of the queen and the

independence of the nation

J. A. (James Aitken) Wylie

Rome and civil liberty
or the Papal aggression in its relations to the sovereignty of the queen and the independence of the nation

ISBN/EAN: 9783742844125

Manufactured in Europe, USA, Canada, Australia, Japa

Cover: Foto ©Lupo / pixelio.de

Manufactured and distributed by brebook publishing software (www.brebook.com)

J. A. (James Aitken) Wylie

Rome and civil liberty

ROME

AND

CIVIL LIBERTY:

or,

THE PAPAL AGGRESSION

IN ITS RELATION TO

THE SOVEREIGNTY OF THE QUEEN

AND THE

INDEPENDENCE OF THE NATION.

BY THE

REV. J. A. WYLIE, LL.D.,

AUTHOR OF "THE PAPACY," ETC. ETC.

THE EIGHTH THOUSAND.

EDINBURGH: ANDREW ELLIOT.

MDCCCLXV.

EDINBURGH : PRINTED BY FAIRLY, LYALL, & CO.

TO THE PEOPLE OF SCOTLAND.

To you, my beloved countrymen, I dedicate the Scotch edition of a work which the generous liberality of an unknown friend in England has made accessible to all of you, and which other motives than those of vanity make me especially desirous all of you should peruse. It is with a deep sense of my own unworthiness, and of the many imperfections attaching, doubtless, to this performance, that I presume on this dedicatory address. But I am moved thereto, in part, by the following consideration :—

Ever since the era of the Papal Aggression the Free Church of Scotland has had in eye the founding of an INSTITUTE in which the youth of our land, and more especially those of them in training in our Universities and Theological Halls for the office of the holy ministry, might receive a systematic initiation into the distinctive doctrines of Popery and Protestantism. A Committee was appointed, charged with this object.* In 1861 the matter was found to be so far advanced that the Free Presbytery of Edinburgh, at its meeting on the 30th October, adopted, and entered on its records, a resolution, from which the following is an extract :—

"The Presbytery did and hereby do appoint the Reverend Dr James Aitken Wylie as Lecturer or Professor in the Protestant Institute of Scotland, it being understood that his tenure of office shall be the same as that of the ministers of this Church."

Accordingly, on the 5th of November thereafter, I was, by appointment of the Presbytery, inducted into my office as Professor to the Institute,—Dr Candlish preaching, and Dr Begg making a statement explanatory of the object ; while the presence of representatives from the other Protestant bodies expressed the concurrence and co-operation

* Of this Committee the Rev. Dr Begg was Convener, and by his great practical sagacity and indefatigable efforts largely contributed towards the realization of the enterprise.

of all the Churches in the erection, as now, by furnishing Directors, they share in the management, of the Protestant Institute of Scotland.

By the blessing of God on my humble labours, the classes in the Institute have steadily increased.   The number of students, session by session, now averages betwixt 100 and 150.   They are drawn from all the Protestant denominations of Scotland ; and they have entered with great enthusiasm and marked success* upon the study of the subject prelected upon.

This trust I regard as one that has connected with it the highest responsibility.   At your hands, my beloved countrymen, have I accepted it ; and for the interests of our common Protestantism shall I ever strive to discharge it.   It is as standing in this relation to you, and bound to devote my time and thought to this question, that I now present you with this treatise.   I earnestly pray you to weigh its facts and reasonings.   They are prompted by no sectarian jealousy.   I speak, urged by love of our native land, by unfeigned devotion to the cause of liberty, civil and religious, and by a supreme desire for the preservation of the gospel, in all its purity, in a country which, above most, it has illumined with its light and enriched with its blessings.

You, the people of Scotland, have ever occupied a conspicuous position in the battle of the Reformation.   You were more purely reformed at the first than any other people.   You pledged yourselves to this cause by solemn oath and covenant ; you endured in its behalf a long and bloody persecution.   In days of darkness you struggled against arbitrary power ; and your contendings largely aided in achieving the Revolution of 1688.   I know that the heroic spirit which of yore spurned "papistry and tyranny" from our borders, still lives amongst you ; and I am confident that, in the crisis that has again arisen, you will act a part worthy of the confessors and martyrs, your ancestors, and of your own hereditary relation to a cause which is nothing less than that of the maintenance of the gospel and of liberty in our country.

* Of the five higher prizes offered by the Protestant Alliance of London, in the competition of 1864, in which the youth of the Three Kingdoms engaged, four of these prizes, and the gold medal, were gained by students in the Protestant Institute of Scotland.

PREFACE.

It is a common error to suppose, because Rome is unchangeable in her dogmas, that she is unchangeable also in the forms of her logic. Society is continually advancing to a higher stage; truth is perpetually receiving clearer manifestations; and this imposes upon that Church which seeks to stereotype the one and to extinguish the other, the necessity of continually devising new modes of assault. The creed of the Church of Rome is immutable: her logic is in perpetual flux: her policy is ever old as regards its ends; it is ever new as regards its phases. In substance, that Church abides unalterably the same throughout the ages; and yet every century sees, as it were, a new Church.

This makes it necessary that every century or so we should re-adjust the argument against Rome. The immortal works of Barrow, Chillingworth, and Stillingfleet, are an exhaustive refutation of the Church which *changes not*, but they are not an exhaustive refutation of the Church which *does change*. They do not, and could not, meet the Papal aggression,—the special phase assumed by the Church of Rome in our century. The following pages are an attempt at a re-adjustment of the argument, so far as that aggression is concerned.

The Papal aggression is here viewed as a whole, from its rise to what may be regarded as well-nigh its completion. The author has been solicitous to extricate the fundamental principle of that aggression, and clearly to explain its implied logic. He has shown the successive stages by which it has been advanced, and the goal to which it inevitably tends. He has, moreover, supported and illustrated his argument by the great facts which form the past dozen years' history of Europe.

The author does not conceal his opinion that the civil liberty

of the country is at this hour in very great peril,—in more immediate peril, perhaps, than its religious liberty ; for it is the
policy of Rome to strike at the latter through the sides of the
former.   The Papal aggression, in the author's judgment, was
a violation of the Constitution of the kingdom as settled at the
Revolution ; and to the extent to which that aggression has been
carried, to the same extent has the throne been betrayed, and
the rights of the subject invaded.   His charge is not that our
statesmen have tolerated the *religion* of the Pope, but that they
have sanctioned the *authority* of the Pope : not that they have
permitted the spread of another faith, but that they have permitted the erection of another Government.

Of all earthly possessions, liberty is the most precious : it is
bought at a greater price, and preserved with greater watchfulness, than any other. Tyranny comes with muffled foot ; it steals
upon us like the night : it deposits, while a nation sleeps, the
seeds of arbitrary rule ; and, under pretence of redressing wrong
or of advancing liberty, it strikes a fatal blow at justice and
freedom.   A somewhat jealous mood is at all times one of the
best bulwarks of a nation's liberties ; but at the present hour,
when the causes of alarm are so imminent, we can scarce be too
watchful against apathy in regard to the public interests, or too
alert to repel the inroads of a tyranny of all others the stealthiest
and the basest.   The Protestantism of Britain, we are told, is
sound, and will bestir itself when the crisis comes.   The crisis is
now : what will come is the catastrophe.

The author earnestly solicits from every lover of liberty, and
especially from every lover of the gospel, a careful consideration
of the facts and reasonings presented in the present volume. The
cause is pre-eminently the cause of our country at this hour ;
and, if the cause of Great Britain, the cause of the world.

EDINBURGH, 1st July 1865.

CONTENTS.

PART I.—THE REFORMATION.

PART II.—THE PAPAL AGGRESSION.

PART III.—ILLUSTRATIONS FROM RECENT EUROPEAN HISTORY.

PART IV.—MAYNOOTH, CONVENTS, CHAPLAINCIES, &c.

PART V.—MISCELLANEOUS

ROME AND CIVIL LIBERTY, &c.

PART FIRST.

THE REFORMATION.

The accomplishment of the Reformation in Britain occupied the better part of two centuries. The first dawning of the light was in 1380. In that year Wycliffe published his translation of the Bible; and England entered, the first of the nations in modern times, upon the glorious path of circulating the Scriptures throughout her realm. Confessors were never wanting to the Gospel from that day in Britain. But the era proper of the Reformation extends from 1516, when Erasmus published his New Testament in England, to 1688, when the ecclesiastical and political constitution of our country was settled on a Protestant basis under William of Orange.

The period embraced by these two dates is the most glorious in our annals. It was fruitful throughout in men of great character, and in events of world-wide influence. More especially was it adorned towards the middle by a constellation of elegant scholars and accomplished theologians, of great statesmen and holy martyrs, who have never

A

perhaps been surpassed in any age, whether of our own or
of any other nation.   Nor did the Reformation develope itself
as a purely spiritual existence.   It made society the com-
panion of its progress and the partner of its triumphs.   The
divine principle at its centre sent the pulses of a new life
through the body corporate, and thus it gave us a new State
as well as a new Church.   Fostering every liberal study,
and encouraging every generous art, it built up around itself
a bulwark of social enlightenment and political freedom.   A
work like this was dearly purchased: it cost the toil and
the blood of two centuries.

Let us run our eye along, and briefly survey the struggles
and the lessons of this most eventful period of our history.
In the retrospect of the past there are two reigns that stand
out with extraordinary prominence.   Let us fix our eye
mainly on these.   If we can profit by the experience of our
fathers, we may be saved the peril of making the experiment over again in our own times.   MARY and ELIZABETH
are the types of the two principles of Popery and Protestantism, as embodied in the government of our country.   These
two reigns are, in fact, the EBAL and GERIZIM or our history.   In them Life and Death, the Blessing and the Curse,
have been set as palpably before the people of Great Britain
as they were set before the Jews of old.   Read in the light
of these reigns, the ascendancy of the one principle means
the promotion of all that ennobles and strengthens a country ;
the ascendancy of the other means, necessarily and inevitably, the extinction of private virtue and the overthrow of
public liberty.   Some there are among us who seem to
think there can be no great difference betwixt a Popish and
a Protestant rule ; or, at least, that no harm can come of
putting the matter once more to the test, and making a
second trial of a yoke which our fathers were not able to
bear.   Well, let us compare Popery and Protestantism, as

exhibited in the reigns of Mary and Elizabeth, and see whether the experiment was not fairly made, and whether the result was in the least doubtful. This may minister guidance in our present circumstances. We have again, as a nation, come to a crisis, and must once more make a choice.

When the eighth Henry went to his grave, the Reformation had advanced but a little way. The supremacy of the Pope had been cast off; the monastic establishments had been abolished ; and a *limited* permission given to the people to read the Scriptures in the vulgar tongue. These, however, were important points ; and the fabric of Rome, wanting these props, yielded the easier to the more systematic and persevering efforts of the Reformers in the next reign. Under Edward VI. the Reformation ceased to be a work of policy, and became a work of principle ; and by the end of that short reign all its main objects had been attained. The churches had been cleansed from images ; transubstantiation was repudiated, the sacrifice of the mass forbidden ; and the Scriptures were freely allowed to the laity of every rank and degree. Tradition ceased to be put in the place of the Bible, and the saints and the Virgin no longer usurped the honour that is due to God. Men no longer prayed in an unknown tongue. The clergy were allowed to marry. Purgatory, indulgences, and all the gainful traffic of Rome, were no longer encouraged. Her wares became unsaleable. But the great point, and that which comprehended all the rest, was, that the doctrine of salvation by *grace*, in opposition to salvation by *works*, was now preached to the people. Not that the work was finished. The great body of the people in the rural parts remained grossly ignorant ; and a full half of the clergy, though conforming outwardly, remained Papists at heart. They had been monks and friars ; and, to save a small annual charge to the new possessors of the abbey lands, they were preferred to livings in the Reformed Church.

Accustomed to nothing but singing the litany and saying mass, they were wretched instructors of the people ; and the atrocities to which they afterwards lent themselves fearfully avenged the avariciousness which had preferred them to livings. So stood matters when the young Edward,—a prince of rare virtue, and beloved by the whole nation,—"in the prime and blooming of his age," went to his grave.

Mary opened her way to the throne by a promise which she violated the moment she was seated upon it. She gave a solemn pledge to her Protestant subjects that religion should remain as in the days of Edward VI. ; but, alas ! her first act after her accession significantly told that she meant to undo all that had been done during the reign of her predecessor, and to restore the Church to the state in which it had existed prior to the days of Henry VIII. Let Protestants learn from this what the oath of a Popish sovereign is worth, and after what fashion promises made before their accession to power are likely to be kept after it. The great men of the former reign, who had guided the destinies of the Reformation, and who were illustrious for their learning and their virtues, for their probity and their wisdom, were hurried off to prison. A Gardiner, a Bonner, and a Tonstal now filled the sees, and wore the dignities, which a Cranmer, a Ridley, and a Latimer had held. All the preachers throughout the kingdom were silenced. Of the sixteen thousand ministers in England, twelve thousand were ejected from their livings, and thrown penniless upon the world. A crowd of needy creatures, whose humble accomplishments extended only to the power "of making holy water, and repeating a lady psalter," rushed in to seize the vacant places. The whole laws respecting religion enacted under Edward VI. were swept away at a single sitting; and this disastrous course was fittingly concluded by the formal submission of the Court and Parliament to the Pope, one member of the House only having courage to oppose this step. The rest crowned their infamy by solemnly giving God thanks that they had been enabled so far to complete the work of their country's ruin and their own disgrace. This was not the end, it was but the beginning, of sorrows, —of dire sorrows to England.

Mary knew that she must go deeper: she knew that she must root out the seeds of religion and liberty which had been sown in England during the days of her predecessors; and her true instincts as a Papist guided her to the only weapon that could effect their extirpation. Argument would never root them out. They must be burned out; and Mary resolved not to spare the fire. She planted a stake in almost every county and county town of England; and she propounded to every professor of the reformed faith, high and low,—to every one, in short, who would not swallow, at her bidding, the doctrine of transubstantiation,—the terrible alternative which came to be expressed in the compendious formula of "*turn or burn.*" She married Philip of Spain; and surely well mated was the "bloody Mary" with the yet bloodier Philip. Sending the sagacious Cranmer and the venerable Latimer to the dungeon, she took into her councils Gardiner and Bonner. With these worthy assistants, the "blessed daughter," as Paul IV. called her, set to work to purge her kingdom of such heresy as Christ and his apostles had preached, and to plant once more the "holy Roman Catholic religion," as a Hildebrand had taught it and a Borgia had exemplified it. The work went on prosperously. The vast zeal of Gardiner and Bonner lagged behind the yet vaster desires of the Queen. She seemed to have a presentiment that her days would be few, and dreaded lest death should overtake her before her work was finished. England became a wide Smithfield. There was no room in the prisons for felons: these were turned loose, to make room

for the God-fearing citizens.   The "coal-cellar" of "bloody
Bonner" has passed into a proverb.   If one wished to hear
good, he went, not to the church, where nothing was to be seen
but contemptible mummeries : he crept stealthily to the grated
window of the martyr's dungeon, and listened to his prayers
and praises.   The Council met oft.   The very unvaryingness
of their decisions is terrible : burn—burn—burn.   Not a week
passed during the last four years of Mary's reign in which
some one was not burned, more commonly two or three ; and
latterly they were brought to the stake in four, six, aye, a
dozen, at a time.   Over all England blazed these baleful fires,
the persecutor, judging of others by herself, hoping to strike
terror into the nation.   Every rank, from the primate of all
England downwards ; every age, from the old man of ninety
who had to be carried to the fire, to the youth of eighteen,
and even the new-born babe ; both sexes ; all conditions,—
the halt, the blind,—all were dragged to the stake, and
passed through the fire.   Their enemies, in their haste and
zeal, did not think it necessary to veil the causes of their
death under any disguise.   They condemned them avowedly
because they could not believe the doctrine of "the real
presence."   They were simply asked by the Bishop, before
whose tribunal they were brought, "Do you acknowledge
that the very flesh, and blood, and bones of Christ, as born
of the Virgin, are present in the Sacrament ?" and when the
martyr answered "No," sentence of condemnation was immediately passed, and he was carried out next morning to
some square, or common, or wayside, and burned.   The roll
is a long one, from Rogers, Vicar of St Sepulchre's, who as-
sisted in the early edition of the English Bible, and who was
burned in Smithfield on the 4th of February 1555, to the
five persons who were burned together at Canterbury on the
15th of November 1558, just two days before the death of
Mary.   The number of persons burned alive during these

four dismal years, as stated by Lord Burleigh, the Primo Minister of Queen Elizabeth, was TWO HUNDRED AND EIGHTY-EIGHT. Besides these, large numbers perished by imprisonment, torture, or famine. Let us weigh the names, as well as count them. They are the brightest of the period. It was the rank, the learning, the virtue, the worth of her kingdom that Mary and her minions dragged to the stake. Nor did she burn them only : she horribly tortured them at the stake. We beg to give a specimen. It is Bishop Hooper that now stands at the stake ; and that stake is planted at the end of his own cathedral in Gloucester. What the reader, mayhap, has not nerve to peruse, the martyr had courage to endure :—

"The hoop prepared for his middle was then put round him with some difficulty, for it was too small. The fire was kindled ; and 'in every corner there was nothing to be seen but weeping and sorrowful people.' His sufferings were very severe. Two horse-loads of green faggots had been piled round the stake : these would not burn freely ; and the morning being lowering, with a high wind, the flame of the reeds was blown from him. A few dry faggots were then brought ; but the quantity being small, and the wind boisterous, the fire only reached his legs and the lower part of his body. During this time Hooper stood praying, 'O Jesus, Son of David, have mercy upon me, and receive my soul!' When this fire was spent, he wiped his eyes with his hands, and mildly but earnestly entreated that more fire might be brought. At length a third and fiercer fire was kindled ; some gunpowder which had been fastened to him exploded, though with little effect ; but after some time the flame gained strength. He continued praying, 'Lord Jesus, have mercy upon me ! Lord Jesus, receive my spirit!' till, as a bystander relates with painful minuteness, 'he was black in the mouth, and his tongue was swoln, so that he could not speak ; yet his lips moved till they shrunk from the gums ; and he smote his breast with his hands till one of his arms fell off ; he continued knocking still with the other, while the fat, water, and blood dropped out at his fingers' ends, until, by renewing of the fire, his strength was gone, and his hand did cleave fast to the iron upon his breast. Then, bowing forwards, he yielded up the spirit,' after suffering inexpressible torments for nearly three quarters of an hour, yet 'dying as quietly as a child in his bed.' "

Mary did all this with the full sanction and approval of

her conscience. Not a doubt had she that, in burning her Protestant subjects, she was doing God an acceptable service. Her conscience did reproach her before her death, but for what? For the blood she had shed? No: it reproached her for not having done her work more thoroughly, and, in particular, for not having made full restitution of the abbey lands and other property of the Church in possession of the Crown. The nearer she drew to her end she but hasted the more to multiply victims; and her last days were cheered by watching the lurid glare of the fires of martyrdom which blazed all over her realm. Is there no lesson here? Does it not teach us that a warped conscience is a much more dangerous thing than any want of conscience whatever?

Mary died in the morning of the 17th November 1558; and by afternoon of the same day all the bells of London were set a-ringing. At night bonfires were lighted, tables were set in the streets, and "the people did eat, and drink, and make merry," illustrating the saying of the old king,— "when it goeth well with the righteous the city rejoiceth, but when the wicked perish there is shouting." The accession of Elizabeth was one of the grand crises of the world. The principle with which she was identified,—Protestantism, to wit,—rose with her, and ascended into the region of influence and government. Instantly the eclipse passed from the realm of Britain; and England was started on a career of commercial prosperity and political freedom in which, with a few exceptional periods, there has been no pause from that day to this. The innumerable social blessings flowing from the Reformation, which now began to be shed upon our isle, we shall more particularly illustrate in the following chapter. Meanwhile it becomes us to acknowledge, with devout and fervent gratitude, the finger of God in an event which called our country from the dust, broke the yoke of tyrants and bigots from off our neck, rekindled

the lamp of truth in our land, raised us from bondmen
of the priests of Rome to the dignity of freemen, and enriched our country with the lesser but still mighty blessings of justice, of science, of commerce, of renown.

Wherever we turn our eyes in Europe, witnesses rise up
to confirm and illustrate our observations. We select two,—
Italy and Scotland.

Of all the countries of Europe, Scotland is the country
which owes most to the Reformation, seeing it has received
most from it. The Reformation found Scotland a country
of inhospitable bogs and moors, and it has made it a country
of gardens and richly cultivated fields. The Reformation
found Scotland a country of wretched hovels and paltry
towns, and it has made it a country of noble cities, which
rival in architectural magnificence and beauty the finest
creations of Italy,—not the poor Italy of the present day,
but the proud Italy of three centuries ago. The Reformation found Scotland a land without letters, and it gave it a
literature destined to endure while the language lasts, rival-
ling in terseness and elegance of diction the purest models
of the Augustan era, and far excelling them in dignity of
matter and grandeur of sentiment. The Reformation found
Scotland a land without arts, and it made it the inventress
of the steam-engine, which has revolutionized the labour of
the world, and is destined, after covering its own soil with
the marvels of industry and of trade, to extend the blessings of commerce to the remotest shores and the rudest
tribes. In a word, the Reformation found Scotland the least
of the European nations, with scarce a name among civilized
countries, and it has placed it, in conjunction with its sister
of England, at the head of the nations of the earth. It was
the birthday of the land : on that day a free State was
born into the world ; and if there was wailing among the
powers and principalities of darkness, the " morning stars" of

liberty sang together, and all the "sons" of freedom shouted for joy.

The relation of Italy and Scotland throughout, ever since the Reformation, has been one of marked contrast. As the night of barbarism and ignorance began to break up in the one country, the day of civilization and knowledge began to wane in the other. As the liberties of the one began to be enlarged, despotism tightened her chains round the other. As the one reverted into a country of morasses and inhospitable deserts, the other put on the cultivation and luxuriance of a garden. The palaces and monuments of the one mouldered into dust; the hovels of the other grew into noble and wealthy cities. Commerce, forsaking the shore she had been wont to frequent, discharged her rich argosies on a foreign, and till then unvisited, strand. Learning quenched her lamp in the halls where it had burned from immemorial time; and art, forsaking the sunny clime where she had loved to dwell, traversed the Alps, crossed the sea, and sought out new abodes in a clime less hospitable, and amid tribes less civilized. Thus have the two countries gone on for three hundred years, pursuing a course the reverse, in all respects, the one of the other. The path of Italy has been downwards, ever downwards, maugre the rich gifts with which nature has endowed it, and the prestige with which power has encompassed it. That of Scotland has been ever upwards, though she has had to fight her way against a hundred foes. The one has been steadily sinking into poverty, social disorganization, foreign dependence, and domestic slavery: the other has been steadily rising in wealth, civilization, liberty, and political influence.

Does any man doubt that the principle which pulled down the one country was Popery, and that the principle which elevated the other was Protestantism? Since the Reformation, have not these two principles been the only ones really operative in the political and religious world of Europe? They have been its two poles; and around one or other have all its governments and nations ranged themselves. These two principles have parted Europe into two worlds: and how dissimilar! Upon the one the sun of liberty has shone, and all that is noble and true has sprung up and flourished in its rays. Upon the other despotism has cast its shadow, as if to wrap up in darkness the melancholy wrecks with which it had filled it,—the ghastly corpses of nations once great, and of men once free.

These mementoes and monitors, so tragic, and yet so instructive, meet us at every step. One other contrast let us cite,—Spain and Britain. Spain,—fallen from the height of power, her noble sierras converted into deserts, her once opulent towns covered with the mould of decay, and her once polished and lettered population debased by ignorance, and delighting only in barbarous and savage sports,—proclaims, far more emphatically than words could proclaim it, the supreme folly of which she was guilty when she chose to rest her greatness and prosperity upon a conscience governed by the Inquisition.

To make the lesson the more manifest and striking, here is Great Britain running precisely the opposite course,—attracting commerce to her shores, constructing magnificent cities, and filling them with the wealth and the treasures of all the regions of the earth; spreading over her land, among the millions' of her people, a purer science and a higher knowledge than Spain ever knew in the days of her glory; and by this career proclaiming, as emphatically as words could proclaim it, the wisdom of her choice when she determined to make freedom of conscience her corner-stone.

Thus does Providence send its instructors into the world to teach by contrasts. Spain and Britain differ, in that each is representative of a different principle. Nevertheless, they agree in teaching—the one negatively, the other positively—the self-same lesson to mankind. They are a "tree of the knowledge of good and evil" to the nations, as really as was the tree in the midst of the garden of old. On the one there has descended a secret dew ; on the other there lies a silent malediction. EBAL, with the curse upon its top, stands over against GERIZIM, with the blessing, like a star, beaming forth from its summit.

We hold, then, that the point at issue betwixt Protestantism and Popery is conclusively decided. The Bible has decided it on the one hand, and the condition of Europe has decided it on the other. The testimony of these two is one,— even that Protestantism is true, and that Popery is false ; that the former is the benefactor of nations, and that the latter is their worst foe. Why, then, are we longer in doubt ? Why does our Government halt betwixt the two systems ? For what do we wait ? For a clearer Bible ? or for facts that shall more awfully confirm it ? If we hear not these witnesses, neither will we be persuaded though others rose from the dead.

THE FUNDAMENTAL PRINCIPLE OF THE REFORMATION, AND WHAT IT GAVE US.

ALL great movements are commonly traceable to one great principle. It is pre-eminently so as regards the Reformation. Its manifold developments, political, scientific, and literary, as well as theological, can all be traced up to one primordial principle. What is that principle ? It is the substitution of a divine for a human authority. This is the primordial truth of the Reformation.

There is a *jus divinum* at the foundation of everything that is true and good. There is a *jus divinum* at the foun-

dation of science ; for all true science is just an induction of
the laws and facts of nature, which are the ordination of
God. There is a *jus divinum* at the foundation of all good
government ; for what is government, but an induction or
codification of the laws and facts of society, which, too, are
the ordination of God ? And there is a *jus divinum* in all
true theology ; for what is theology, but just an induction of
the laws and facts of the Bible, which are the revelation of
God ? The Reformation was a return to the *jus divinum*
of God, in opposition to the *jus divinum* of man, which, in
fact, was nothing else than a *jus humanum.*

We are accustomed to say that the doctrine of justification through faith alone is the fundamental principle of the
Reformation. This is true if by the Reformation we simply
mean a system of theology standing in contradistinction and
opposition to the theology of the Roman Church. But if by
the Reformation we mean a great movement, extending over
the entire area of human life and action, beginning, no doubt,
in the religious sphere, but developing itself immediately
thereafter in the political and social,—a movement enlarging
and elevating all the rights and relations of man, and communicating new powers and privileges to human society,—a
movement, in short, which gave us a new State as well as a
new Church,—then, we say, the fundamental principle of the
Reformation was the substitution of a divine for a human
authority. This principle is first in order : it is a deeper
principle than the other, and of greater breadth of application. Luther must have seized upon it, consciously or un-
consciously, before he dared to open the Bible, and interpret
for himself the Word of God, and accept the *divine righteousness* of the Bible, instead of the *human righteousness* of
Rome, as the ground of the sinner's justification. This principle is applicable to every department of human thought and
action : it is as applicable, in its own way, to the business of

politics and of science, as of religion.   The first discoverers,
we maintain, of this great principle in modern times were
the Reformers of the sixteenth century ; and they, too, were
the first who had courage to act upon it.   From them the
statesmen and philosophers who came after received it ; and,
working with it, each in his own department, they have
come, in the course of three centuries, to educe that marvellous and unrivalled combination of political power, social
order, scientific and mechanical skill, and commercial prosperity, which at this day is seen embodied in the empire of
Great Britain.

*The Fundamental Principle of the Reformation gave us a
Scriptural Church.*   The Church of Rome put herself in the
room of God.   She said to man, I am the one infallible authority upon earth.   With the Bible you have nothing to
do : with God you have nothing to do.   It is with me, and
me alone, that you have to do.   Whatever I teach, that you
are to believe : whatever I enjoin, that you are to do.   And
to that claim the conscience of man yielded for ages.   This
was mere human authority ; but upon that authority was
founded the mighty Babel of monstrous dogmas and burden-
some ceremonies under which the world groaned.   The Reformation shook that Babel to the ground, by undermining
the authority on which it rested, and substituting a divine
authority,—the Bible, to wit.   It said to man, this is a perfect and sufficient revelation of the will of God : this is a
complete and authoritative directory of all you are to believe,
and of all you are to do, in the matter of religion : this is
God speaking to you.   And when man came back to God as
his one Teacher, and to the Bible as his one storehouse of
divine truth, mere human authority fell, and the monstrous
superstructure of error of which it had served as the foundation fell with it.   " God alone," said the Reformers, " is
Lord of the conscience."   That was the truth that made

Europe free. At the hearing of these words, a world of slaves shook off their fetters,—a world of dead men arose, and stood upon their feet. Thus did the Reformation substitute the authority of God for the authority of man. Loosed from their shackles, men now betook them to the Word of God. They searched its pages with earnestness, with prayer, with dependence upon the Holy Spirit. They no longer inquired, What does this doctor teach? What does that Council decree? What has this Pope decided? Their one question now was, What saith the Bible? This was the unrolling of a black fog from the face of heaven; and men saw with astonished and ravished eyes those eternal lights which God had placed there, but which tradition had so long obscured. Now arose a holy temple, whose foundations were the twelve apostles of the Lamb, Jesus Christ himself being the chief corner-stone. The pattern exhibited in the Mount, of the New Testament, which had so long disappeared from the earth, and which some of the better spirits of former ages had sighed over as lost for ever, was again beheld. The Church had become a brotherhood, whose various members were knit together by the same spirit, in the profession of one faith and the enjoyment of one baptism. Salvation was again the free gift of God. And the Church, without the intervention of any intercessor save the One Mediator, had free access to the throne of God and of the Lamb.

The Fundamental Principle of the Reformation gave us a Free State. The right constitution of the Church was immediately followed by the right constitution of the State. Both grew out of the same principle,—the substitution of divine for human authority. All true government,—the government of the State as well as of the Church,—is founded on a *jus divinum*. But that *jus divinum*, or right divine, is not the right of one man to govern the rest. This last was the great political axiom universally received before the

Reformation. It passed as a truth indisputable and unquestionable ; yet was it at bottom nothing better than government by mere human right ; for it manifestly resolved itself, as a basis of power, into the capricious, arbitrary, and irresponsible will of one man. The Reformation came, preaching the true *jus divinum,* when it taught the right of society to govern itself according to those eternal principles of justice, equity, and order which God has graven on the natural conscience. Just as the Reformation exploded the right divine of the priest to teach and rule in the Church by his own infallible and irresponsible authority, so it exploded the right divine of kings to legislate and govern in the State by their tyrannical and irresponsible will. It taught that all power is by delegation from God,—that there ought to be no government but by law,—that law ought to be the expression of the popular will,—and that this will ought to be enlightened and controlled by right reason, and by the principles of Revelation. Thus did the Reformation substitute a really divine basis of government in room of the mere human basis, which had served but as a pedestal to tyranny. Thus were Liberty's everlasting doors open to the nations.

In the sixteenth century, the Reformation and Liberty made the circuit of the European nations hand in hand, and knocked at the gates of the several countries. Those nations that were so happy as to admit the one, admitted at the same time the other : those that closed their gates upon the Reformation, by the same act shut out Liberty. This was not so apparent at the time ; but three centuries have sufficed to make it palpable to the whole world. Every year that has since elapsed has but widened the immense distance betwixt the Reformed and the Unreformed nations of Europe. The one have steadily pursued a career of ever-expanding greatness ; the other have as steadily kept the downward path of decadence, and at every turn have sunk deeper and deeper into slavery and barbarism. And now, look at the contrast! BRITAIN, at home the abode of order and peace; abroad covering the world with her laws, her arts, and her literature: ITALY, the birthplace of revolutions. Since the fatal day on which the Papal nations rejected liberty, how often have they agonized to attain it! They have sought to woo it with tears; they have sought to buy it with blood. But all in vain. Tears and blood have been rejected as its price. No! Revolution cannot make liberty take root: the sword cannot make it grow. Liberty comes only in the wake of the Bible.

The Fundamental Principle of the Reformation gave us our Inductive Philosophy. All true philosophy is divine. God is its author, inasmuch as he ordained the laws of matter, and endowed every body with its special properties and powers. All true science is just the knowledge of those divinely-ordained laws and properties. Before the Reformation there was a human philosophy, just as before the Reformation there was a human religion. Instead of consulting nature, men sat down in their closets, and by the working of their own fancy constructed a system of natural truth, which had no relation whatever to the existing laws and properties of bodies, and which, of course, could form a basis for no useful art. It was the very error repeated over again in the department of science which had been committed in the department of religion. Instead of consulting the Bible, men endeavoured, out of their own vain heart, to invent a system of religion which was as useless for spiritual and eternal ends as the anti-Reformation philosophy was for temporal and earthly ones. Bacon seized upon the grand principle of the Reformers; and in his hands that principle wrought the same revolution in science it had already wrought in theology. The Reformers said, if you wish to know the will of God, you must go to the Bible. So Bacon said, if you would have

B

a really true and useful science, you must go to nature,—
you must study her laws,—you must observe her workings,
—you must put her to the question,—you must sit down at
her feet, and become her disciple, and listen reverentially to
her voice.   Thus did Bacon substitute a really divine authority in science for the mere human authority of the middle
ages, which had yielded only guesses and illusions, instead of
scientific truth.   But mark ! the principle of the Reformers
was the key by which Bacon opened the path to true science.
It was now that the philosophy of the middle ages vanished
as vanish the mists at sunrise ; and what a glorious world
unfolded itself to the eye of man !   The heavens stood un-
veiled ; every star unfolded the law by which it is hung in
the vault above ; every flower, and crystal, and piece of
matter, animate and inanimate, organic and inorganic, dis-
closed its secret properties, affinities, and uses.   Then arose
the sciences of astronomy, of chemistry, and others, which
are the foundation of our arts, our mechanics, our navigation,
our manufactures, our agriculture.   Man found himself suddenly re-invested with that dominion over nature which was
his birthright, but of which his fall had robbed him, or rather
put in abeyance.   As sinful, man, instead of being the lord
of the elements, had fallen under their dominion : when he
rebelled against God, they rebelled against him.   But in re-
turning to God, he found he had at the same time returned
to his primeval sovereignty over nature : he was crowned a
second time.   Here were a hundred servants, aforetime all
in mutiny and insubordination, now waiting to do his bidding ;—the stars to guide his barque over the trackless ocean,
—steam to bear his burdens,—the lightning to run on his
errands,—the hidden mine to furnish materials for the arts,
—and the resources of chemistry to enable him to change the
desert into a garden, and replace the brown moorland with
the golden grain.   In short, out of that principle first pro-

claimed by the Reformers has come the whole colossal fabric of our industrial skill, mechanical power, agricultural riches, and commercial wealth.

But not only do our men of science and industry owe to the Reformers their master-principle : they are indebted to them farther for the power to use it. Rome had planted her anathema at the gate of science, just as she had planted it at the portal of religion. Each new discovery she denounced as a heresy, and rewarded with a stake ; and had not the Reformers previously struck the bolt from her uplifted hand, she would have crushed science at its birth ; a dungeon had been the fate of Bacon and of Newton, as it was the fate of Galileo ; and the scientific and mechanical power of Britain had never been.

It was the Fundamental Principle of the Reformation that gave us our Literature. Before the Reformation, mind had slept for five long centuries. It would never more have awaked, had it not been touched by the spear of Ithuriel in the hands of the Reformers. Thought was compelled to move in the rut of ages ; and many centuries had passed without so much as one noble work, or, we might say, one really new or useful idea, having been given to the world. The human soul had drunk the opiate of superstition, and lay benumbed and stupified ; or, if it waked at times, it was only to rave deliriously, as one who had quaffed an intoxicating cup. But the calm daybreak of the Reformation, the holy light welling once more from its Divine fountain, healed man's sorely wounded spirit, and soothed his troubled mind, so long distracted and maddened by frightful night-visions. Not only did the Reformation rend the shackles from the human soul ; —it opened new fields in which it might expatiate. The imprisoned eagle, escaping from the murky cell of the monk, into the open vault, its rightful inheritance, soared upwards on joyous wing, and basked in the glorious sunlight. It is true, that a feeble dawn preceded the Reformation, occasioned mainly by the fall of Constantinople, which compelled a few learned men to seek asylum in the West, bringing with them the treasures of Greek lore ; but that dawn Rome would have speedily extinguished, had not the Reformation come in time to save it. But, grateful as was this revival of letters, it was as nothing compared with the intellectual outburst that followed the Reformation. In all the Reformed countries mind opened out into an amplitude of faculty, and exhibited itself in a comprehension of judgment, a subtilty and force of reason, a richness, boldness, and brilliancy of imagination, of which the world till then had seen no example. The brightest era of classic times pales before it. The human mind had a second youth. All the leading Reformers as far outstripped their contemporaries in their literary accomplishments as they excelled them in their theological attainments. One of the most elegant Latin writers since the days of Cicero was our own Buchanan. Knox excelled all the writers of his country in graphic vigour and idiomatic purity. In the hands of Luther the German language attained at once to classic terseness and rhythm. Need I mention the galaxy of great thinkers and writers which illuminated the horizon of England in the days of Elizabeth ? By one quality were all of them marked in common,—great creative power and mental boldness ; but that boldness and power they owed to the Reformation. But for the Reformation, not one of these deathless names should we ever have heard of, and not one of their immortal works should we ever have possessed. Bacon had never opened the path to true science ; Newton had never discovered the law of gravitation ; Shakspeare's mighty voice had been dumb for ever ; Milton had never sung ; Taylor and Barrow had never discoursed ; or Watt invented the steam-engine.

But, after all, these great names and immortal works are

the least part of the service which the Reformation rendered
to knowledge. Not only did the Reformation give us learned
men;—it gave us institutions of learning. It gave us arrangements by which the lamp of learning, like the lamp in the
temple of old, might never go out. The Reformation gave
us an educated nation, or would have done so had it not been
hindered. The idea of educating the masses,—of putting a
whole people to school,—had no more dawned upon the
middle ages than had Newton's discovery of gravitation.
Even in Papal countries to this day the masses are scarce
more educated than are the brutes; and yet Knox three
hundred years ago produced a scheme of education which
not only would have suited the Scotland of his own day,
but would suit the Scotland of the present hour,—would, in
fact, be a mighty boon to it. All the great educationists of
our times are but following in Knox's steps, whose nobly
comprehensive plan they have never exceeded in theory, as,
unhappily, they have never reached it in practice.

These are a few of the benefits, and but a few,—for time
would fail to tell all,—which the Reformation has conferred
upon us. Besides our holy faith, with its Sabbaths, its sanctuaries, peace in our land, virtue and love at our hearths,
hope at our death-beds, and the blessed words of inspiration
dispelling the gloom above our graves;—besides all this,—
and how much all this is worth, eternity only can tell,—we
owe to the Reformation every generous art which distinguishes
our nation. If law now reigns where violence formerly prevailed,—if the lamp of learning now burns where darkness
formerly brooded,—if noble cities now rise where hovels
aforetime stood,—if the ocean is whitened with our ships,
and the land is covered with our factories and our workshops,
—if our flag floats on almost every promontory of the earth
and every island of the sea,—and if our population is flowing
outwards in mighty waves, and peopling the ample regions

of Canada and Australia,—these are but the developments of the Reformation,—the workings of that mighty and still unspent impulse communicated to our nation three centuries ago.

But the Reformation is not completed : its work as yet is but half-accomplished.   The pause that has occurred has made some misdoubt the power of its great principles, and their adaptability to modern times, and to talk of seeking somewhere for some new and mightier moral forces.   Instead of being led away by this hallucination, which tends only to retrogression, let us arise, and, assured that the Reformation is but another name for Christianity,—Christianity come out of its sepulchre of a thousand years,—and believing that its principles are for the whole world, let us strive to send its regenerating and healing influence downwards among the masses of our own country, and outwards to the very extremities of the earth.   Completed the Reformation never will be till it has made every country under heaven what Britain now is, and more than Britain now is.   Completed it never will be till it has laid prostrate every tyrannical throne, rooted out every idolatrous Church, razed every dungeon, broken every fetter, emancipated every nation and tribe that dwell beneath heaven's cope, and assembled them all in one ransomed and glorious throng before the throne of the Lamb, to join their voices in the song, never again to cease upon the earth, as it never will cease in heaven,—"Blessing, and honour, and glory, and power, be unto Him that sitteth upon the throne, and unto the Lamb, for ever and ever "

PART SECOND.

THE PAPAL AGGRESSION.

PLEASANT CHANGES IN THE DISTANCE.

WHAT matters it, many say, and more think, though the Church of Rome should regain her ascendancy in Great Britain? What harm would it do us? or what great change would it work upon the country?

It would change, of course, the national creed, and modify the forms in which our devotion is expressed; but the devotion itself it would not impair. Nay, so far from impairing it, the likelihood is, that by ministering certain helps and stimulants to it, which it lacks at present, our devotion would become a far warmer, and certainly a far more æsthetic, thing than it now is. The dominancy of the Roman faith would leave untouched the essence of our morality, the form of our government, and the substance of our liberties. No one political right of the least consequence would it abolish; and no one of our social customs on which we put any value would it set aside. We would be the same energetic race we are at this hour. Our air would be as pure, our soil as fertile, our arts as prosperous, our commerce as vast, and our empire as great.

Nay, there are some who think that the restoration of the ancient faith would work a very pleasing and a very beneficial change, at least upon the exterior of society. It would relieve the tameness which the Reformation superinduced, and render the country, in its outward aspects, much more picturesque. Would it not mightily improve our ecclesiastical architecture? How proud should we be to see those majestic cathedrals, with their oriels, their rich tracery, their airy pinnacles, and their stupendous towers and domes, which are the pride of Continental cities, rising in the midst of us, and attracting the traveller's eye at many leagues distance. And then, to enter these august edifices and say one's prayers, looking up, the while, into the face of the Madonna, or kneeling before some saint in marble! How ravishing! Instead of sleeping under the drowsy sermon of some preacher, would not the whole æsthetic principle within us be vivified and roused to a holy intoxication by the priest's chant, the organ's mighty voice, the mystic rites, and the fragrant fumes of the flashing censer, aided by the sobbings of the devotees around us, overcome, like ourselves, by these powerful spells? Then indeed should we know what devotion is.

The ascendancy of the ancient faith would also greatly enliven our sober costume. What a change would pass upon our streets by the appearance upon them of the conventual habits of southern Europe! How delightful to see holy men, and holier women, trundling along in their gown of serge, their scapulars, their girdle of rope, their sandalled feet, their cowl, their crucifix; in short, tricked out in the whole of that mysterious gear which now we see only in pictures, where they look so pretty, seeing one can put in all the poetry, and keep out all that is not! Would not such importations tend to shame us out of our national demureness, and help to make us emulate that vivacious gaiety which is thought to follow in the wake of a religion which teaches its votaries to masquerade on Sabbath, and to pray only amid the glories of statuary and painting?

What a fascinating change would be wrought, too, on the interior of our churches! The pulpit, that "drum ecclesi-astic," with its sombre trappings, and its Bible theology, which so unmannerly disturbs the conscience of the sinner in its quiet sleep, would disappear, and in its place would come the snow-white marble altar, with its gorgeous furni-ture of gold and silver vessels, its chalice, its crucifix, and its candles burning at noon-day. Our higher clergy, the equals of temporal princes, would perform their ministrations "clothed in fine linen, and purple, and scarlet, and decked with gold, and precious stones, and pearls." And instead of sanctuaries with unadorned wall, humble roof, and monoto-nous rows of wooden pews, our congregations would meet amid the solemnities of nave, and aisle, and pillar, with the rich light falling in many-chequered hues upon the marble floor. If we can buy all this grandeur for a few dry dogmas, do we not well to strike a bargain? True, our theology would be somewhat more meagre; but what our theology would lose our worship would gain. The splendour of our rites and the fervour of our piety would more than make up for the meagreness of our divinity.

Some few changes, too, would the full realization of the Papal aggression introduce into our every-day life. We should get much into the habit, doubtless, like all devout people abroad, of wearing little dangling crosses, and of say-ing our prayers with the help of a string of beads. We would contract a liking for chrism and holy water. We would carry about with us bits of rotten bone, and other precious relics, instead of insurance tickets, as a protection against accidents and evil spirits. Small and tastefully-decorated shrines to the Madonna would adorn the corners of our streets; and Calvaries would rise beside our highways. Our vintners would sell their ale under the sign of this saint, and our craftsmen ply their trade under the sign of that

other.   Our cabmen would swear by St Anthony of Egypt,
and our fishermen by St Anthony of Padua.   Every week
we should have a fête-day, on which no servile work must
be done, although on Sabbath that prohibition would be re-
laxed.   A few such quiet and harmless changes, and there
the matter would end.   When all was over and finished, we
would be astonished to find how easily we had slid into the
true fold, and how comfortable we were now under the crook
of the shepherd of the Tiber.

Meanwhile the country would go on as before.   The Queen
would open our Parliament every session.   The two Houses
would meet, and debate, and legislate, as now.   The courts
of law would try causes and administer justice by the old
laws.   We should have our newspaper every morning, and
our conversazione or lecture in the evening.   We would
go on laying down railroads, building steamships, and buying and selling with all the earth.   We would shoot grouse
in September, and make merry at Christmas ; and our relish
for the sports of the one season and the festivities of the
other would be none the less that we were under Papal
rule.   In short, Scotland would be Scotland still ; and old
England would be old England still ; and, it might be, a
little more so.

Such is the picture which many draw of what would be
the results of the triumph of Romanism in Great Britain.
It might work, they think, a few changes on the surface of
society, but it would fail to go deeper.   Our books, our public meetings, our factories, our commerce, it would leave us.
The great business of this world would go on as before ; and
the only difference would be, that men would travel to another
and a better world by a new road.   The body of British law,
British toleration, and British liberty, would remain intact
and entire.   How great a delusion this is, the following pages
are intended to show.

THE RECONNOITRE, OR FIRST STEPS.

THE shock of the French Revolution convinced the Church of Rome, that in the slumber in which she had passed the eighteenth century, she had rested her mitred head upon hidden fires, and that she must rouse herself, and strike for her old dominion, or be swept out of existence. Accordingly, so soon as peace had returned to Europe, the Jesuits came forth from their hiding-places, and concocted that plan for reducing Britain under the yoke of Rome which they have ever since been pursuing with great astuteness and most astonishing success.

That plan may be gathered from various hints dropped by Dr Wiseman, in his book on the "Four Last Popes," and, in particular, from his conversations, there recorded, with Gregory XVI. and the Abbé Lemennais. A great work was to be done ; and the first step was to prepare the proper instruments for the doing of it. With this view the English College at Rome was restored. This was the deed of Pius VII. and his well-known Minister, Cardinal Consalvi. This college had been closed for the period of a generation. On the 18th of December 1818, a small band of youths entered that college, and took possession of its long-deserted corridors and chambers. Who were these youths, and from what country had they come ? They had come from Great Britain. They had been selected with great care, and sent to Rome to be educated under the keen eye and the skilful hand of the Jesuits, that, when their education was finished, they might come back to England, and begin their work of reconquering Britain to the Roman faith. Of this number was the future Cardinal (Wiseman). One can scarce refrain a smile when he contrasts this little army of six with the greatness of their allotted task. But Rome can foresee great results from apparently insignificant causes.

From Rome the scene now shifts to Britain. These youths were in due time educated, and sent back to England. The implements fashioned abroad were now employed in fashioning other implements at home. The first object was to reduce the Catholic laity and priesthood of Ireland thoroughly under Jesuit control. With this view the College of Clongows was erected, filled with Jesuit professors, and opened for the youth of the middle and upper classes of Ireland. The next step was to reduce the priests of Ireland under Jesuit influence. Dr Kenry was sent from Rome, and appointed Principal of Maynooth. Its chairs were filled with Jesuits from the College of Clongows; and thus was the priesthood of Ireland brought completely under Jesuit control. The priests were under Dr Kenry, the head of British Jesuitism; and Dr Kenry was under General Roothan, the head of the Jesuitism of the world. And now, headed by a man of no principle but a good deal of rough eloquence (Mr O'Connell), that political agitation was commenced which resulted in the great Romanist victory of 1829. By the Act of '29 the doors of the British Legislature were opened to the subjects of another potentate, and a right was conceded to the members of a foreign community to legislate for a State whose law is not their law, and whose sovereign is not their sovereign. This done, the next step was to bring the lay adherents of their Church in England under Jesuit control. The College of Stoneyhurst was erected, and filled with Jesuit professors; and into that college was gathered the youth of the old Catholic families in England, to receive an education and polish fitting them to take their place with effect in English society. Thus was the whole Catholic body, lay and cleric, in Great Britain and Ireland, subjugated and made ready to be wielded by Jesuitism.

Having taken proper measures with her own members in Great Britain, Rome next turned her attention to the Protestants. Her first measure was to seize upon the universities. On the idea that a plan had been formed for perverting Britain, where should we expect that plan first to discover itself? Why! where but at Oxford and Cambridge? These are the twin fountains of influence in England. From thence do the pulpit and the bar of England draw their supplies. There it is that our future legislators, Cabinet Ministers, and Privy Councillors, are educated. Romanizing teachers were placed in certain of the chairs of these seats of learning; and thus were the seeds of Popery deposited in many a young and unsuspecting mind.

About the year '33 the next step was taken: the "Tracts for the Times" began to be issued. In this, Rome showed that great practical sagacity and quick discernment in which she so much excels. She did not sit down and write a ponderous volume: she knew that few would buy, and still fewer would read, such an exposition. Oxford produced, by the thousand, four-paged tracts, and into each tract she put the substance of a volume; and Rome turned them to good account. Some philosophers have held that matter is so compressible that the whole universe might be put into a nutshell. However this may be, the whole Papal system was so compressed as to be put into these nutshells,—these little tracts, which were showered like snow-flakes over the country. They were, to borrow a figure from the military art, the gunboats of the Papal invasion. While the volume was lying unbought on the bookseller's shelf, or unopened on the drawing-room table, these tracts, written with great apparent unction and much logical acumen, were passing rapidly from hand to hand. They could be thrown into a railway carriage, circulated in the baron's hall; in short, they penetrated society, where large volumes could not enter; and deposited seed destined to bear an early and plenteous harvest.

A short period indeed divided that seed-time from its harvest ; and accordingly, the next stage of this development was the appearance of Puseyism in the Church of England. Several busy years had been passed in sowing Roman seed. Within the Universities it had been largely scattered ; outside the Universities it had been scattered still more largely ; and now the fields began to be white unto harvest. The pulpit was now heard to speak with a Roman voice ; and by and by, ministers of the Church of England began to go over, very scantily at first, to the Church of Rome. The process by which their perversion was accomplished was a skilful and subtle one. They were made to feel as if, in becoming first Tractarian, and next Romanist, they had adopted no new creed, but had only followed boldly and logically to its natural issues a creed they had always held. And now the number of secessions to Rome among the clergy amounts to more than two hundred, and to a number still larger among the nobility, gentry, and middle classes.

The next step in advance was the abolition of the statute forbidding the introduction into the country of bulls and rescripts from the Pope. The penal statutes against Popery were abolished in 1778. They were framed by our fathers, not to oppress Papists, but to protect their own liberties against Popish machinations. They were extremely mild, when we consider that, when they were framed, the gibbets on which the Protestants had been hanged were but newly taken down, and the ashes of the fires in which they had been burned were yet scarce cold ;—mild, especially, when we compare them with the statute "De Comburendo Heretico," framed in the time of Henry IV., and always acted upon so long as the government was in the hands of Papists. Whatever may be thought of these statutes, the opposition to their

abolition was rested on the ground that the Church of Rome
was not so much a religious society as a political confederation hostile to the liberties of this country.

After the abolition of these laws, there remained the inhibition against bringing bulls from Rome. We are prepared
to defend such inhibition, as in harmony with the great principle which is every man's birthright, which we claim for
ourselves, and are prepared to give to every human being,—
freedom of conscience, to wit. A Papal bull is no matter of
religious profession,—it is a matter of civil obedience. The
question it raises is, not whether a Church shall have the right
of communicating with its members on matters of doctrine,
but whether a foreign prince shall be at liberty to send his
edicts into our country, enjoining upon the consciences of his
adherents, under the highest penalties, matters both temporal
and spiritual. France concedes no such power to the Pope.
No rescript from Rome can be published in that country
without permission of the Government. It is the same in
Spain and Austria ; indeed, in every country of Continental
Europe, Protestant and Popish. But in Great Britain this
statute was repealed in 1846, so far as regards the penalties
attached to the 13th of Elizabeth, prohibiting the introduction of letters apostolic from Rome. As regards the older
statutes, in especial that of Richard II., Government has declared that it will not now prosecute upon them; so that the
abolition of these prohibitory enactments is virtually total.
The Papists said, " Why do you keep these enactments on
your statute-book ? They are a relic of the times of bigotry :
they are a disgrace to you, and an insult to us. We have
no intention of doing what these statutes forbid. For your
own credit, if not for our sake, repeal them." This reasoning
prevailed. The gates of the country were opened to import
and to publish all and every edict from Rome. Thus another
great point was gained,—a point indispensable for what was

to come after. That an eye in the Vatican was all the while watching this movement, is evident from a conversation of Wiseman with Gregory XVI., recorded in his " Four Last Popes," in which the Pontiff refers to a certain obstacle in Great Britain which must be removed before an organized aggression could take place in that country.

That obstacle was now out of the way ; and speedily came the *denouement,*—the Papal Aggression of 1850. That Aggression was the fair and full launching of the whole scheme. It exhibited the complete machinery of Rome set up in our country, openly and avowedly, from the red cardinal to the barefooted monk. By these wary and well-weighed steps did the Church of Rome steadily advance to her crowning measure.

THE EDICT FROM THE FLAMINIAN GATE.

In 1850, Cardinal Wiseman, arriving from Rome, published in England an " Edict from the Flaminian Gate." The form of the deed was imperial, and its import was not less imperial than its form. By the same formality did old Rome signify to the countries which her legions had overrun, that they had passed under her yoke, and were become part of her empire. Adopting the style of the haughty mistress of the Old World, the yet haughtier mistress of the New told England that she had been taken back into the empire of Catholicism, and was henceforward to hold herself the subject of the pontifical see. The " Edict " joined Great Britain to the Seven Hills. Such was held to be its legal import. All law, authority, and rule in the country opposed to that of Rome, or not holding of it, was virtually abrogated, although meanwhile suffered to exist. The only valid authority in Great Britain in the eyes of Romanists henceforward was the Vatican.

The first intimation given to the nation of the new Roman policy was in the *Tablet* of October 5th, and was to the following effect:—"It appears now next to decided, that Cardinal Wiseman will return to England for a short time, and will hold a Synod, and *establish the hierarchy.*" This, of course, meant that the mask or guise which the Popish bishops in Britain had long worn as merely "missionary bishops" of "Melipotamus," "Trachonitis," "Limyra," and so forth, would be thrown off, and Romish territorial sees established in the country. We next learnt from the *Gazetta di Roma*, that on the 30th of September a consistory was held in the Vatican, that a Cardinal's hat was bestowed on Dr Wiseman, that the city of Westminster was erected into an archbishopric, and placed under the new Cardinal, who was appointed to govern the kingdom with the aid of twelve suffragan bishops, among whom England was distributed into territorial dioceses! An entire change had been decreed upon the Popish Church in Great Britain.

The selection of Westminster as the seat of the government of the new Cardinal had an arrogant and offensive look. Westminster is the spot of all others most associated with the glories of our past history. Within its time-honoured precincts are the tombs of our kings, the monuments of our statesmen, the trophies of our warriors. There our Parliament sits, and our courts administer justice. It had never been a bishopric in Papal times, but simply a monastery. But the offence lay not in that this act disturbed the cherished associations of the nation, but in that it encroached upon the country's independence. It bore the character, not of an ecclesiastical arrangement, but of a temporal usurpation.

Semi-regal fêtes celebrated the event at Rome. The new owner of the purple held a levee in the Quirinal, the Princess Doria doing the honours. Princes, ambassadors, and consuls crowded the anti-chamber of the Cardinal. After this, departing from Rome, not now as when a simple student, but full of honours, and charged with a great mission, he travelled by easy stages to England ; and, resting on his way at the despotic courts of Tuscany and Vienna, he slowly approached our shores.

In the end of October the Cardinal and the "bull" appeared in England together. The document was immediately published. The essential truculence of the "bull" was masked by an affluence of high-flown professions of tender solicitude for "the flock of the Lord in England." Under the guise of deepest spiritual humility, it aimed only at earthly power. In it the Pontiff informed us that, having "besought the assistance of the blessed Virgin Mary, Mother of God, and of the saints whose virtues have made England illustrious," to be enabled to help us, he now, in virtue of that "plenitude of apostolic power" entrusted to him "by our Lord Jesus Christ, through the person of St Peter, Prince of the Apostles," "decreed the re-establishment in the kingdom of England, and according to the common laws of the Church, of a hierarchy of bishops deriving their titles from their own sees." The bull went on to partition England into territorial dioceses, and to appoint bishops in each, with jurisdiction,—the full and complete jurisdiction of the Roman Church,—the same which she exercises in the most Catholic countries. "In the sacred government of the clergy and people," said the bull, "and in all that which concerns the pastoral office, the archbishops and bishops of England will enjoy all the rights and faculties which bishops and archbishops can use, according to the disposition of the sacred canons and the apostolic constitutions." The government now set up was declared to be "such as it exists, freely exists, in other nations." And, added the Pope in conclusion, "we likewise decree that all which may be done to the contrary *by any one, whoever he may be, knowing or ignorant, in the name of any authority whatever, shall be without force."* So far the edict from the Flaminian Gate.

We do not possess the gift of infallible interpretation. It is equally undeniable that Cardinal Wiseman does. Therefore, instead of offering any opinion of our own, let us hear the Cardinal on this great edict of annexation. Here, at least, he cannot err. He was present when Infallibility took counsel in this matter; he knows its secret purposes, which are hidden from ordinary mortals; and he is entitled to all credit when he interpets the mind of the Pontiff, as embodied in his bull. A "Pastoral Letter" from "Nicholas, by the Divine mercy, of the Holy Roman Church Cardinal Priest, Archbishop of Westminster, and Administrator Apostolic of the Diocese of Southwark," instantly followed the promulgation of the pontifical bull. "WE GOVERN," quoth Nicholas of the Holy Roman Church, "and shall continue to govern, the counties of Middlesex, Hertford, and Essex, as ordinary thereof, and those of Surrey, Sussex, Kent, Berkshire, and Hampshire, with the islands annexed, as administrator with ordinary jurisdiction." Let us mark the words of "Nicholas," not spoken at random, but spoken in the full foresight that they would be carefully weighed and narrowly criticised; and therefore, we may be sure, selected because they were the terms of all others best fitted to announce the fact of his assumed jurisdiction, without appearing unnecessarily to insult our independence or ignore our rights. But, cautious as the terms are, the FACT stands out in unmistakeable prominence. "We govern," said the Cardinal, not the members of the Roman Church in the counties of Middlesex, &c., but the counties themselves. "We govern, and shall continue to govern, the counties of Middlesex, Hertford," &c. The Cardinal knows nothing of any other authority, from that of the Queen down to her humblest functionary. All

comment of ours is superfluous. "Peter" hath spoken, and
"Nicholas" hath interpreted. The Cardinal and his suffragans govern, not English Papists, but England.

To show that he regarded his acquisition as neither vision-
ary nor ephemeral, but, on the contrary, solid and durable,
this man in purple lifts up a pæan of triumph so loud, that
the whole realm rings again. We seem to hear the shout
of some old warrior, as, dragging his captives after him, he
slowly climbs the Capitol. So sits Cardinal Wiseman in his
triumphal car, as he proudly climbs the "Capitol" from
which he was to sway the sceptre of *government.* He drags
behind him an illustrious captive,—England ; and he sees
the celestial hierarchy bending from their seats to gaze on
the grand spectacle which made this a day of glory to his
Church. "Truly," he continues in his Pastoral, "this day
is to us a day of joy and exultation of spirit, the crowning
day of long hopes, and the opening day of bright prospects.
How must the saints of our country, whether Roman or
British, Saxon or Norman, look down from their seats of
bliss with beaming glance upon this new evidence of the
faith and Church which led them to glory ! and all those
blessed martyrs of those latter ages which have fought the
battles of the faith, how must they bless God, as they see the
lamp of the temple again enkindled and re-brightening,—as
they behold the silver links of that chain which has connected
their country with the see of Peter in its vicarial government, changed into burnished gold !" Let it be marked that
it is the *country* which is bound to the see of Peter, although,
adds the Cardinal considerately, not with a chain of steel, but
of "burnished gold." Ah ! fetters ! But then they are of
"gold." It were unreasonable, surely, to complain of such
fetters.

Equally jubilant were the notes pealed forth in the Romish cathedral at Birmingham on occasion of the enthroni-

zation of one of the "twelve" (the same number as of old, seeing it is a second planting of Christianity), Dr Ullathorne, now styling himself "Lord Bishop of Birmingham." The preacher was the English pervert, Dr Newman. "The mystery of God's providence," he exclaimed, "is now fulfilled. I do not recollect of any people on earth but those of Great Britain who, having once rejected the religion of God, were again restored to the bosom of the Church. But what has God done for them? It is wonderful in our eyes. The holy hierarchy has been restored. The grave is opening, and Christ is coming out."

We give but one specimen more of those vauntings, regarded as hallucinations at the time, the fumes of Roman pride, the maunderings of Papal dotage. Alas! it has since been found that the maundering was on the side, not of Rome, but of some of our own statesmen and ecclesiastical dignitaries, who then spoke and wrote some very valorous things, but afterwards could find nothing to back up their *big* words except *little* deeds, or no deeds at all. "The Pope," said the *Tablet* of that day, "has made Westminster an archiepiscopal see; and he has given to Dr Wiseman, now a cardinal, jurisdiction over the souls of all men living within the limits of his see, excepting Jews, Quakers, and unbaptized Protestants."

Thus did the Romanists, holding that a work of this sort so well begun was as good as finished, deem that the schism of three centuries was now healed,—that the hydra of British heresy was crushed,—that the first sovereign on earth was virtually converted into a subject of the pontifical throne, and the mightiest of existing empires legally annexed to the empire of Rome.

Fifteen years have since passed away. Do these vauntings now appear groundless? Have these hopes been shown to be illusions? Has Rome slackened in the work; and, having

begun, does she despair of making an end ?   Have the foundations of the new Papal temple in Britain, laid in 1850, been
razed by the authority of British law and the strength of British Protestantism ?   Are they rotting in the ground amid
the faint hearts and feeble hands of the Romish builders ?   Far
from it.   Whoever has retreated, these men have not.   Their
hopes are as high and their boastings are as bold at this day
as they were then.   And with reason too ; for the building
then begun has neither been stopped nor gone back, but is
advancing to its completion from one day to another.

THE PARTITIONED LAND.

WELL, but what avails, it is asked, this fine scheme of a restored hierarchy ?   It is a scheme, and nothing more.   It
looks very pretty and very imposing, extended on Papal parch-
ment, and seen in grand perspective, dressed out with many
an artistic illusion ; but one thing it lacks,—tangibility, and
reality even.   The Pope has but reared an empire in the air.
He has left the solid earth to us ; and so long as we are
masters of *it*, we make the Pontiff heartily welcome to con-
struct as many kingdoms in the clouds as he pleases.   *His*
kingdom and *ours* lie far apart : they are, in fact, in different
worlds ; and the two never can come into collision.   In partitioning England, he might, for that matter, as well have
mapped out the moon, or crossed and re-crossed our country
with chalk-lines, or written with his own apostolic finger,
"I govern, and shall continue to govern," upon the sea-shore
when the tide was out.   In Wiseman and his twelve suffragans we have but a repetition of Sir John Falstaff and
his men in buckram.   The red hat of the Cardinal has not
yet converted England ; and the throne of Victoria still
stands, despite the "Edict" hurled against it by the man on

the Seven Hills. Why should not the Papacy take a som-
nolent fit, and fall a-dreaming? and what vision so likely to
visit its pillow as that of mighty England, with sackcloth on
her loins and ashes on her head, doing obeisance before the
Papal throne, and, in token of profoundest penitence for her
sins of three hundred years, soliciting permission to kiss the
Papal toe? But the Papacy will awake, and find that it is
but a dream. We daresay the *Times* expressed very fairly
the general mind of England on the point when it said, in
some such words as the following,—that the return of Dr
Wiseman to our country, with all his high-flown titles and
his bravery of office, need give us no more concern than if it
had been the pleasure of his Holiness to bedeck and bedeco-
rate the editor of the *Tablet* in style equally gorgeous, and
assign him the puissant rank of " Duke of Smithfield."

It was natural for us to reason in this manner. Our unquestionable superiority in science, in material wealth, and
in political power,—the creation, as we boast, of our own skill
and courage,—has given us an overweening sense, more perceptible to foreigners than to ourselves, of self-sufficiency and
self-importance. We are the men. The love of liberty is
in our blood. Our freedom lies safely entrenched within the
double fortress of law and usage, of our social instincts and
our political forms. The Pope, of course, puts his own meaning upon his own acts ; but the question is, not what he understands by them, but what we understand by them. This
reasoning, we grant, is very specious ; but it is, we maintain,
and will endeavour to show, thoroughly fallacious.

It is true, Great Britain is not yet converted to the Popish
faith. No one—not even Rome herself—expected that this
would happen in a day. But Great Britain is at this hour
nearer conversion—very considerably nearer—than at the
period of the Papal aggression. The more one reflects, the
more one is astonished at the great change which a very short

time has sufficed to bring about.   The Roman deposit, like
a crystallizing salt, has been adding layer after layer, and
expanding silently, yet continuously, from one day to another.
Look at it now : what solidity of nucleus and what goodliness
of bulk,—and all within a few years !   The Church of Rome
has nearly quadrupled her priesthood.   She has quadrupled
her members, quadrupled her funds, quadrupled her edifices.
She is now as good as endowed, and every year the country
is acquiring a more Roman look ; and yet we console ourselves by saying, "England is not converted."   England's
Government is in the hands of the Roman Catholic members
of the House of Commons ; these, again, are in the hands of
their priesthood ; and to that priesthood neither pension,
money, nor money's worth, can be denied.   The nation, in
both its religious and its worldly sections, is sleeping its quiet
sleep.   To any one who would rouse it by unwelcome prog-
nostications it mutters in its sleep, "Go thy way, bigot, for
this time. Come back and call me when England is converted."

Nor will this be long.   What with the continual flow of
Romanists from Ireland ; what with the increasing manufacture of Papists in the Puseyite camp ; and what with the
recoil in favour of Rome from infidelity,—for to weak and
frightened minds that Church will appear the only real protection from, and the only effectual bulwark against, a universal scepticism,—the progress of Romanism will go on,
not simply in an arithmetical progression ;—it will proceed
in geometrical ratio.   The balance numerically is still in our
favour ; but from one hour to another it tends towards equi-
poise.   The Roman community, like the cave of Cacus,
exhibits many a foot-print going in, but it shows *nulla vesti-
gia retrorsum*.   One pervert to-day, a dozen to-morrow, an
hundred the day after ; and with whom will the majority be
found very soon ?   "And surely the mountain falling cometh
to nought, and the rock is removed out of his place."   And

when the mountain of our Protestantism has fallen with this ceaseless corroding and trickling down of its substance, and we go back, and cry to a slumbering nation, "Awake, arise!" we shall be answered, "It is too late now: England is converted."

The question is, not what the Pope understands by the restoration of the hierarchy, but what we understand by it. So do many most confidently argue, as if this were decisive of the whole matter. This, doubtless, is a true canon of interpretation in ordinary cases. But those who so oracularly enunciate it, and so confidently rely upon it, in this case totally misapply it. They fail to take into account, because they do not, or will not, understand it, the peculiarly subtle genius of the Church with which they are dealing, and the marvellous efficacy which she attributes to all her arrangements. The Church of Rome is a Church of *shams* in one sense, but in another she is, above all other Churches, a Church of *realities*. As a moral and spiritual organization, she is a *sham;* as a political and earthly confederation, she is a compact, energetic, terrible *reality*. There is not under the sun a greater contrast than there is betwixt the necromantic and illusory character of the agency which she employs for her spiritual ends, and with which, nevertheless, she leads a great many clever people, as we say, by the nose, and the intense common sense, and the almost, indeed we may say the altogether, superhuman knowledge of human nature, especially of its weaknesses, with which she labours to attain her political and worldly objects. She never does anything without a meaning, and that meaning she almost always contrives to make good. And we may depend upon it, that whatever Rome understands by the Papal aggression she will compel us too to understand by it in the long run: what she holds to be its *legal* import she will eventually oblige us to recognise as its *actual* import. We maintain, therefore, that the question is, not what we understand by the restoration of the hierarchy, but what Rome understands by it. What, then, does she understand by it?

And, first, to determine this question, it is not enough to look at the form of the act. The fundamental and primary consideration here is the character and constitution of the Church whose act it is.

It has been said with great plausibility, that the Episcopal Church parcels out Scotland into dioceses; that the Free Church partitions it into Presbyteries and Synods; and that the Wesleyan Conference, and other religious bodies, map and over-map, cross and re-cross, with their ecclesiastical lines, the surface of England. In fact, you can conceive of Great Britain as covered from sea to sea with these ecclesiastical arrangements, lying one above another, like the coatings of a bulb or the reticulations of a plant. Rome comes, and adds one more to those previously existing. You have not said a word about the former: why object to this last? We object because the two cases are widely dissimilar.

Other denominations are purely spiritual societies. They exist for only spiritual objects: their organization is spiritual; and the power they wield is solely spiritual: therefore any mapping out of the country on their part is, and only can be, spiritual. They all recognise, practically as well as theoretically, the two great jurisdictions, the temporal and the spiritual; and while they claim full liberty of action within the one, they as expressly disclaim all right of entrance into the other. Any attempt to exercise a particle of temporal jurisdiction would amount to a flagrant violation of their most fundamental principles, and would speedily result in their destruction. But the Church of Rome differs radically on the point in question from all other Churches. She is not a pure, but a mixed society: the secular element enters as largely as does the spiritual into her constitution. Her jurisdiction must be of the same kind with her constitution. In constitution, we have said, she is a mixture of temporal and spiritual power; and of the same mixed kind must be the authority she wields. She can advance no claim, and make no arrangement for giving that claim scope, which does not embody the temporal quite as much as it does the spiritual element. It would be not less in violation of the fundamental principles of this Church to forego the temporal jurisdiction than it would be in other Churches to claim it. And when Papists ridicule the idea of their Church seeking to exercise temporal jurisdiction, and speak of her confining herself to spiritual power, they are simply presuming on Protestant ignorance, and, for the good of their Church, are concealing and denying her fundamental principles.

But, second, the restoration of the hierarchy has in it a *new spiritual claim.* That spiritual claim is rested on a territorial basis. Beforetime we had, no doubt, Popish bishops in the country; but let us mark the difference. They were here, not in their character of bishops, but in their character of missionaries. They bore titles taken from other countries, and from old extinct bishoprics. Dr Wiseman, for instance, was Bishop of Melipotamus, and Dr Gillis of Edinburgh was Bishop of Limyra. At Rome these ecclesiastics were viewed as having a territorial relation to these places, wherever they are, and episcopal jurisdiction over all their inhabitants, if they have any; but in our country they were simply missionaries, or missionary bishops. To England they had no territorial relation; and they had no episcopal authority, save only over the members of their own Church in the land.

But the Papal aggression brought this state of things to an end. It gave us bishops with territorial titles taken from our great cities,—for the law prohibiting the assumption of the titles of existing bishoprics was evaded,—and so it gave us bishops with a territorial relation to Great Britain, and episcopal jurisdiction over every baptized man and woman in their several dioceses. Instead of a mission, henceforward we had a regularly constituted Church, with territorial relations, and episcopal authority, not over Romanists only, but over all. The Papal aggression rooted the Roman Church in the soil, and gave it infeftment, as it were, of stone and earth. The Pope stamped his seal upon Great Britain as his own,—his own to distribute territorially, to teach doctrinally, and to govern by direct spiritual power and indirect temporal power. There is neither Church nor Christianity in Great Britain, in the eyes of the Church of Rome, but herself.

Not to go back upon the specimens of Papal vauntings already given as decisive of the light in which the Papal aggression, to this hour steadily prosecuted, was held by its authors, we adduce only the figure of Dr Wiseman. "Catholic England," said he, in his "Pastoral," "had been restored to its orbit in the ecclesiastical firmament, from which its light had long vanished, and begins anew its course of regularly adjusted action round the centre of unity, the source of jurisdiction, of light, and of vigour." Who or what was this unhappy planet,—this "Son of the Morning," which had long been fallen from heaven? Not the Romanist body in England, surely? It had never strayed from its "orbit:" its light had not "long vanished." This fallen star is, without doubt, —indeed, there is a heresy in the Cardinal's words should we interpret them otherwise,—Great Britain, the whole body of the people, which for three centuries had strayed in the gloom of Protestant night; but which, by the grace of the Pope, and the omnipotence of Infallibility, is now restored to its orbit. It was upon the British people *as such* that Rome fastened this claim, which she holds to be legal and valid to all and every effect with territorial bishoprics in other Catholic countries, and to be enforced as such, when circumstances

shall permit, by the powers and penalties for that end made
and provided.

But, third, this partitioning of the country is manifestly
an usurpation of the powers of the Sovereign. To erect territorial sees, and appoint, is, in virtue of the ecclesiastical
supremacy, the Queen's sole prerogative. So has the Constitution of the country decreed. But here comes a foreign
potentate, and does what the law declares the Queen, and
the Queen alone, has a right to do. Is not this to insult
the Sovereign, violate the law, and degrade the nation?

We are aware that there is a difference of opinion among
ourselves as to this part of our Constitution,—the ecclesiastical supremacy, to wit. But the question is not, whether the
power of the head of the State to appoint the officers of the
Church be right or wrong morally considered, but whether
it is right or wrong legally and constitutionally considered,
—whether, in short, the Queen's ecclesiastical supremacy be
according to law. This admits of but one answer : most
undeniably it is. Right or wrong, the nation has so ordained.
If we wish that the laws of Great Britain should be changed,
we will change them ourselves. We give to no foreign Power
on earth,—we give to neither Pope nor Kaiser,—right to step
in and alter our laws. But this man in purple has claimed
a right to alter the law. What the Queen could not do, for
she has no dispensing power in the matter,—what the nation
would not permit any of its own courts or servants to do,—
this legate of a foreign prince has done. We maintain that
he has committed an usurpation upon the Queen's prerogative, and offered an affront to the nation's independence and
dignity. That we put no forced interpretation upon this act,
but that, on the contrary, Rome held that this was the real
meaning of the Papal aggression, we may quote the words of
the Paris *Univers* of that day. The *Univers* distinctly tells
us that the "Edict from the Flaminian Gate" effaced all

previous territorial sees in England, and put down all ecclesiastical dignitaries set up by the Queen. The chairs of York
and Canterbury were no more.	"From the promulgation
of the brief," said the *Univers*, "there exists neither see
of Canterbury, nor of York, nor London, nor any of the
sees established anterior to the Reformation. The personages
who shall for the future assume the titles of Archbishop of
Canterbury and Bishop of London will be mere intruders,
schismatic prelates, without any spiritual authority. . . .
In England it is sought to calm apprehension by comparing
the new dioceses and divisions to those of the Episcopal
Church of Scotland or the Methodists ; but nothing can be
more false than such a comparison.	The Methodists have
never pretended to attack the spiritual authority of the Anglican Bishops, or, in dividing the dioceses of London or
Oxford, to abrogate the authority of those sees, and render
void and without effect all acts emanating from the Anglican
prelates who occupy them.	We prefer, since the Holy See
has thought fit, in its wisdom, to take this grave step, to avow
plainly and openly its bearing, to attribute to it all its importance, rather than weaken it in order to calm the irritation
of the enemies of the Church.	Yes ; the act of supremacy
just exercised by Pius IX. denies the existence in England
of all other spiritual authority save his own."

And, last of all, the greatly enhanced splendour and prestige which the restoration of the hierarchy has thrown around
the Popish Church in Great Britain is not unworthy to be
taken into account.	Rome knows well that the great mass
of mankind are more governed by show than by reality.
None knows better the value of the *ad captandum* argument.
She has here employed it to purpose.	Instead of a Church
in humble serge, she has given us a Church in cloth of gold.
Instead of a little missionary staff, with outlandish titles,—
men from Truchonitis and Sardiac,—she has sent us bishops

from the very foot of the throne of the Vicar of God. Instead of a nondescript body, half-missionary, half-episcopal,
standing on two countries at once, having one foot in Melipotamus and another in London, one foot in Limyra and
another in Edinburgh, we have now a regular and complete
hierarchy, bedizened with titles secular and spiritual, full to
the very brim with apostolical authority and virtue, singing
its masses and reciting its litanies in magnificent cathedrals,
and, with coquetish air, now showing itself in all the bravery
of gilded chariots in our streets, and now hiding from public gaze, which it courts while it seems to shun, amid the
shades of the cloister,—a full hierarchy, rising rank on
rank in spiritual pomp, from the sandals of the capuchin to
the red hat of the cardinal. Thousands who passed it by
unnoticed aforetime will now stop to gaze, and fall down to
worship.

With all our advancement, real independence of mind is
still rare. The world, to a large extent, still worships shams.
Even in quarters where complete emancipation from everything like superstitious thraldom is loudly vaunted, how often
are we astonished to find a sneaking reverence for the Church
of Rome ! We discover this weakness peering out in a hundred quiet ways,—many of them so well known that we need
not enumerate them.

A BATTLE THAT WAS NOT FOUGHT.

HARDLY had the foot of the man in purple touched our shores
till the storm began to mutter. But when he had entered,
and thrown the gauntlet down before the Queen and the
nation, then indeed did the tempest burst. The thunders of
popular wrath awoke, and were heard to roll fearfully, and
apparently were concentrating their terrors around the mitred

head of him who, in evil hour for himself, as was believed, had so wantonly provoked them. Some there were who even went the length of commiserating the man who, together with his too bold project, stood, as they thought, upon the brink of annihilation.

In that peculiar symbolic style which it pleases Rome to employ, and which is so meaningless to him who understands it not, but so fraught with meaning to the man who can read it, Wiseman told the people of England and of the world, that the Pope, his master, regarded the Queen of Great Britain as but his vassal, and that no deed of hers had force or validity till countersigned in the Vatican. By an unmistakeable act, he intimated that the land was his, to do with it as he pleased,—to divide and subdivide it, to put down whom he would, and to set up whom he would,—that, in short, the deity of the Seven Hills had extinguished all the lights of the ecclesiastical firmament of England, and had rolled it together as a scroll, and folded it up as a garment ; seeing that, having been woven by heretical hands, it was incurably tainted with Protestant pravity ; and that the same power had spread forth a new ecclesiastical heavens, and created a new ecclesiastical earth ; and that it behoved every dweller on that earth,—every baptized man and woman in England, —to account himself henceforward a "good Catholic," under peril of having to answer to Rome at a future day ; and no sooner had this been intimated to us in the symbolic deeds and metaphorical words of Rome, than, after the first pause of astonishment—the first few moments of deep musing and marvelling at the insolence of the man and the haughtiness of his language—was over, the blood of the nation rose to repel the insult.

The Prime Minister of the day, Lord John Russell, indited his Durham letter. He spoke with energy and courage ; —every sentence, flashing and fiery, went to the mark like an arrow : but he had spoken for the first and last time. In this one effort Lord John had expended his whole stock of Protestant zeal, and henceforward had neither heart nor hand for effectual resistance to the invading foe. The prelates and clergy of the Church of England, whom Rome had so summarily unfrocked, placing them in the same category with the muftis of Islam and the fakirs of Hinduism, rose in defence of the validity of their orders and the Biblical character of their faith. The people of the land, whom Wiseman had taken captive with his " Edict," and led, as it were, *en masse* to the baptismal font, loudly protested against being *catholicized* against their will, and vowed to defend their liberties as citizens of an independent country, and their rights of private judgment as rational beings. The whole nation was in motion.

Even Tractarianism, which for years had been marching with steady but stealthy steps towards the Seven Hills, quickening its speed the nearer it drew to that centre of mysterious but potent attraction, suddenly stopped, and, pausing a moment to bethink itself, turned its face in the opposite direction. It blew out its candles, took down its crosses, attired itself in vestments a little less fantastic, and learned to do its devotions with some abatement of that exuberance of genuflexion and grimace in which it had found so much spiritual edification aforetime. It now beheld a greater than " York," a greater than " Canterbury," in the land. Like the old man who had prayed to Death to come to his aid, and, when the grim spectre stood before him, prayed yet more earnestly that he would depart, so was it with the Tractarians, or, as they now began to call themselves, Anglo-Catholics. This body had invoked Rome to come and rescue it from the fetters of Protestantism ; and when it saw Rome standing over it,—when it felt the light of its red eye, and heard the tones of its voice, still husky by reason of old ana-

themas,—it faltered before the terrible presence, and prayed
Rome to depart from it—for a season.

Leaving for a while the debates of the senate and the
weighty cares of the judgment-seat, learned and eloquent
statesmen, donning their armour, hastened to do battle alongside of their fellow-citizens. " Protestant England,"—so
spoke the Lord Chancellor at the inaugural banquet of the
Lord Mayor in Guildhall,—" Protestant England is informed that she has now come under a Catholic hierarchy. The
hymn of triumph for admission to equality in civil liberty
has given place to the note of insult, triumph, and domination, announcing that you have come under a Roman Catholic hierarchy. Considering the language of the document
to which I refer, and considering the truly Roman construction which some attempt to put upon the oath of supremacy,
it would seem as if some were acting in anticipation of the
fulfilment of an ancient prophecy, which represents a cardinal's cap as equal to the crown of the Queen of England.
If such be anticipated, I answer them in the language of
Glo'ster,—

> "' Under our feet we'll stamp thy cardinal's hat,
>   In spite of Pope or dignities of Church.' "

The Lord Chief Justice of the Queen's Bench, speaking for
all the Judges, refrained from touching on this topic,—the
one topic to which he found that large and brilliant audience
would listen,—only because he anticipated the appearance of
his " Eminence" the Cardinal and his " Holiness" the Pope
before his tribunal some of these days, to answer for their
misdemeanours ; "and Pius IX., with triple crown," his
Lordship said, "should receive the same justice from him as
if he were a simple parish priest." These valorous sentiments
were re-echoed by the city magistracy of London, who, to
encourage the rulers of the country in their steadfast resolution to maintain the independence of the throne and the

ancient liberties of the kingdom, said that, "whether Ministers led or followed, one thing was certain, that Britons never
would be slaves either to Puseyism or to Popery."

Satire, as well as grave argument, was called into requisi-
tion on this great national emergency. Reason, speaking
through the higher organs of the press, laboured to prove that
the claims of the Pontifical Court were unfounded and treasonable; and laughter, finding vent in the lighter journals,
strove to render them ridiculous. The shafts of irony grazed
the Cardinal's hat. It was announced with great mock formality, that his Eminence Cardinal Pantaleone had arrived
at the Golden Cross, Charing Cross, and that he was bearer
of a message to the chief of the British Government, demanding the usual acknowledgment on the part of the Sovereign
of Great Britain, which has been always, and from all time,
a fief of the Holy See. In case of obstinate recusancy (which
was not apprehended), his Eminence was commissioned to
proclaim the Prince of Lucca sovereign of these islands,—the
Prince being direct and undoubted descendant of those legitimate monarchs of England who were driven by rebellion,
the one to death and the other to banishment, from their palace
of Whitehall. It was also announced that the Holy Father
had appointed Monsignor Snooks, with the title of Marquis
Saint Bartholomew, Lord Chancellor of England, *vice* Lord
Truro, who had not resigned; that the palace of Bedlam
would be occupied by the new primate until the palace of
Lambeth should be vacated by the (titular) Archbishop of
Canterbury, Mr Sumner, to whom the office of parish beadle
had been offered; that the Cathedral of Westminster would
immediately be taken possession of by its rightful owners;
that the heathen temple erected on the site of the old Basilica
of St Paul's would be given to Madame Tussaud, who was
in treaty for it; and that, in fine, the statue of Saint Mary-
Axe, opposite the Post-Office, had on the previous Wednes-

day begun to wink with its left eye in so convincing a manner, that thirty-three letter-carriers, and two commercial gentlemen staying at the Bull and Mouth, were instantly converted.

Thus the movement appeared to be truly national. It extended to all parts of the kingdom. It embraced all classes and ranks, from the Prime Minister downwards. It included all bodies, from the hierarchs of England to the Methodists of Wales and the Presbyterians of Scotland,—from the corporation of the metropolis to the town councils of the provinces. Memorials were presented to the Queen, and petitions were sent to Parliament. The country presented the appearance of a vast spiritual camp ; and the din of spiritual war rung over the whole land. A touch of the melo-dramatic was thrown into what appeared to be fast becoming a tragedy, by "the Right Reverend Father in God, William, Lord Bishop of Brechin." This prelate was heard to lift up his voice in the midst of the commotion, and protest against the Papal aggression on the ground of its being an unbrotherly act. It was, he held, an invasion of the rights of one bishop by another bishop. It was—oh, monstrous and unheard-of usurpation !—the Bishop of Rome intruding into the diocese of his brother the Bishop of Brechin.

The only practical measure which resulted from all this amount of protestation was the Ecclesiastical Titles Act. As a measure of resistance to the Papal aggression, that act was miserably inadequate. As originally drafted, it contained some clauses which might have helped to defeat one main object the Church of Rome had in view in the aggression, namely, the more easy accumulation of property from death-beds. The original draft, after prohibiting, under a penalty of one hundred pounds, the assumption of ecclesiastical titles taken from any place in the united kingdom, except in the case of the dignitaries of the Established Church, went on to declare null and void all deeds executed by persons bearing

the prohibited titles ; and it provided, moreover, that all lega-
cies and gifts bequeathed to persons with such titles, or for
their purposes, should be confiscated to the Crown. Even
had the bill passed with these provisions, so necessary for the
protection of the subject, and especially of the dying Papist,
means would easily have been found to evade it. Simply by
omitting the *quasi* title in a deed of gift, or by substituting
one particle for another,—an *at* for an *of*, for instance,—the
bill would have been rendered inoperative, and the death-bed
of the Papist thrown open to the invasion of the priest. But
before the bill had passed,—indeed, before it had been brought
in,—these clauses were struck out. *

All that now remained of the bill was its opening clause,
forbidding any one to assume an ecclesiastical title taken from
any city, town, or county of the united kingdom, and visit-
ing the offence with the formidable penalty of one hundred
pounds. This was all the fruit of the great agitation which
had prevailed in the country for a full half-year before the
passing of the bill. The act was utterly powerless to prevent the erection of the hierarchy, or to hinder the synodical
action that was meant to follow. The Government believed,
at least they maintained, that synodical action would be impossible under the bill; but obviously and undeniably there
was nothing to prevent Dr Wiseman changing *of* into *at*, and
assembling his suffragans in synod the very next day. The
bill did not deal with the cardinalate,—the first, the most
offensive, and the most easily disposed of part of the affair. A
prince of another State, he was permitted to reside and to
exercise dominion, in the name of a foreign potentate, in the
Queen's dominions. The Papal machinery imported with

* This year, 1865, the Lord Chancellor of Ireland has declared a legacy
illegal for the support of two Dominican priests, on the ground that by
this Act (which is in substance that of 10 Geo. IV.), it was illegal for
any of the order of Dominicans, &c. to come into Great Britain or Ireland. The same would apply to Romish Ecclesiastical Titles.

the Cardinal, or to be imported in years to come, into the
country, could be worked without check or challenge. What,
then, had the country gained by the bill of the Government?
It had gained this, and only this,—that as soon as the measure should have become law, Dr Wiseman would be obliged
to subscribe himself Archbishop *at* Westminster, instead of
Archbishop *of* Westminster.   Practically the country has
not gained even this small advantage; for, slight as was the
change required to satisfy the law, Dr Wiseman did not put
himself to the trouble of making it.   He has gone on from
that day to this subscribing himself Archbishop *of* Westminster; and his suffragans have followed his worthy example, just as if no Ecclesiastical Titles Act were in existence.   We do not recollect a single attempt on the part of
Government to put in force their own act.   It was passed,
put upon the statute-book, and there the matter ended.

    Had the Papal aggression taken place in the times of the
Commonwealth,—an occurrence which it is not easy to conceive of as happening while the Lord Oliver was at Whitehall,
—Cromwell would not have so dallied with it.   The Cardinal
would never have been permitted to see his brave see of Westminster.   His red hat, if not hung up at his point of de-
barkation, as a terror to all similar invaders of the nation's
independence in time to come, would, ere two hours had
elapsed, have been hurried across the Channel.   Admiral
Blake would have been under weigh for Civita Vecchia; a
battalion of Ironsides would have demanded explanations in
the Vatican, and, if they found them unsatisfactory, they
would to a certainty have brought the Pontiff, not as Lord
Campbell, in a figure, but in actual fact, to answer in his
own proper person before Cromwell's Lord Chief Justice;
and they might have brought away, at the same time, Peter's
chair, deeming it likely that there was no farther use for it
at Rome, and that its more appropriate place was the British

Museum, alongside the great bull of Nineveh and other kindred curiosities.

We live in a different age. Still, betwixt what would certainly have been the decisive and summary proceeding of the statesmen of Queen Elizabeth or of Cromwell, and the abortive expedient of the British Government in our day, there was room, surely, for a measure which, without trenching on conscience, would have vindicated the independence of the nation, and shielded the Queen from the traffickings of the Pope and the Cardinal.

Meanwhile Wiseman stood firm. The realm of England appeared to rock to and fro beneath him : still he moved not. Nay, when the storm was at its loudest, he found courage to speak a few quiet but very daring words. He knew well how unflinching the spirit, and how immoveable the purpose, of Her who stood behind him. He had also taken the measure, with tolerable accuracy, of the sincerity and strength of those who brandished their weapons in front. He waited, therefore, until the storm should subside, that he might go on with his work.

Thus did the trumpet summon the nation to a battle which, alas ! never has been fought. The noise we made but deceived ourselves : it did not deceive Rome.

THE EMPIRE WITHIN THE EMPIRE.

WHEN the earthquake had subsided, and the ground, which had heaved like the ocean in a storm while the shock lasted, was again still, the Cardinal proceeded with his edifice. The severe but short-lived hurricane had taught him a lesson, which he was wise enough not to disregard. He occupied himself heart and hand with his work ; but, if he laboured as energetically as ever, he said less about it than before.

He no longer proclaimed what he was doing from the house-
top. The building prospered none the less that it proceeded
in silence.

The materials of which the new Roman edifice in Great
Britain was to be constructed were already all fashioned.
The great stones with which this second Pantheon (for the
Reformation had thrown down the first) was to be reared
had been blocked and chiselled by the cunning artificers of
other days. They lay ready to the Cardinal's hand in the
great quarries of the Pontifical theology and casuistry ; and
all that Wiseman had to do was to send and fetch them, and
pile them one upon the other, according to the instructions
for that end framed by the great builders of this and of former
ages. There was no need to alarm any one by a noise of
axes and hammers. Like a temple of a very different sort,
erected in early times, the Cardinal's building rose in silence.
We pray our readers to lend us their understandings, while
we try to describe to them the fashion of the house, the
height of its walls, its length and its breadth, its going out
and its coming in.

The real object and aim of the Papal aggression plainly,
as briefly stated by Cardinal Wiseman, was to introduce
CANON LAW. This announcement awakened little alarm,
for this reason, that its real significance was scarce perceived.
The sound struck upon the nation's ear, but the sense failed
to reach its understanding. Had the Cardinal said that he
came to claim pontifical jurisdiction over every baptized person in Great Britain, and to compel submission, in time
convenient, by fine, by imprisonment, and by death, the announcement would have startled us. Or even had he said
that he came to introduce into England the common law of
the Roman States, first over a sixth or so of her Majesty's
subjects, and ultimately, as he hoped, over them all, the intimation would have awakened our fears. But the Cardinal

warily avoided a plainness of speech that would have been
so very dangerous. He quietly let fall, as if they had been
words of course, the harmless intimation, as it seemed, that
he had come to inaugurate canon law.

Canon law, it was believed by most, was a purely spiritual
code, noways different from the disciplinary rules of other
dissenting bodies, and would, just as little as theirs, interfere
with the prerogatives of the sovereign and the rights of the
subject. Can there, it was asked, be greater danger to Liberty in the Church of Rome carrying out her discipline, than
there is in the Protestant Church carrying out hers? If it
shall be found, it was further argued, that there is a civil
element in canon law, which will bring it into conflict with
the Constitution of the country, how easy will it be for us to
confront and repel that element by the application of the law
of the land! Surely the ghostly authority of the Cardinal
can be no match for the material and temporal power of the
kingdom. If the Cardinal directs the conscience, we govern
the body. His hat cannot overtop Victoria's crown, and
canon law must go down before British law. We had the
Church of Rome in the country before : we have that Church
in the country still ; only her bishops, instead of pretending
to govern us from Babylon, or from Trachonitis, or from
some other far-off, and, it may be, fabulous region, have now
done us the honour of assuming the designations of our own
cities. So did the most part reason ; and, reasoning thus,
they felt very much at ease in prospect of the new regime :
another example of that security which arises from ignorance.

It is to be feared that our people still very imperfectly
understand the tremendous inroad that is made upon our
Constitution, when a Romish bishop presumes to assume the
title of an English prelate. We have not the slightest objection to a Romish bishop as such. Roman Catholics are,

and have long been, as much entitled to have their bishops
as the Church of England and Ireland to have hers. Further,
too, they are quite at liberty to style themselves, if they
please, Roman Catholic bishops in Liverpool, Birmingham,
or elsewhere ; but when Dr Ullathorne starts up Lord
Bishop of Birmingham, he assumes a title which only the
Queen can bestow, and with it a legislative function which
no sovereign can bestow without the sanction of Parliament.
The Queen herself cannot create new bishoprics ; for the
simple reason that, according to the English Constitution,
they govern in spiritual things the diocese over which they
are placed. They exercise magisterially spiritual powers, and
are, indeed, entitled, with the exception of the junior bishop,
to a seat in the House of Lords. When, therefore, Dr Ullathorne proclaims himself, or, which is the same thing, permits
Roman Catholics to proclaim him, to the world as Lord Bishop
of Birmingham, he means to inform us that he has a full
right to the territorial government of Birmingham in spiritual
things. The law by which he has a right to govern is the
canon law of Rome ; and it is thus he gives us the polite information, that he hopes and intends one day to take under-
neath his fostering wing not only the clergy and laity of the
Church of England, but the congregation of the revered Angell
James, those of the Wesleyan ministers, the Scotch churches,
and all other heretics, of whatsoever name.

If we had weighed the real significance of the Cardinal's
words, we would have been the better able to gauge the quiet
but irresistible power that lay hid in his acts : we would have
seen that the Church of Rome in Great Britain had undergone a great transformation ; that it was no longer what it
had been for a century and more ; and that the Cardinal had
deposited at the bottom of it a principle which necessitated
that from that day forward it should grow, should encroach,
and should at last precipitate itself in open conflict upon

British liberty and law. The die had been cast as regarded the future relations of his Church to the empire of Great Britain. The truce which had lasted for a hundred and sixty years betwixt the two was at an end ; and war was again proclaimed.

Now, we pray the reader to pause and reflect. What is there wanting here which a temporal kingdom should possess ? We do not say a spiritual kingdom. We affirm that here we have the entire organization of a temporal dominion set up on British soil, and alongside the throne of our Queen. We have, in the first place, a *king ;* we have, in the second place, a *law ;* and we have, in the third place, a pretty numerous body of *subjects.* A king, a law, subjects : this is a kingdom.

We grant all this, say some ; but then, is not this just what may be said of any other Church or ecclesiastical body in the country ? Have not they a king or head ? Have not they disciplinary rules, or a law? And do not their members or subjects in some cases amount to millions ? Is the Church of Rome any more an empire within an empire than they are ? It is at this point that men go wrong. It is at this point that Rome comes in with her great deception ; and, imposing on men by that deception, she proceeds, unchallenged by us, nay, even with our aid, to introduce a *civil* element into the nation, and to erect a temporal kingdom, which insults the independence of the country, and, by silent and subtle means, undermines its liberties. Her political aims are masked by spiritual pretences, and pushed forward by spiritual agencies. That renders them the more formidable. Her true character, nevertheless, is of easy demonstration, would men only admit what is demonstrated to them. Rome wields a vast power of deception ; but the better half of that power lies in the fact that men are so willing to be deceived. Great is her adroitness, perfect her jugglery, con-

summate her craft.   Still, it were easy to unmask that craft,
to lay bare that jugglery, to defeat and disarm that adroitness, were men but willing to listen to proof, or ready to
follow up what is proved by corresponding action.

Once for all, we say, so far as Rome is a Church, let us
tolerate her : so far as she is a monarchy, let us resist her,—
in the name of liberty let us resist her, and by every means
in our power.   This, as it appears to us, is our true ground
as citizens.

As Christians, our relations to Rome are somewhat different.   In our character of Christians, we are bound to resist
even what is spiritual in Romanism.   Rome is, and these
twelve hundred years has been, the grand opponent of the
blessed gospel.   Its Author she affronts, and the souls of
men she destroys.   We cannot therefore, without heinous
guilt, view with indifference the continuance of such a system, much less its progress.   And just in proportion as we
love the souls of men shall we with earnestness and vigour
oppose that which destroys them.   But to do so by pains and
penalties were persecution.   It were bootless, as well as tyrannical.   The spiritual can be resisted only by the spiritual.
However erroneous we may deem the opinion of the Papist,
he has the most incontestible right to hold it, so far as man
and human governments are concerned.   We have no more
right to forbid to him a belief in any one of the dogmas of
his Church, from the Immaculate Conception downwards,
than he has to enforce such a belief upon us.   Up to the
point where he encroaches on the rights of others, or invades
the statutory liberties of the country, he may profess and worship as he pleases, without challenge from man.   If we combat
his errors, it must be with argument only.   It is with the
light that we can make war upon the darkness.

But as citizens our conduct must be regulated by other
considerations.   Our first duty in our character of citizens is

the safety of the State.   We are solemnly bound to conserve
its independence, to protect its liberties, and to uphold unim-
paired and whole the authority of its Sovereign.   If a jurisdiction is introduced which strikes at the jurisdiction of the
Queen and the independence of the nation, in fact, ignores
both,—it matters not by whom, nor under what specious
pretexts and disguises,—the loyal subject has but one course
left him: he must resist by the means competent to him as
a citizen; that is, he must meet the political attack by a political defence.   He betrays his country, and he violates the
fealty he owes to his Sovereign, if he does not.   He connives
at invasion: he becomes a traitor to liberty.

But the Court of the Vatican has made such an invasion.
It has installed in Great Britain another king; it has proclaimed over the nation another law; that king and that
law claiming, not simply jurisdiction over the souls of *all
baptized persons* in Great Britain, but also a divine and infallible right to define their duties as subjects, to control their
actions as citizens, and to dispose of their goods on the plea
of religious obligation; forbidding all appeal from its enactments, and declaring null and void all authority whatever—
whether that of Queen, or Parliament, or magistrate—which
shall interfere with its decisions; and it is proceeding to
gather under the wing of its alien jurisdiction a large body
of subjects, all of whom own the validity of its authority, and
yield themselves to it, so far as the yet superior power of
British law will permit them.   This is not a Church: this
is a monarchy, established, no doubt, under spiritual pretences, and by spiritual weapons, but not a whit less political
on that account.   Shall we permit this alien kingdom to grow
up before our eyes?   The least we can demand in regard to
it is, first, that so far as it is political, we shall resist it by
legislative means; and, second, that so far as it is spiritual,
we shall refrain from endowing it.   If we do the latter, we

.in against God : if we neglect the former, we sin against our country.

Let us sketch a little more in detail the organization and growth of this new Roman kingdom.

THE KING OF THE NEW KINGDOM.

In giving a rapid sketch of the Roman kingdom which is rising amongst us, our first attention is due, of course, to its king. He does not, indeed, bear the name, but most assuredly he assumes the office. Nor does he wear a crown: his symbol of authority is a red hat. He announced his advent amongst us, like other sovereigns, by the use of the royal pronoun; and he opened his mission in terms right royal and imperial. "We govern, and shall continue to govern," said this potentate in scarlet and fine linen, as he stepped upon the shores of a country which he deemed much more his Master's than the Queen's.

But Cardinal Wiseman* is but a sovereign-depute. Behind him stands the Pontiff. Pius IX., the king of the Roman States, is present with us in the person of Cardinal Wiseman. He is the real head of the new kingdom which is rising on the soil of Great Britain. The power by which it is upheld, and the authority by which it is ruled, emanate from him, and are his; and every subject of that kingdom, looking beyond the Cardinal, recognises in the Pontiff his supreme lawgiver and king. But inasmuch as the Cardinal is more immediately before us, and is the ostensible head of this kingdom, we shall give to him the prominence, in our observations

* Since this chapter was written, Cardinal Wiseman is dead. No doubt we shall be favoured with another Cardinal. It is therefore unnecessary to change the name, which would occasion some delay.

upon the nature and arrangements of this new and rival monarchy in Great Britain.

The first question here is, Who is Cardinal Wiseman, and what is his rank? The man himself is an ecclesiastic, but his rank and title as Cardinal are purely temporal. He is a senator of Rome, a member of the Electoral College, a prince of the Roman States, and, last and highest of all, having regard to his status in our country, as that status is viewed at Rome, he is the representative of the Sovereign of the Roman States.

The next question is, What kind of authority is it which he exercises in our country, and from what source does he draw it? Is it the case with the Cardinal, as with every other judge, magistrate, and official in the realm, that he derives his authority from the Queen, and that he exercises it in subordination to the law of the land, and is amenable to that law? It is not so. The Cardinal's authority is drawn avowedly from a foreign source,—that source the sovereign of another State; and it is wielded without subordination to the Queen or to the law. The Cardinal is accountable to the Pontiff, and to the Pontiff alone. He is an independent ruler in the realm. As Cardinal, he knows neither Queen nor law. He is a vice-king in the right of his designation by the Pope.

But may it not be said that the supreme courts of judicature in the various religious bodies exercise a jurisdiction which, like that of the Cardinal, is not drawn from the Queen, and is not amenable to the law? There is a wide difference betwixt the two cases, which we pray our readers to ponder. The jurisdiction of these bodies has its source *within* the kingdom: the source of the Cardinal's jurisdiction is *without*. These bodies exercise a purely *spiritual* jurisdiction: the full half of the Cardinal's is *temporal*. The jurisdiction of these bodies is an integral part of the *Constitution*, and is accord-

ant with the *law* of the land, inasmuch as it is based upon
the Bible, which is part—indeed, the most fundamental part
—of the Constitution of the realm and its statutory law.
The Cardinal ignores our Constitution, our law, and our Bible,
and knows only the *ex cathedra* edicts of the Popes, dead and
living,—the canon law. Our spiritual courts submit their
sentences, as regards their civil effects, to the revisal of the
civil courts, to which they themselves are amenable in all
things civil,—rendering to Cæsar the things that are Cæsar's,
and to God the things that are God's. The Cardinal knows
no distinction of things : his jurisdiction confounds all, and
subjects all to the Pontiff, who is to him God on earth. The
members of our religious courts have each of them sworn
allegiance to the Queen, and are her subjects. The Cardinal
has sworn unconditional allegiance to the Pope, and therefore can in no true sense be a subject of the Queen or a
member of the nation ; and if, meanwhile, he must in some
respects act as if he were, he submits himself to the "powers
that be," not "for conscience' sake," but "for wrath's sake."
His acts of submission are done virtually under protest.

So full, independent, and supreme is the authority which
has been arrogated, and is now being exercised, by the new
king, who has set up his throne by the side of that of our
Queen, and is creating a Roman kingdom in the heart of
the British one. Accordingly, his first act, as we have seen,
was an exercise of that royal supremacy which the nation
has vested in the Sovereign, whereby he declared void all
the ecclesiastical arrangements of the kingdom, and annulled all ecclesiastical titles and offices, creating others in their
room, in virtue of his own plenary supremacy, given him by
the Pontiff.

The position of the Cardinal at the head of the Roman
body in Great Britain has accomplished not merely a change
on the exterior relations of that Church, but a change also,

of no little importance, in her internal structure and working. Formerly the Popish community in our country was governed by bishops. Being without a head, their action was spasmodic and fitful, and not unfrequently conflicting. But this evil has now been cured by the substitution of a prince of the Roman States, in whom the whole authority of the Roman Church in Britain is centred, and by whom its whole action is wielded. The Cardinal is the Pope's *alter ego*: he speaks and acts with the weight of Peter himself; thus bearing down all opposition, extinguishing all division, and giving greater combination and power to the Roman Church than it has had for centuries, or perhaps than it ever had; seeing the kingdom in our day is more open than in almost any former age to the free importation of Romanism in both its spirit and its edicts. In the Cardinal, Rome has been brought to Westminster, Peter's chair has been set up in Great Britain, and the Vatican has been transferred from the Tiber to the Thames. The old spasmodic and divided action of the Roman Church amongst us has been replaced by an action that is steady and systematic, and which is skilfully directed upon one great and well-defined object, namely, the seizure of the country, together with the appropriation of its wealth, and the prostitution of its power, to the Pontifical See.

If it be good that we should serve a foreign priest, let us no longer be the subjects of Queen Victoria. We may be well assured that both we cannot serve. If slavery be the better part, let us be slaves. But if we prefer to be ruled by the Sovereign of our own choice, and to be judged by the law of our own making, then let us halt no longer betwixt two masters. Let us be a little more decided, and dally no longer with our Queen's prerogatives and our own liberties.

F.

THE TWELVE THRONES.

In speaking of the new monarchy that is growing apace amongst us, we have given, as was right, precedence to its monarch; and now it is fitting that we should speak of his inferior rulers. In Cardinal Wiseman we behold the great apostle of this second planting of the Church in Britain. But the Cardinal did not come alone : he was attended by a goodly following of twelve suffragans, who were to take part with him in this great work. These are the princes of his kingdom : these are the apostles whom he and his master have appointed to sit on thrones, judging the twelve tribes or dioceses into which the nation has been divided. Thus has the new kingdom received at once unity and diffusion : unity in the Cardinal ; diffusion in the twelve suffragan bishops.

The twelve territorial bishops form an organic machinery, which renders the now centralized authority of the Roman Church practically available for the government of Romanists in our country. The grand object of the Propaganda in the erection of territorial dioceses, and the appointing of a bishop over each, with jurisdiction, was "synodical action." This was much insisted upon at the time. It was pleaded in defence of the Papal aggression, because, without bishops with territorial status and titles, synods could not, according to the rules of the Church of Rome, be convened, and without provincial synods the government of the Church could not be carried on. The real drift of "synodical action," and especially its bearing on the independence of the nation, was not then very clearly perceived ; but events have since helped to make it exceedingly plain. Provincial synods are holden ; they pass decrees touching the government of their Church ; these decrees are sent to Rome ; at Rome they receive the sanction of the Pope ; and, when so ratified, they are returned to Great Britain, having all the authority of Papal bulls.

The monthly importation of bulls from Rome, and their public proclamation in the country, would have awakened alarm, would have raised troublesome questions, and might have led eventually to the revival of some of the old securities against the traffickings of foreign priests ; but these difficulties are dexterously avoided by the contrivance of synodical synods, whose edicts, ratified by the Pope, are, in fact, Papal bulls, and, as such, receive implicit submission from the conscience of every Papist. There is thus established a great manufactory of Roman law on the soil of Great Britain.

Should we grant that these resolutions, passed in synod, and afterwards ratified at Rome, are mainly about spiritual matters, it is nevertheless true that they are spiritual in such a way as to imply the control of the body and the disposal of the goods of the Romanist. In truth, these synods charge themselves with the regulation of all matters appertaining to their flocks as a social and political community. For instance, they can place certain classes of schools under ban, or enjoin certain modes of political action on their followers. It is about such matters, much more frequently than about matters of faith, that these synods legislate. And thus, under the modest name of "synodical action," a new order of judges and courts is springing up, exercising a species of hybrid rule, partly spiritual and partly temporal, over a large portion of those who ought to be her Majesty's subjects, but who, in fact, are the subjects of Cardinal Wiseman. Thus is the wedge being silently introduced which is intended to withstand the authority of British law, and to rend in twain the British nation.

We have already explained the change which passed upon the Popish Church in Britain at the period of the Papal ag-

gression.   From the Reformation downwards that Church
had existed amongst us as a missionary institute : in 1850
she ceased to be a *mission*, and became a *Church*,—a Church
with as complete an organization, and as plenary an authority, as in Austria or in Spain, or even in Italy.   A few
words will make the nature of the change very plain, and
bring out at the same time its bearing on the country.   The
Pope's division of the globe is exceedingly simple and compendious.   In the first place, the whole world is his ; for
" the earth and the fulness thereof " has the Father given to
the Son ; and " the earth and the fulness thereof " has the Son
given to the Pope, his vicar.   Looking down upon it from
the Seven Hills, he sees that part of the world owns his sway,
and that part disowns it.   The first he calls Christendom ;
the second he styles Heathendom.   Corresponding to this
division of mankind, he has two sets of bishops.   He has territorial bishops for the Christian portion of the earth, where
his sway is owned ; and he has bishops *in partibus* for the
pagan and infidel portion of it, where his sway is rejected.
Previous to the Papal aggression he sent us bishops *in partibus*, which was a clear token that he regarded us as forming
no part of the holy land of Catholicism, but that, on the contrary, he viewed us as dwelling afar in those gloomy regions
where the light of the Vatican has not yet shone, and the
apostolic foot of territorial bishop has not yet come.   Here
our portion had been assigned us with pagans and unbelievers.   But, now that the Pontiff has sent us bishops with
territorial status and titles, it is an equally clear token that
he regards us as rescued from our deplorable estate, as brought
into the clear light of Catholicism, as annexed to the Christian division of the world, and as sharing equally with other
Christian lands in the undoubted privileges, and the yet
more undoubted obligations, of government by canon law.
At Rome, then, the aggression is viewed as embracing not

merely our souls, but also our bodies, nay, as extending to the very soil of our country.

The Pope, then, has resumed, in all its fulness, his supremacy over our country. Already we have tasted its sweets in the partitioning of our land, in the appointing of judges, and in the erection of courts to administer his temporal and spiritual jurisdiction. His government extends *de facto* over those who own his sway; it extends *de jure* over every baptized man and woman in England. In a hundred points will his rule conflict with the Queen's. In questions touching education, marriage, wills, mortmain, and a great variety of other matters, will the pontifical tribunals come into collision with the British courts; in many cases openly, but in a great many more privately and secretly. We shall have a continual battle betwixt the two jurisdictions. We shall have a persistent invasion upon the one authority by the other. Quiet the nation will not be permitted to know. Its patience will be exhausted and its spirit broken by ceaseless and bitter wranglings. It will be disturbed and agitated by never-ending strivings for authority and rule betwixt two empires, which will be seen struggling for predominance, where one only ought to reign in peace.

THE LAW OF THE NEW KINGDOM.

THE next question touching the new kingdom is, By what law are its affairs administered and its subjects governed? We answer, by CANON LAW,—"the real and perfect code of the Church," as Dr Wiseman styled it.

It is essential to the right understanding of our subject that we form a clear notion of canon law. It is the heart of the Papal aggression; it is the soul of the new empire; and as is the law, so will be the kingdom which will spring

from it. A glimpse into canon law will show us how largely
the Papal aggression was political, and how inevitably its development must fill and absorb the whole realm of Britain,
expelling all, annihilating all, and becoming the one sole,
all-controlling power in the country.

The two grand characteristics of canon law are, first, it is
an infallible code. It is not merely infallible : it is the one
infallible authority in the world. All other codes are subordinate to it, and must be modified by it. The Bible itself
is to be interpreted according to it. It is the organ through
which an infallible Church speaks to the Papist. The voice
of canon law is to him the voice of God. It governs his
conscience with the power of omnipotence.

The second characteristic of canon law is, that it is the
code of a body whose head is as really a temporal as a spiritual prince. Being the common law of the Roman States,
—for none other is there known,—it must necessarily rule
as well political and social rights as religious, and be the measure, not of spiritual privileges only, but of temporal also.
It must apply to all matters that appertain to men as citizens as well as Church members; in short, it must take
under its one compendious jurisdiction all that in other
countries is embraced under two,—the spiritual and the temporal, to wit. This, indeed, is the fact. Cardinal Wiseman
came to inaugurate, not a part only, but the whole, of this
code ; for it cannot be cut in two. It is easy, then, to conceive how much homage is left to the Queen, and how much
obedience is reserved to the law, on the part of a community
placed under a code which requires of them that they shall
love and serve their Lord and Sovereign the Pope with all
their heart, and all their conscience, with the unqualified devotion of their persons, and the unlimited surrender of their
goods.

Keeping these two characteristics of canon law in eye,

let us next inquire what is the range over which its authority extends. As laid down by Popish jurists, canon law embraces three departments:—1, Doctrine; 2, Morals; 3, Discipline. There is not much in these words to alarm one. But let us weigh well their import. The Roman Church has a wonderful faculty for embodying the hardest meanings in the mildest terms. Let us lift up our eyes, and survey, in the length thereof and the breadth thereof, the territory over all of which canon law is the one supreme, infallible authority. It is, in truth, a territory wholly without limits.

The first department is doctrine. Canon law infallibly prescribes what the Romanist is to believe. With this, it may be said, we as Protestants have nothing to do. We therefore pass it, and proceed to the second department,—Morals, to wit. By morals, Roman theologians mean absolutely all actions whatever. Protestant divines are accustomed to distinguish, under the head of morals, betwixt offences which a man may commit as a citizen, and faults which he may be guilty of as a Church member,—betwixt crimes which are punishable by the civil authority, and sins which fall under the jurisdiction and discipline of the ecclesiastical judicature. The jurists of the Church of Rome ignore this distinction. They include under morals all actions, of whatever kind, which a man, in whatever capacity or relation, can do ; and therefore in every action they hold him amenable to the Church's discipline. From every action, say they, there flow good or evil consequences to the Church ; and therefore over every action of man it is requisite that the Church should stretch her disciplinary control. To canon law,—that is, to the priest who administers it,—it appertains to say to what school a man is to send his child ; with whom his son or daughter is to contract marriage ; with whom he is to buy and sell ; what opinions he is to hold on all political and social questions ; what party he is to sup-

port by his vote ; when he may obey the law peaceably, and
when he must meet it with riot and insurrection ; when he
may account the sovereign of the country in which he resides
legitimate, and when he must hold his title invalid ; and,
especially if he be a rich man, does it minutely instruct him
in all matters appertaining to a death-bed, not unfrequently,
as the widow and the orphan have cause to know, adding to
its letter of direction the personal and watchful superintend-
ence of its priests.   There is not, from the cradle to the grave,
an act done by the man, or an office filled by him, in which
canon law does not come in with its infallible supervision
and control.

The third department embraced by canon law is Discipline.   Discipline is a mild term.   It signifies in the Protestant sense only spiritual inflictions ; but in the Roman Church
it has terrors unknown to us.   The theory of the Church of
Rome under the head of Discipline is, that the Church, being a perfect and complete society, must possess within herself everything necessary for the ends of government.   But
the power of punishing breaches of its law, the power of re-
straining and coercing refractory members, is necessary to
these ends ; and therefore this power the Church must possess.

No doubt, the Protestant Church says, in terms, the same
thing.   She equally holds that the power of discipline is inherent in her as an independent spiritual society, and that its
exercise is essential to her welfare.   The difference lies in
the *discipline* exercised.   The Protestant Church holds that
this punitive power must, like the Church herself, be exclusively, and in every case, spiritual.   Not so holds the Church
of Rome.   Rarely indeed are her sentences, even in their
form, exclusively spiritual ; and in no case do they end within
the spiritual sphere.   They always embody a civil element ;
they almost always inflict a corporal and temporal penalty ;
and they are ever, when resistance is offered, to be carried

out by the civil arm. That Church accounts it not enough
to warn, exhort, rebuke, and, in extreme cases, to visit with
deprivation of spiritual privileges. Her discipline runs on
through the ascending stages of fine, imprisonment, confiscation of goods, loss of political and social rights, up to its last
and extremest penalty, which is death by burning. In the
rear of her Church courts stands an array of physical penalties,—the rack, the dungeon, and the scaffold. Such is the
ecclesiastical discipline of Rome. Such is her ecclesiastical
discipline as prescribed in the canon law, as exercised in its
whole extent at this hour in the Roman States, as exercised
in France, and Spain, and other Popish countries, to all the
extent to which Rome has been able to extort permission by
her concordats ; and such is the discipline under which the
whole Romanist body in Great Britain has now been placed,
to its whole extent *in theory,* and to an extent *in fact* that
is already large, and is daily widening.

This makes sufficiently plain what is, and only can be, the
real position of the Romanist body in Great Britain. They
are under canon law ; and by that law they are cut off and
separated from all around them. The moral force of all other
authority and law is completely evacuated as regards them.
They form absolutely, in political as really as in religious
matters, a distinct and different community. There are two
nations on the soil of Britain : Queen Victoria the sovereign
of the one ; Cardinal Wiseman, as the representative of the
Pope, the sovereign of the other.

It may be said, intolerable as is the slavery of canon law,
still, if the members of the Church of Rome are willing to
bear that yoke, it is no right or duty of ours to object to
their doing so : grievous as this bondage is, it does not affect
us. This is a view of the case wholly fallacious. For, first,
the very proximity of slavery is dangerous to liberty. The
glacier, amid the sunshine and flowers of a Swiss valley, gives

an icy chill to the air, and dwarfs surrounding vegetation.
So great an organized system of slavery, mental and bodily,
on the free soil of Britain, as we now unhappily have in the
case of the restored hierarchy, must necessarily cool down the
political and social atmosphere, and, by familiarizing us with
the spectacle of bondage, must, insensibly it may be, but not
the less really, blunt our nice appreciation of liberty, and
tend to make us less jealous of our rights, and less prompt
in repelling aggression upon them.   This we hold to be no
small evil, even though we had ample guarantees that in all
time coming the operation of canon law should be restricted
to the members of the Church of Rome.

But the authors of the Papal aggression are at no pains to
conceal, that neither on the ground of expediency nor on the
ground of duty can they consent that the operation of canon
law, and the pontifical supremacy founded thereon, should be
confined within the narrow limits of their own community.
They plainly enough avow that their object and aim is to
make canon law universal,—that they will not rest till it
has become the one code of the empire, and till the supremacy of Queen Victoria has been displaced *de facto*, as they
already hold it to be *de jure*, by the supremacy of the Pontiff.   This is the only logical issue of the Papal aggression ;
and stop it possibly cannot, nor is it intended that it should,
till it has reached this issue.   Towards this issue have its
promoters been pushing it with an adroitness as logical as
it is persistent, and with a most unscrupulous and daring
courage.   Their efforts have been crowned with a success
which is as encouraging to them as it is formidable to us.
They are nearing the goal day by day ; and from one year
to another the great kingdom of Papal bondage is spreading
wider, and waxing higher, in the midst of the free kingdom
of Great Britain.

Let us suppose that the Emperor of France sends across a

marshal of the empire to inaugurate the Code Napoleon, and form a little community of Frenchmen in Great Britain, and that, for the better effectuating of his design, he partitions the country, and appoints an inferior officer in each district, with power to hold courts, and administer the new code to all who wish to enjoy its benefits. And let us suppose farther, that the marshal admits into this "little France" not only all born Frenchmen, but persons of British birth willing to be denaturalized, and to make profession of Voltairianism. Or let us suppose that the Czar of Russia deputes a grandee of his kingdom to inaugurate " Peter's Testament," and form a "little Muscovy" on British soil, under the modest pretence of being simply a Church of the Greek rite. Or that the Sultan of Constantinople should commission to Britain a chief mufti, with a tail of twelve suffragan muftis, to form a community owning and obeying only the law of the Mohammedan empire, but professing all the while to be a company of the "faithful," who swear by Allah, and believe that Mahomet is his prophet. Would we have any difficulty in seeing what was meant in these supposed cases ? Should we not quickly distinguish betwixt the belief of Voltairianism and the Code Napoleon,—betwixt the Greek rite and the rule of the Czar,—betwixt the faith of the Prophet and the government of the Prophet's successor ? In vain would the one plead his descent from " James," and the other his commission from " Gabriel." In the name neither of apostle nor of angel should we permit the independence of the country to be attacked. There is not a particle of essential difference betwixt the cases we have supposed and the Papal aggression ; nor is it a whit more difficult to distinguish—were we but willing to make the distinction—betwixt the *religion* of the Pope and the *authority* of the Pope. The religion of the Pope, like the religion of the Prophet, is still one of the superstitions of the world. The one superstition as well as

the other will invade our country and find adherents. These
we must tolerate. But the authority of the Pope, which
canon law has imported whole and entire, is a different affair.
It we cannot recognise : it we cannot endow. To endow, or
even to recognise it, is to betray the independence of the
nation and the sovereignty of the Queen.

CANON LAW VERSUS BRITISH LAW; OR, A BATTLE FOR MAGNA CHARTA.

CANON law, then, bears on its front a claim, in the Pope's
behalf, of a supreme, a universal, and a divine sovereignty.
This sovereignty embraces both the spiritual and the temporal jurisdictions. To be sure, there is a distinction here
in law, but not in fact,—a distinction all but unknown to
canon law, though maintained by modern canonists, between
the spiritual and temporal jurisdictions, which go to make up
the one supreme, irresponsible, and infallible sovereignty of
the Pontiff, of which it is but fair to give our opponents the
benefit. His spiritual jurisdiction he possesses and exercises,
say such, *directly:* his temporal jurisdiction he possesses and
exercises *indirectly.* But even these writers admit that the
Pontiff's supreme spiritual power extends to all temporal
matters which involve *duty;* and as there is no matter in
which duty is not involved, so there is no matter into which
the Pontiff's power does not penetrate, and which falls not
within his *indirect* temporal jurisdiction.

The Pope, then, according to canon law, and even according to the admission of recent jurists, is the temporal as well
as spiritual chief of the world. He is the one sovereign, and
all other sovereigns can claim only those prerogatives, and
exercise only those powers, which are compatible with the
supreme, the all-comprehending, and divine sovereignty of

the Pontiff. Canon law saith expressly, "the constitutions
of princes are not superior to ecclesiastical constitutions, but
subordinate to them; and still more plainly, "the Emperor
ought to obey, not command, the Pope." As the power of
a chieftain over his clan is necessarily regulated by the paramount jurisdiction of the sovereign, who can absolve them
from their obligation of feudal service to their immediate superior, so canon law gives consistently to the Pope an analogous power. "The Bishop of Rome," it says, "may excommunicate emperors and princes, depose them from their
States, and assoil their subjects from their oath of obedience
to them." In Reiffenstuel's Text-book on the Canon Law,
published at Rome in 1831, it is stated, "The Pope, as
Vicar of Christ on earth, and Universal Pastor of his sheep,
has indirectly a certain supreme power, for the good estate of
the Church, if it be necessary, *of judging and disposing of
all the temporal goods of all Christians.*" This is very plain.
That the Popes understood canon law in its literal meaning,
as conferring upon them a most comprehensive temporal jurisdiction, the whole history of Europe since the tenth century testifies.

What, then, does canon law mean as applied to Great Britain? It means, in the first place, the transference of the
sovereignty of Britain from Queen Victoria to the Roman
Pontiff. It means, in the second place, that the right of
Parliament to legislate, unless in complete subserviency to
every requirement of canon law, shall cease and determine.
It means that priests shall not be amenable to the civil tribunals; and that, when accused of treason, or of murder, or
of any crime whatever, the ecclesiastical courts only shall have
power to try them. It means that the Pope shall be entitled
to appoint to every ecclesiastical living in the country. It
means the restoration of the Church lands, aye, to the very
last acre. It means that Protestantism is punishable with

confiscation of goods, with imprisonment, and, finally, with death, at the hands of the civil magistrate; and that every suspected man shall purge himself to the satisfaction of a severe and vigilant tribunal, or die by fire. It means that those who die not in communion with the Church of Rome shall not have Christian burial.

Canon law, then, though based on a great religious dogma, namely, the Vicarship of the Roman Pontiff, is mainly a civil and political code. The prerogatives it claims are of a civil and temporal kind, namely, supreme jurisdiction over persons and lands. The punishments it inflicts are of a temporal sort,—confiscation of goods, banishment, imprisonment, and death. We hold, then, and we challenge any Romanist to disprove our position, that any society formed on such a basis, and governed by such a code, is not a religious, but a political association; and that the man who attempts to introduce such a law into Britain throws down the gauntlet to the Queen. He, in fact, engages in an open attempt to overthrow the Constitution of the country, and to abrogate all laws, all rights, and all privileges, which do not emanate from canon law. We maintain that the Papal aggression as much contemplates the overthrow of our Constitution, and the subversion of all our liberties, as if the standard of open revolt were unfurled, and arms and armies raised to effect the enterprise. Every man who puts himself under canon law deserts his Queen, throws off the authority of British law, and places himself, body and soul, under a foreign domination.

Such is the constitutional aspect of this question. It is not a question of Church, or a question of creed, but it is a question, first of all, of national independence. It is a trial of strength between the Queen and the Pontiff, which shall govern the realm of England; and no one can make a concession to the Pope without becoming a traitor to the Queen. We are aware that in this light our statesmen have not been

brought to view it, else surely they would not help forward
rebellion.   They persist in looking on the matter simply as
a religious controversy.   Their mistake, however, cannot alter
the nature of the case, which indisputably is an attempt—the
more dangerous since it is covered by religious disguises—
on the part of a foreign power to obtain supreme civil and
spiritual jurisdiction within the realm.   Every favour conferred on the priesthood, every penny given to Maynooth,
is a contribution on the part of the nation to help to overthrow itself.

Some few shreds of British law might remain, such as did
not come into collision with the inexorable claims of canon
law ; but they would be utterly worthless as a defence of
our liberties.   Every jot and tittle of British law not in harmony with the ghostly enactments of canon law would be,
ipso facto, cancelled ; and our noble code would become a
poor, shrivelled, palsied thing, without life or vigour.   Even
if the form of constitutional government were suffered to
exist, and Parliament allowed to assemble, its legislative
functions would be reduced to a dead letter.   It could not
legislate about a college, or a school, or a convent ; it could
not make laws about a new book, or extend a new privilege
to the subject, or impose a new tax, or make a railroad, or
form a treaty with a foreign government, without being told
that in every one of these matters the Church had an interest, and that Parliament must guide itself by canon law, in
other words, surrender the whole legislative powers of the
country into the hands of the Church.   Every social, as well .
as every political right, would come to be regulated by canon
law : our right to educate our families, our right to trade,
our right to speak, to publish, to read, our right to marry,
our right to be buried, would all be regulated by this code,
that is, they would be swept away altogether.   To all this
extent have we seen the Pope attempting to interfere in

Piedmont ; and to all this extent do the concordats framed
with Spain and Portugal, and other Continental States, go.
Those who think that the triumph of Romanism will bring
with it only a few slight changes on the surface of society,
simply labour under a hallucination. No : it will lay the axe
to the root of the British Constitution ; and that noble tree,
which shelters alike the Queen and the peasant, the noble
of Britain in his ancestral hall, and the poor Indian on the
banks of the Ganges, will fall, and at the sound of its fall
the earth will shake.

THE SUBJECTS OF THE NEW KINGDOM.

This, it may be said, is mere abstract law.   Stringent as its
enactments may be, and treasonable as its object undoubtedly is, unless it has some way of embodying itself in fact,
it cannot endanger the rule of the Queen, or destroy the
unity of the nation. So far true. But we ought to bear
in mind, that there is daily growing up in the midst of us
a concrete body, from whom this law receives unquestioning
and implicit obedience.

In ordinary cases the kingdom comes first, and the law
afterwards ; for the law is made for the subjects, and not the
subjects for the law.   But this, which is the natural and
usual order, has been reversed in the case of which we are
speaking. First came the law ; and that law created subjects
for itself.   This order obtained not in the most absolute
sense ; for even before the arrival of the Cardinal from the
Flaminian Gate, nay even before the Emancipation Act of
1829, there was a considerable body of Romanists in the
kingdom, who furnished standing ground to canon law, and
were made the fulcrum on which the lever of the Papal aggression was rested.

But latterly this body has been rapidly increasing in numbers and in strength. This is to be ascribed to a variety of causes : to Anglo-Catholic perversions, to the systematic and skilful working of the Romish hierarchy, and last, but by no means least, to the vast immigration from Ireland. Previous to 1829, Ireland was confined to the western side of St. George's Channel ; and all the Popery, well-nigh, of the British islands was included betwixt the two points of Giant's Causeway and Cape Clear. But since the period of the Emancipation Act, Ireland has burst her bounds, and diffused herself all over Great Britain. Again and again we have seen the gates of the country suddenly open, and its sons issue forth in hundreds of thousands. We have witnessed corresponding transformations, as if by enchantment, in not a few localities of our own country. An Irish town has risen here, and an Irish parish has emerged there. After the fashion of the house of our Lady of Loretto, and it may be by the same agency, whole villages of Irish cabins, with all their accompaniments, have been, as it were, carried across from the wilds of Kerry and the shores of Galway, and safely deposited on this side the Channel. This has happened, in part, we doubt not, at the wish and by the arrangement of the priesthood ; but in still greater part, we are persuaded, it has arisen from causes over which the priesthood had no control, and which neither they nor any one else could have foreseen. But we have to do, not with the cause, but with the fact, of this extraordinary diffusion of the Irish race, and the lasis which it furnishes, so opportunely for Rome, but so disastrously for us, whereon to rear and set a-working the machinery of canon law.

Thus, a great variety of concurrent causes,—famine in Ireland, the railway enterprise of Great Britain, improvements in agriculture, and the increased demand created thereby for unskilled labourers,—legislative measures,—all acting toge-

ther have opened the flood-gates of Romanism, and brought
a deluge over the face of the whole land. No longer is the
Popery of the British islands confined, as it was but a few
years ago, to one division of our empire,—Ireland, to wit.
We now behold a systematic and universal distribution of it
over the three kingdoms. It is encamped in our great cities.
There its adherents are counted in fifties of thousands; and
in some cases, as in the commercial capital of Scotland, and
the great trading and manufacturing cities of England, they
amount to hundreds of thousands. We find the Romanists
in considerable force in all our secondary towns. They form
an item,—in some instances a large one,—in the population
of our rural villages; and they are scattered by twos and
threes of families over many of our rural parishes. These
small outlying colonies, individually viewed, are not formidable; but viewed as parts of an organized body, which one
spirit animates, which one will wields, and which one voice
can on emergency bring into action, their importance is great.
They swell the numbers and augment the power of the aggre-
gate body.   Thus do Roman colonies dot our country, afford-
ing foothold, at every short distance, to canon law.

When we take into account the unchanging character of
the Church to which this vast body, now distributed amongst
us, belongs, the essential antagonism of that Church to free
institutions, the necessity that is laid upon her to wear down,
and ultimately root out, British liberty,—when we think of
the ignorance and turbulence of the Irish Romanists taken
in the mass, the peculiarly malignant type of Irish Popery,
and the use which the Church of Rome in past ages has ever
found for such mobs,—we may well tremble at the danger
to which the order and peace of the nation is exposed.   As
hangs the avalanche on the mountain's brow, or as rested the
sword of Damocles above the head of its victim, so hangs this
formidable body above the nation.   It may not fall imme-

diately, nor for some little time : it must grow as the avalanche grows ; it must rest as the sword of the tyrant rested ; and, while it is waiting its hour, it will toil in our service, and be to the nation a hewer of wood and a drawer of water ; but as certainly as the avalanche descends at last, so swiftly one day will this moral avalanche descend in thundering ruin upon the order, the trade, and the liberty of Great Britain.

Is it we only who say so ? Do not Romanists themselves proclaim the same thing, and openly boast that their adherents are distributed over Britain as soldiers are posted on a battle-field ? In the November following the Papal aggression, Father Ignatius (the Rev. Mr Spencer) perambulated Ireland, addressing large meetings on the conversion of England, the people pressing about him, eager to kiss the hem of his cloak, and share in the virtue of the holy man. Among other inflammatory harangues by which he sought to rouse the hopes and the passions of the Irish Romanists, he was reported as having spoken at Londonderry as follows :—" He assured his audience, in the first place, that if Napoleon had had the advantages enjoyed by the present crusader, he would infallibly have invaded and conquered England. For there are two hundred thousand Irish in London, in a garrison, as it were, impregnably entrenched ; there are eighty thousand in Manchester, the same number in Birmingham, and in other towns in like proportion. Then, in Ireland itself, there is the grand army of six millions,—*God's chosen people.* If Napoleon had had such forces in the enemy's country, would he have hesitated for a moment ? Certainly not."

Father Ignatius was not alone in his sentiment. Others were found, not among the priests only, but even among the laity, as fiery and warlike as the *padre*,—ready, if plots should fail, to propagate their faith by arms. For instance, there was published at the time an extract from a letter from Mr Ambrose Lisle Philips of Grace Dieu, to Lord Shrews-

bury, in which the writer thus expressed himself :—" There
will be no flinching on the side of the Catholic Church."
"The decree of our Holy Father the Pope has gone forth,
and it will be upheld by every faithful Catholic, from the
greatest to the least, though Protestant violence should con-
vulse England to its very centre." "You are on your way
to the holy city. Pray our Holy Father to bestow again
and again his apostolic blessing on his children here, who
are ready to combat for his sacred rights." "The Holy
Father may count upon us : we are the children of the crusaders : we will not falter before the sons of Cranmer and
John Knox." The children of the "crusaders !" This recalls the days of Simon de Montfort, and the frightful tem-
pests which swept the south of France and the valleys of the
Alps, exterminating in blood the Albigensian confessors. It
does not tend to re-assure us, to find the Catholic so fondly
clinging to the hope that the era of the crusades is not yet
closed, that the future will produce its Simon de Montforts,
and that the holocausts of the Alpine valleys may yet be
repeated in the cities of Great Britain. About the same
time, or, to be a little more precise, on the 12th November
1850, a public meeting of the Roman Catholics of Manchester was held, at which, as reported in the prints of that day,
a Mr Henry Turley, who deserved to be made a bishop,
moved, and prevailed on the meeting to adopt, the following
resolution :—" That the Protestant heresy of this country, as
a religion, is dangerous to the peace and morals of society,"
—the very plea on which the Protestantism of five centuries
ago was assailed by the terrible violence on which the Catholic imagination so loves to dwell. The Irish masses lo-
cated in our great towns are Rome's arsenals,—the "treasures
of the hail," which she has "reserved against the time of
trouble, against the day of battle and war."

Some little foretaste have we already had of what this force, that now sleeps so quietly in the midst of us, or rather labours so patiently for us, will do when fairly roused. The riots of Belfast, of Birkenhead, and of Hyde Park, were on a formidable scale. They attacked a right which we had thought was indisputably established, and which no party at this time of day would dare to challenge,—that, namely, of free discussion. They were attended by wrecking, conflagration, and bloodshed; yet were these riots only insignificant and premature skirmishings, compared with what we are fated to see if matters proceed for a few years as at present. We imagine that we have found a mine of wealth in the thews and sinews of the Irish Romanists; but we must be permitted to ask, "Will" this "unicorn be willing to serve thee, or abide by thy crib? Wilt thou trust him because his strength is great? or wilt thou leave thy labour to him? Wilt thou believe him that he will bring home thy seed, and gather it into thy barn? Wilt thou make a covenant with him, and take him for thy servant for ever? Lay thine hand upon him: remember the battle; and do no more."

Most obvious, as well as just, is our punishment herein. Great Britain has treated her sister Ireland very cruelly indeed; and now the cry of her wrongs has gone up to heaven. But in what lay our injustice and cruelty to Ireland? Was it in that we closed for so many years the doors of Parliament against some dozen or score of Popish representatives? Alas for the idea! Our crime has been in that we have left Ireland these two hundred years sitting in darkness; and now that darkness invades our own shores. We might have filled Ireland long ere now from one end to another with light; and how different in that case would her history have been! The genius of her sons, and the vast resources of her soil, would have made her one of the chief glories of the British empire, and one of the main bulwarks of our liberty. Instead of this, her lost millions living in beggary, and, dying in a superstition that hides from them the Saviour, form the opprobrium of British Protestantism. *

Let us bestow a rapid glance on the organization of this force. In our country, as everywhere else where she exists, Rome strives to make visible her presence and power by imposing architectural efforts. Splendid cathedrals are being built in our leading towns. These, of course, will be immediately followed by the formation of chapters, with canons, prebendaries, and so forth. Funds would appear to be easily forthcoming for the erection of these edifices, and the permanent endowment of the foundations connected therewith. The younger sons of the aristocracy will be chosen to fill these stalls, and for two reasons. First, because in this way provision will be made for the lower branches of those families which may be disposed to enrich the Church with the gift of land or money; and, second, because the prestige attaching to the birth and social rank of these officials will be reflected upon the Church herself. As a proselytizing agency, this will possess no small power; for the number of persons is still large who prefer to worship in a gorgeous temple, and to have their devotions led by titled dignitaries in splendid vestments. In his petition to the House of Commons, we find Mr Alfred Smee stating that he had seen his Grace the present heir to the dukedom of Norfolk, with his Grace's brother, assisting, in ecclesiastical garments, in the public performance of services on the 16th July 1863, at the Catholic chapel of the Oratory at Brompton, in conjunction with the

* In the above censure, the author includes all the Protestant Churches of Great Britain. All have been chargeable with a common negligence, and all are now suffering a common infliction. At the same time, the great difficulty of evangelizing Ireland must be borne in mind; with a priesthood always exciting to murderous attacks on the lives of Protestant readers or zealous clergymen, of which a friend of the author's, a clergyman of the Church of England, had ample proofs laid before him while in Ireland a few years ago.

priests of the Oratory, and also subsequently on the same day
at the garden of the house called St. Mary's at Sydenham.
As soon as it shall be lawful for Popish processions to take
place in public, we shall see lords figuring as the train-bearers
of priests, and marchionesses doing duty as the carriers of
lighted candles.

After the cathedral, with its chapter and titled dignitaries,
come the chapel, with its staff of priests. There is scarce a
town of any importance in Great Britain in which there is
not now a Popish congregation. We confine our view to
Scotland, often accounted the most Protestant part of the
three kingdoms. In all our great cities, in all our manufacturing towns, and in many of our rural villages, new Romish
edifices attract the eye, and Popish congregations have been
formed, or are in course of being so. In the town which had
the honour of giving birth to Knox there is now a large Popish
congregation, although only a few years ago there was not a
single Papist in the place. One characteristic of this distribution is specially note-worthy. It centres mostly round
the site of the old cathedrals and abbeys. It would seem
as if a virtue lingered in the old walls, and in the very
soil, which attracts the Romanist, and draws him to the spot
where, three hundred years ago, dwelt his ancestors in the
faith. Of course, the priest is careful to represent himself
and his religion as the lineal descendants of these men, and
the rightful heirs of the possessions of which the Reformation deprived them, unlawfully as he holds. How amply has
this justified the sagacity of the national reformer of Scotland, who, although he did not counsel the pulling down of
these strongholds of superstition, consoled himself for their
loss, when dismantled by an outburst of popular indignation
which he could not control, by saying that, now the nests
were pulled down, the rooks were not so likely to return!
Wherever they were left standing, the rooks have returned,

and are now seen hovering on sable wing around the venerable and ruinous towers which in former ages sheltered the same dark brood.

The Popish congregation once formed, becomes of course the centre of a machinery which acts steadily and systematically upon the surrounding district. There is first the priest. The priest in our country is not the vulgar, illiterate person which he often is in France and Italy, or even in Ireland. In these countries, it is enough that he is a priest: the oil of consecration is to him instead of all other gifts and acquirements. He can awe his flock by his scowl; or, if refractory, he can reduce them to obedience by the rod, and administer discipline with the horsewhip. In our country, on the contrary, and especially in our great cities, he is a man not unfrequently of good address, of fascinating manners, and sometimes of truly amiable and obliging dispositions. He possesses a little knowledge of letters, is well informed on a variety of subjects, and in the drawing-room can talk on works of art, exchange thoughts on politics and business, or retail the gossip of aristocratic families. He ever bears about him a vast profession of charity. There is no character he so much abhors as a bigot: he wonders how such a being can exist in this the nineteenth century; but drop an allusion to Spain and its Bible-readers, and he quickly changes the subject.

In our rural towns he is less a gentleman and more a priest. That man with face so cadaverous, with glance so quick and restless, with foot so stealthy, and whose whole figure conveys the idea of a perpetual struggle on the part of its owner to pass from substance into shadow, and to become viewless as a spirit; or that man of just the opposite type, —large, bulking, with bold defiant face,—is the priest. He may be seen at times hovering on the skirts of a revival meeting, and scaring away some member of his flock who wishes to place himself within ear-shot of the preacher. Occasionally, on prayer-meeting night, he plants himself opposite the church-door ; and, gathering round him a few congenial friends, he fires off his gibes in a tone of voice so loud, that they reach the ears of the subjects of them. This proceeding is noways fitted to increase the audience on such occasions, and perhaps it is not intended to have that effect. In other instances the priest lives in all good neighbourhood, and contrives so to ingratiate himself with all, that he passes, in common *parlance*, as " one of the ministers of the district."

To the action of the strict ecclesiastical machinery we are to add the influence of Romanist congregations on the population around them. The latter is even more disastrous than the former. The district speedily becomes familiarized with irreligion and vice in their multiform aspects. Its quiet is invaded by frequent brawls : its sobriety is undermined by scenes of intemperance. Sabbath profanation, horrible oaths, foul deeds, improvidence, idleness, and rags, begin so to deform and darken it, that the community puts on a new face, and becomes totally unlike its former self. Although there should not be a single perversion, there is nevertheless a state of things created, in the lowered tone and deteriorated morals of the district, which is highly favourable to the future success of the Popish Church in the community.

Thus has the Papal aggression given us, not a king only, not a law only, but subjects also. Rome's army of fighting men are in our country. They have not merely pitched their tents, they have built their barracks, in our land. They are here with their generals, twelve in number ; and over them is a general-in-chief, who directs, step by step, the progress of the invasion. Each year finds that invasion with a more extended front, and sees it occupying a line in advance of that which it occupied the year before.

It is, too, very note-worthy, that Popery in Great Britain

has infused itself into the whole framework of our national organization, and is at this hour acting through all the main channels of our national life. It has possessed, as it were, the whole fabric of corporate Britain,—Parliament, the army, the prisons, the schools, the reformatories, and the poorhouses: in all, and through all, it operates. Thus has our national life and action become to a large extent a ministration of Romanism. Though still numerically the minor party, Popery has made itself imperial. It has expanded itself to the dimensions of the nation by borrowing our national organization, and using it for its own purposes. Like the prophet who stretched himself upon the dead body of the child, putting " his mouth upon his mouth, and his eyes upon his eyes, and his hands upon his hands," so has the Papacy stretched itself upon the body of the nation, putting its mouth upon the nation's mouth, its eyes upon the nation's eyes, and its hands upon the nation's hands, not that, like the prophet, it may breathe life into the nation, but death.

So perfect and complete is the organization of Romanism in Great Britain. We behold it with a centre of temporal and spiritual authority in the Cardinal ; with a machinery for the diffusion of that authority in the territorial bishops and the provincial synods ; with numerous communities through whom that authority becomes a living power and a solid kingdom in the midst of us ; and, lastly, with an engrafting into the framework of our empire ; so that it has got an imperial status, and wields an imperial power. Out of the one kingdom of Great Britain two kingdoms are emerging. The subjects of Queen Victoria diminish from one day to another, while those of the Pontiff continually multiply.

ROMANISTS DECLARING THAT THEY WILL NOT OBEY THE LAW.

SCARCE was the ink in which the Ecclesiastical Titles Bill was written dry before the Papists declared that they would not obey it. A plain and unmistakeable declaration to that effect appeared in the *Tablet* of the 26th July 1851, the organ of the more respectable Roman Catholics. The article of the *Tablet* breathed a spirit of deep-rooted hostility to British rule, and of fierce and determined defiance to British law. It declared that the voice of the Pope is the voice of God, and that there cannot be a moment's doubt as to which of the two—the Pope or the Queen—is to be obeyed. The laws of a heretical Parliament it stigmatized as not *laws*, but *lies;* they were not to be obeyed, but spit upon. And it plainly declared that the law in question *must* not, and *will* not, be obeyed; that it must be "rigorously disobeyed" by all Roman Catholics in England and Ireland. But we shall allow the *Tablet* to speak for himself :—

"Lord Truro, indeed, pathetically asks,—'Is it to be said that the Roman Catholics of Ireland would not obey the law?' We answer with the most perfect frankness, that it both has been said, and is to be said, and that it will be done. Neither in England nor in Ireland will the Roman Catholics obey the law, that is, the law of the Imperial Parliament. They have, or are likely to have, before them two things called laws, which unhappily (or happily) contradict each other. Both cannot be obeyed, and both cannot be disobeyed. One of them is the law of God ; the other is no law at all. It pretends to be an act of Parliament ; but in the ethics of legislation it has no more force or value than a solemn enactment that the moon is made of green cheese. It is not a law, but a lie,—a Parliamentary lie,—which its very utterers know to be false, and which they deliberately put forward as a falsehood, careless of contempt and ignominy, so that they can retain their hold of office. Of these two things, we need hardly say which will be obeyed and which disobeyed. The law of God, that is, the Pope's command, will be, or rather has been and is being, carried into effect : the Parliamentary lie will be spit upon, and trampled under foot, and treated as all honest men treat a lie that is rigorously disobeyed."

How oft and loudly did Papists reiterate the assurance that the aggression had in it no element hostile to the genius of our Constitution, the independence of our throne, and the integrity of our liberties! and yet a measure based on the grand primal element of our Constitution,—THAT THE POPE HATH NO JURISDICTION IN THIS REALM,—and in the mildest possible manner asserting and applying it, the Papists tell us they cannot obey. Could we imagine a more severe condemnation of their projects as embodied in the Papal aggression? Have not Romanists in this threat unmasked themselves before the nation? Do they not confess that British liberty and their designs cannot stand together; that canon law can be planted only above the ruins of British law; and that the throne of Cardinal Wiseman can attain its full development only when the throne of Queen Victoria is in the dust? Who can have forgotten how oft and how solemnly the Pope's legate in London asserted that the rescript which he brought into the country carried only spiritual effects, and that what he said about dividing and governing the Queen's counties meant only a purely spiritual jurisdiction? Well, here is a bill which gives him full latitude in spirituals, and only forbids the assumption of secular titles and the exercise of secular jurisdiction; and yet it cannot be obeyed.

Had Dr Wiseman's object been, what he affirmed it to be, the government, by spiritual means exclusively, of the members of his own Church, what possible quarrel could he have had with the Ecclesiastical Titles Bill? It does not declare penal the holding of the most unintelligible and monstrous of the Papal dogmas; it does not forbid him to believe in purgatory or in the infallibility; it does not seek to punish him for celebrating mass or praying to the Virgin; it does not decree the shutting up of confessionals or the pulling down of cathedrals. We grant to Dr Wiseman what Dr Wiseman would not grant to us,—liberty to hold any opinion he pleases, and to preach it too from the house-tops, provided it does not endanger the peace of society. Nay, the bill grants him leave to assume any ecclesiastical title he pleases, provided it be not also a territorial title. This is what the bill does ; and Dr Wiseman's organ tells us that it cannot be obeyed. Could anything more completely falsify all the former assertions of Romanists ?

Let us mark how the *Tablet*, in the passage cited above, utterly ignores the Queen's authority and the Parliament's jurisdiction. In the true spirit of the canon law, which declares that the decrees of the Pope are superior to the constitutions of princes,—in the true spirit of the infallible jurist Liguori, who recognises only one authority and one jurisdiction in the world, the Pontifical,—in the true spirit of that ultramontanism which is taught by the help of British money at Maynooth,—the *Tablet* declares, " Both (the Parliament's bill and the Pope's bull) cannot be obeyed, and both cannot be disobeyed. One of them (the Pope's bull) is the law of God ; the other is no law at all. It pretends to be an act of Parliament ; but in the ethics of legislation it has no more force or value than a solemn enactment that the moon is made of green cheese. It is not a law, but a lie." It emanates from a body which has no real authority,—so the *Tablet* holds ; for both Parliament and the Queen are cut off from the one true source of jurisdiction in the world ; and what Parliament does not possess it cannot impart. There is not a law in the statute book which has a particle of force with a Catholic conscience, unless it is countersigned in the Vatican. To disobey such a law is no rebellion. In truth, it is the Parliament and the Queen which are the rebels. They are in rebellion against the Pope, and that is to be in rebellion against God ; for the *Tablet* assures us in so many words, that

the *command of the Pope* is the *law of God.* We do not
blame the *Tablet* for holding these opinions ; and farther, we
admit that in carrying his purpose of rebellion into effect he
will act most consistently and logically. Believing the Pope
to be God on earth, and both Parliament and the Queen in rebellion against God, how can he act otherwise ? Were we
enlightened and honest Papists, we must act in the same way :
we should feel that we could not, without renouncing our
principles, and being condemned by our consciences, obey in
matters which violated the revealed and declared will of God.
And the *Tablet* holds that the Ecclesiastical Titles Bill is in
violation of the revealed will of Deity ; for the Papal aggression is the express and revealed will of God, because it is the
command of the Pope, and the command of the Pope is the
law of God. The *Tablet*, then, and all honest Papists, have
it in their choice to submit to the law of Britain, and so disobey God, or to follow the dictates of conscience, and so disobey the Queen. We do not, we say, blame the *Tablet* for
holding these opinions. What we wish is, that the public
should be aware that these opinions Papists *do* hold,—that,
if honest and consistent, they *must* hold them ; and not only
must they hold them,—they *must* act upon them.

The *Tablet*, we say, is the organ of the more respectable
Catholics. We find the same sentiments expressed with more
emphasis and violence of language, though not in tone more
firm, by the *Catholic Vindicator :—*

" Rather than that our loyalty to the holy apostolic see should be in
the least degree tarnished, let ten thousand kings and queens (and Queen
Victoria included) perish (*as such*),—*i. e.* let them *be deposed from their
thrones*, and become mere individuals, as we have lately seen in the case
of a Catholic sovereign. We should not of course have spoken so strongly
as this under ordinary circumstances. But when the Pope and the Queen
are placed in antagonism to each other, as has been done lately, and it is
intimated that her Majesty will not accept a ' divided allegiance,' we are
compelled to say plainly which allegiance we consider the *most important ;* and we would not hesitate to tell the Queen to her face, that she

must either be content with this 'divided allegiance' or *none at all* (so
far as Catholics are concerned) ; for it is perfectly certain that (come
what may, even the rack and the torture,—the instruments used by her
Majesty's predecessors in their conflict with ' Popery'), we shall never
do otherwise than strictly obey the Sovereign Pontiff, *whoever* may presume to forbid it, and, in their puny insignificance, pronounce the acts
of the Vicar of Christ ' null and void.'"

One of the first acts of Cardinal Wiseman after his return
from Rome was to remove from the canon of the mass the
prayer for the Queen, and to cause all the missals of his diocese to be changed, in order that the obnoxious passage might
be expunged. The only ground he assigned for this proceeding was, the impropriety of having the name of a heretical
prince mixed up with that of the Pope in the mass. So far
as ourselves are concerned, we are thankful that the honoured
name of our Queen should be rescued from a companionship
so questionable. Still, the act of the Cardinal is none the less
significant on that account. It clearly shows that in his
opinion the title of Victoria is invalid, and that her throne
is as good as vacant. However, while Papists avow their
hostility against the Queen in her character of Queen, they
entertain, they tell us, charitable feelings towards her personally ; and while they omit her name in their public devotions, "because she is not a member of the Christian Church,"
and does not rank with Catholic sovereigns, and, *de jure*, is
not a sovereign at all, yet she has the benefit of being prayed
for by the priests of Rome in a general and inferential way,
that is, along with "other heathens, publicans, and heretics,"
as the following paragraph from the Catholic *Vindicator* testifies :—

" How does *the Church* regard Queen Victoria and other heretical
sovereigns ? Has her name much prominence in her services ? Nay, is
it there at all ? Did not the Cardinal Archbishop of Westminster omit
the prayer for the Sovereign (which is only intended for a *Catholic* sovereign) at Southwark Cathedral on Good Friday ? *Of course* he did, for
the simple and very obvious reason, that Queen Victoria is not a mem-

ber of the Christian Church,—of that Church which if we refuse to 'hear' and obey, we are at once classed with '*heathens and publicans,*'—(they are the words of Almighty God); and hence Queen Victoria is only prayed for *generally* (in the prayer for 'heretics and schismatics') with other Protestant unbelievers. Let us, then, act as our holy mother the *Church* does in the matter; and whilst we have none but charitable feelings towards the Queen *personally*—(and most certainly wish her no greater harm than that she may one day be received into the Christian Church, even though it be at the cost of her throne),—let us never forget that, whatever her boasted authority may be, it is *as nothing*, and less than nothing, compared to that of the Vicar of Christ."

These deliverances are in perfect harmony with the current stream of Papal dogmatic teaching. They are simply fair and legitimate applications to the point in hand,—the relations, to wit, of the Romanists of Great Britain and Ireland to the Sovereign,—of what the canonists and doctors of the Church of Rome have taught on that head. And does not this most conclusively show that modern Papists are neither ashamed of their doctrines, nor unacquainted with them; and that, instead of being permitted to slumber in musty tomes, or to lie hid in the darkness of some unfrequented library, they are diligently studied by them, that they may be reduced to practice? Not only are these doctrines taught from the chairs of Maynooth: they are proclaimed from all the Romanist printing presses of the country. Not only do the youth in training for the priesthood receive them as the foundations of their theology: the journalists and civilians of the Church adopt them as the guiding maxims of their politics, and enjoin them on all Romanists, as an ethical code, which is as incapable of change as is the religious creed of Rome, and which must, with certain modifications of form, be inflexibly carried out in substance in every age and in all countries.

The doctrine, then, so pithily inculcated upon the consciences of the Romanists of the empire in the above extracts just amounts to this, that the globe is but the footstool of the priesthood. The relation of the Pope to the outer world is that of its absolute and supreme master; his relation to the inner or spiritual world is that of its sole and infallible director. Thus he stands with one foot on the bodies of men and the other on their souls. According to the Roman canonist, Liguori, for instance, the world is under a theocracy, having the vicar of the universe at its head. Kings are but the mere lieutenants of that one divinely-appointed and infallible ruler; and their thrones are but mushroom seats compared with Peter's chair.

By the side of a polity ordained and administered by the Almighty, through his vicar on earth, adding the force of spiritual and eternal sanctions to the terrors of earthly punishment, the strongest human government dwindles into insignificance, and is shrivelled up into utter feebleness; and the obligations which these governments may lay upon their subjects, when the Pontiff speaks, become but as the green withes upon the arm of the strong man. According to the doctrine of Liguori, the first obedience of the *baptized*,—the only obedience from which no power can absolve them,—is due to their spiritual sovereign. There is only one obligation which is unalterably binding, and it is this. Other laws inconsistent with that one paramount and unalterable obligation are not binding *in foro conscientiæ*. It may be a wise policy on the part of the *"faithful,"* their great doctors teach to submit to such laws; but, as Bellarmine frankly confesses, it is the want of power alone that justifies that submission; and a more modern and more popular, if not more authoritative doctor, namely Liguori, has said that pernicious laws are no laws. Apply these doctrines on the subject of civil allegiance to the condition of the "faithful" in Britain, and we should be forced on some startling conclusions. In our country, the "faithful" live in the midst, if not of *their* enemies, yet of *God's*. They are governed by statutes framed by heretical

G

legislators, which, doubtless, are the most pernicious of all
pernicious laws.   Liguori teaches that such laws are no laws;
and Bellarmine says that want of power alone justifies submission to them.   The authority that administers these pernicious laws falls yearly under the anathema of the Pope;
and in the jurisprudence of Rome an anathematized sovereign
is virtually a deposed sovereign.

ROME'S SAPPERS AND MINERS.

THE weapons with which the Papacy maintains the conflict
in our country are different indeed from those with which
it is fighting so resolutely abroad.   It dare not employ the
dungeon, as in Rome, as in Naples, as in Tuscany.   It cannot exchange concordats with the British Government, declaring the faith of Rome to be the only recognised and
tolerated religion in the country, and calling on the magistrate to assist in expelling all heretical books, as in Spain.
It cannot launch excommunications at dying Ministers of
State, forbidding a grave to their ashes and paradise to their
spirits, as in Piedmont.   It cannot claim exemption from
the secular tribunals in behalf of its priests, as in Austria.
It cannot close schools and colleges, or do what is tantamount,—teach in them only the glories of Mary and the
virtues of chrism, as in France and Ireland.   But it is
fighting resolutely nevertheless, and with the more success,
doubtless, that it dare not here employ those coarse weapons
which it is wielding with such hearty energy and good-will
abroad.

Here it plies silently, but ceaselessly, the mattock and spade.
It works, mole-like, under ground, and hour by hour is advancing its trenches nearer our walls, and sinking its mine
deeper under our Constitution.   It besieges death-beds; it

erects nunneries, to which, like certain teachers in ancient
times, it "leads silly women captive, laden with" pelf, and
.ouses them comfortably for a consideration. It opens schools
for Christian instruction, in which it takes care to initiate the
youth in that one fundamental point of Christianity, as a
living writer on the Papacy calls it, the "primacy of Peter;"
and strives to impress them with the prosperity that may be
expected to attend them through life if they early begin the
habit of praying to the Mother of God. It is attempting to
engraft itself upon the literature, the arts, and the fashionable amusements of the age, that so it may inject its "leprous
distilment" into the mind unawares. It sends its spies into
Protestant families; it circulates industriously the tale of
scandal; it labours to sow strifes in families; and, through
the confessional, it moulds the declamation of the mob orator,
and regulates the speeches and the vote of the senator. It
builds magnificent cathedrals, rich in the glory of nave and
transept, of painted glass and silver shrines; and enacts within,
    " Scenes not unworthy Drury's days of old,"
in the hope that some who have come to gaze may retire to
pray,—to the Diana of Rome.

It has poured a swarm of Italian priests, of all orders and
garbs, into our island,—some in scarlet hats and some in
cowls,—some shod and some bare-footed,—some decked with
surplice, and others begirt with hempen cord. It has sent
among us, too, the high-bred and scholarly Jesuit, whose business it is to penetrate into the drawing-rooms of the great,
and to talk with equal grace and intelligence on all subjects,
from the mysteries of canon law down to the newest novel
or the last painting. Each has his place assigned him in
Rome's invading host, and each has his part to play, and,
what is more, he takes care to play it to purpose. Thus, by
a plan of systematized efforts, by which British Protestantism
is attacked simultaneously on all points, is Rome pushing for-

ward her aggression. And Britain is worth all the efforts which that Church is now concentrating upon her. Popery discerns clearly that it is here that the great conflict now waging all over Europe must be decided. The Church of Rome may triumph in Spain or in Austria, and yet lose the day ; but if she triumphs in Britain, she triumphs everywhere : the world is at her feet once more.

Rome has two kinds of soldiers. One division of her army she stations in the open plain, conspicuously in view of the enemy, marshalled under banner and ensign. But she has her sappers and miners also. These carry neither banner nor ensign, and certainly they never think of notifying their movements by sound of trumpet. Their modest post is under ground, where they ply shovel and pickaxe, working steadily but stealthily at the foundations, while the Protestant, secure in the strength of his ramparts, is sound asleep. By and by the crash of a falling tower, or the yawning of some hideous rent, suddenly awakens him He becomes aware that his position has been attacked, by finding that it is already carried. Thus the untitled Jesuit has it often in his power to do greater service to his Church than the titled cardinal. He costs her less, and he gives her more. The one struts his hour in purple splendour in the cathedral : the other is unostentatiously busy in the school, in the workshop, or in the drawing-room. The one burns his incense, chants his mass, preaches his homily on St. Anthony or St. Patrick, and closes the show : the other comes in the modest character of the scholar, or of the tutor, or of the friend, or of the lover, or, it may be, of the household servant. The mitred functionary takes aim at the mass of society : the Jesuit selects his victim ; he is Rome's rifleman, and seldom does he miss his mark. It is on her sappers and miners that Rome's main reliance is placed for the furtherance of her schemes in our country.

Few things tend more to the success of Popery than the

fancied impossibility of its succeeding. Popery, say those who cherish this delusion, revolts the intellect quite as much as it contradicts the Bible ; and in an age like this, when everything is brought to the test of reason, and nothing is accepted on mere authority, how impossible that Romanism should find believers, save among enthusiasts and simpletons ! It is sufficient to reply, that thousands in England have of late become converts to it, who are neither enthusiasts nor simpletons. However we may account for it, there lies unquestionably some mysterious and potent power somewhere in this system, which, when once it has seized upon the conscience, bows down the strength of intellect, the subtilty of logic, and the pride of learning, even as the tempest bows down the reed. Unhappily the instances are numerous of men of splendid gifts becoming Romanists. In science, and all similar departments, intelligence is a sufficient guarantee against the belief of demonstrable absurdity ; but, as the whole history of the world testifies, intelligence is no guarantee against absurdity in religious matters. Here reason is as weak as in other departments it is strong, and as prompt to embrace error as in other cases it is quick to reject it. Nor is it difficult to account for this anomalous working of the intellect in the religious sphere. The whole bias of our nature is towards ceremonialism, seeing the conscience finds a singular satisfaction in resting in the performance of a positive rite ; and the more painful the rite, the greater the satisfaction. On the other hand, nothing is more difficult than the act of simple faith. To realize and rest upon the Unseen, and by that resting to lay hold upon an unseen good, without rite, or ceremony, or service of any sort interposed, is difficult intellectually, and to fallen man impossible morally, save by the aid of the Divine Spirit. Spiritual Christianity must ever contend at great disadvantage against a splendid and pretentious ceremonialism like Popery. Hence the predominance in every past age of ritualism, and the apparently incurable tendency of mankind to lapse into it.

There are two classes for whom Popery possesses great attractions, and who will consequently be an easy prey to the sappers and miners of the Roman Church. The first are those who have arrived at old age with a conscience burdened with past sins. With the judgment-seat before, and a long array of accusing crimes behind, the priest appears to the man overwhelmed with remorse and terror, a very angel of light, sent to shut the gates of hell, and open to him the door of paradise. He is but too thankful to be permitted to atone for the sins of a whole life by spending his short remaining term in austerities, and buying salvation with a portion, or even with the whole, of that wealth which he can no longer enjoy. The worn-out debauchees of either sex, seeing no other refuge at hand, are fain to throw themselves into the Church's arms, without a moment's doubt or inquiry as to her power to make good all she promises.

The second class who stand peculiarly exposed to the arts of the spiritual seducer are those who aim at being at once fashionable and devout. In times like our own, when there is a perceptible increase of religious warmth in the air, this class is apt to be a somewhat numerous one. They abound mostly in aristocratic circles, and the priest must seek them in the drawing-rooms of the rich. The door of such places is open to him. Handsome in person, it may be ; of courteous manners ; of good birth, or known to be on familiar terms with those who are ; *au fait* of all the gossip of fashionable society ; equally at home in criticising a new picture, in discussing the comparative merits of foreign watering-places, or in assisting at the performance of a piece of music,—how delightful to have such an accomplished and agreeable person at one's party of an evening ! While the Protestant minister is toiling in his study, or at the bed-side of the sick, and permitting himself only rare intervals of relaxation, the priest is enjoying the good things of the dinner table, or figuring at a concert, or acting the connoisseur in the galleries of art, or guiding the conversation in the saloons of the aristocracy, and all the while has the satisfaction of thinking that he is very effectually plying his sacred vocation, and making proselytes for his Church.

Admission into Protestant families once gained, the next object of the priests is to select their victim. They usually begin with some weak young man, or some gay young lady. If, in addition, the selected object of attack is of a sentimental turn, or if inclined even to occasional seriousness, so much the better. Nor will it greatly disconcert the *fathers* should the person hold what he himself deems very decided views on religious subjects. And, the more effectually to disarm their victim, they may even encourage the hope that he may win them over to a better opinion. They leave themselves unacquainted with nothing in the character and habits of the person that may aid them in their intended conquest. With inimitable wariness and skill is the assault gone about. The blows dealt at first are amazingly gentle. The person must not be made alarmed. To fly at him all at once with a piece of grave argumentation would be to spoil the whole business. The work of sapping and mining is commenced with a jest or a sneer. Ridicule, not argument, is employed to assail names which the person has hitherto been accustomed to hold in reverence, and truths which aforetime he has deemed most surely established. Doubt is gently insinuated rather than boldly propounded; and not till it is seen that the foundations of the person's belief are beginning to be loosened by these light weapons, is the heavy artillery of argument brought into play.

The assault now becomes bold and uncompromising. The man, already shaken in his belief, is perplexed by difficulties

which are speciously propounded, and dazzled by sophisms
boldly and skilfully maintained   The avenues to his heart
have already been gained by a well-counterfeited show of
concern for his highest welfare ; and he cannot but listen,
even though as yet he may be unable fully to assent, to one
who so sincerely, as he believes, wishes him well   A fever-
ish state of mind is gradually induced, singularly unfavour-
able to calm inquiry.   The intellect becomes enfeebled and
dissipated at the very time when it ought to be vigorous and
concentrated.   The priest sees and pursues his advantage.
He gives his victim no pause to inquire, or to weigh the real
force of the arguments brought against him.   He literally
hurries him, by the whirlwind of excited fears, and an enfeebled and dazzled reason, into Catholicism.   A bold appeal
to the authority of the Church completes the process.   After
such a tempest of agitating and tormenting doubts as that
through which the person has passed, he welcomes peace,
though at the expense of bowing his neck to a yoke which
there is but small chance of his ever afterwards being able
to throw off.

The person so ensnared is next made the instrument of
ensnaring others.   With this view two forces are straightway brought to bear upon him,—the authority of the confessional and the fear of purgatory.   Instead of the elysium
into which he expected to enter, the unhappy man finds
himself environed for life with the gloom of ghostly direction.
What a transformation has the priest undergone in his eyes !
He who aforetime was dressed in smiles is now clothed with
terrors ; and yet, much as he dreads, he dare not renounce
his dominion.   At any cost of toil or suffering he will do his
bidding.   He will labour to convert his relatives, doomed,
as he believes, to eternal perdition ; and if he cannot succeed,
he will sever the dearest ties, and renounce family and kindred.   All that he possesses on earth he will give up, if,

haply, he may work himselt out of the terrible bondage that weighs upon his soul, and rise to the assurance of paradise. It is so with him all through life. There is for him no parting in the black cloud,—no escape from the ghostly fetter. He finds himself at last on his death-bed ; and beside him, like unto a demon, sits the priest. When he first encountered him in some aristocratic saloon, he was radiant as an angel, and he won him to listen by pouring into his ear the blandest and most persuasive words. Now he hovers above him, a thing all talons and stings, hoarsely urging extortionate demands, and pointing, the nearer he comes to his last breath, the more emphatically, by way of enforcing these demands, to a purgatory of blazing flames opening to receive his soul.

To these operations, one chief theatre of which are the saloons of the aristocratic circles, we must add a host of others, which also come under the category of sapping and mining. We can bestow only a single glance upon them, still reserving certain of them for fuller consideration to an after part of our work. There is first the secret society. The headquarters of these societies are on Continental Europe ; but their affiliated branches are widely spread, and are perseveringly although stealthily active, in Great Britain. Their members are mostly Jesuits. The more scholarly of the body lay themselves out to cultivate the acquaintance of the gentry and nobility, and carry on the operations we have already described ; others make it their business to interpolate our literature with Popish principles ; while others hang on about our newspapers, in the capacity of reporters, or of regular contributors, or even of writers of occasional paragraphs. In a hundred instances does the pen of Jesuit meet the eye of the public, while the public suspects no such thing. Others ply the trading and working classes,—for Rome is taking hold of society by its two ends,—sometimes doffing the clerical vestment, and courting disputation on the streets, espousing at times the side of Protestantism, that by their weak defence they may do it more deadly damage than they could possibly do it by their strongest attack.*

Then there is the school.   That same Church which has grossly neglected the education of Italy and Spain professes in our country to be a great educator.   Abroad she loves the darkness : here it suits her to be a patron of the light. The amount and kind of education which are communicated in the Popish school depend altogether on circumstances.   In the neighbourhood of a vigorous Protestant school the Church educates well, striving to outdo the Protestant teacher, and draft his pupils into her own school.   Where competition does not exist she generally takes care not to create it.   In Poland the Jesuits adopted the plan of communicating to their pupils some fragments of knowledge without teaching them to read.   The plan is pretty generally followed in the Jesuit schools on the Continent at this day, where the youth are taught their catechism by rote, but not their letters, lest, when they grow up, they should read bad books. There is some reason to fear that the same peculiar mode of instruction is practised to some extent, where circumstances will allow, in Great Britain.   An illustrative instance once fell under the author's eye.   He chanced to visit the nuns' school, supported by Government money, in Belfast, and found a class of some dozen pupils, standing primer in hand.   Picking out one boy of the age of eight or thereabouts, the author asked him to read the page which he held open.   He read it with all ease, but with more than the ordinary rapidity.   The

* This plan, to the author's knowledge, is now being adopted at Rome. It is not uncommon for the priests to hold public disputations in the churches,—one taking the Popish, another the Protestant side.   The Protestant champion is, of course, always defeated.   The author has been told of cases in our great cities which leave no doubt that the same tactics is being pursued in our country.

author turned over a few leaves, and requested the boy again to read. He did so a second time, with the same ease and the same great rapidity. On examining, the author found that the pupil, instead of reading the page now open, which, indeed, he appeared to be unable to read, had simply recited the former page. The author could hardly resist the conclusion that the boy had conned this one page by heart, and stood there prepared to recite it to any visitor who might chance to drop into the school.

Then there come reformatories, and hospitals, and prisons, in all of which Rome professes to be giving intellectual or spiritual instruction. It is simply a grand sapping and mining enterprise carried on at the nation's expense. By these measures Rome seeks to persuade the world that she is a great spiritual regenerator, and that she is deeply concerned about the highest welfare of society ; while, in fact, she is but displacing the only true regenerator of the world, which is the gospel.

ROME'S GRAND MISSIONARY INSTITUTE.

WE are disposed to view the whole state and condition of the Irish race as presenting a ground of greater anxiety to the friends of truth, and a source of greater peril to the Protestantism of the empire, and, indeed, to the Christianity of the world, than any other that at this moment exists on the face of the earth. In the degradation of that race the Church of Rome has found a lever of tremendous power for aggrandizing herself. What that Church accomplished in other days by the arms of France, by the wealth of Spain, by the statesmanship of Italy, she is now doing, and doing more successfully, by means of the mental debasement and physical destitution of Ireland. In short, Ireland in her hands has become a great missionary institute. The swarms of emigrants in rags which are cast upon our shores, which crowd our cities, which burrow in our poorhouses, and swelter in our jails, are just the missionaries which that great institute is sending forth to spread the superstition and the dominion of Rome over the empire. No weapon comes wrong to the hand of Rome; and, while dreading her power, as well we may, we are compelled to admire the genius of a Church which can so adapt her policy to every age and to all countries.

That Church has seen deeper into the matter of Irish destitution than any of us. True, she has raised a mighty outcry about that destitution: she has made the world resound with her lamentations over the sufferings of the Irish race and the oppressions of their Saxon tyrants. And she has managed to get credit for full sincerity in her well-simulated sorrow. Most men have thought that the Church of Rome was in very deed overwhelmed by the sight of a race so degraded and so miserable; and that if the priesthood had the power, by word or sign, of annihilating that misery, it would be instantly ended, and to-morrow's sun would rise upon Ireland a flourishing and happy country,—trade filling its cities, cultivation clothing its fields, and abundance of bread gladdening all its dwellings. We must take leave to doubt whether, though the priesthood could simply by a word charm Ireland into a happy country, they would speak that word. Have the priesthood a motive to annihilate the misery of Ireland? Have they not rather a motive to perpetuate it? Were they to annihilate the degradation of the Irish race, would they not to a large extent shear the locks of their own strength, and dry up a source of power which far transcends any other instrumentality at this hour in possession of their Church for spreading their superstition and ascendancy over the earth?

Let us illustrate our point by taking a single instance. We all know that, among the other orders of men in her service, Rome keeps an order of monks. For some of her clergy she provides a splendid palace, a luxurious table, and a robe of purple. Others she attires in a hair shirt, a girdle with iron spikes; and, throwing a wallet over their shoulders, she sends them forth, with naked foot and shaven crown, to beg from door to door. That mendicant monk renders as effectual service to the cause of the Church as that princely cardinal. The cloak of serge and pilgrim staff of the one are as essential to the good of the general body as the purple robe and gilded chariot of the other. And why may not that Church which serves her interests so effectually by maintaining this gradation and variety among her clergy, serve her interests no less effectually by maintaining a similar gradation and variety among the nations subject to her? Why may not that Church find it for the general good to keep a mendicant nation? Ireland is that nation. The Irish are the monks of the Papal world. She takes them fresh from the sod, all unwashed as they are; and, without putting a single patch upon their garments, or a single loaf in their wallets, she sends them forth, their outer man all aflutter with rags, and their inner man all on fire with zeal, to beg, for the love of the Virgin and the glory of the Church, among the wealthy heretical nations of Christendom.

We all know the sad history of those poor Italian boys whom we see at times upon our streets. Torn from Italy, with the tint of Italy's sun upon their cheek, and the music of Italy's tongue upon their lip, they are compelled to grind in our cities for their avaricious masters. Rome is doing the same thing on a vastly greater scale. She has taken the poor Irish race,—so amply endowed with native genius, so rich in generous sympathies and in loving and trustful dispositions, —and she is leading them about over the world, to grind sad

music indeed, and all for pennies to fill her coffers. Most
indulgent mistress! most compassionate Church! When they
have gathered a crowd, and attracted notice by their doleful
strains, sung upon their harp, which has so long been attuned
only to sorrow, lifting up her voice, she cries aloud, "Behold
the woes of this once glorious country! pity the sorrows of
this noble but downtrodden race!"—accompanying her words,
the while, with floods of tears as copious and as sincere as ever
rolled down the cheek of crocodile. In this way does Rome
work her great mission institute; for the real Propaganda
at this hour is not at Rome; it is not at Lyons: it is in Ireland; it is where the Atlantic surge breaks high on the bleak
coast of Galway, and the black bog stretches drearily out to
the horizon in Connemara.

And then we must bear in mind that the Church of Rome
runs no risk by letting her people down into this frightful
pit of moral debasement and physical wretchedness. Were
the Protestant Church to let her people down into such a
depth as this, she would lose them altogether. But superstition will cling to a man where Christianity would forsake
him, just as a man may retain a belief in ghosts after he has
cast off all belief in the existence of God; and superstition
will permit a race to remain from generation to generation
where the gospel would not suffer them to abide for a single
hour. Were the gospel to lay hold of men in the state of
the Popish Irish, how soon would it pull them out of the
gulf! It would wash and clothe them; and, kindling the
spark of intelligence in their bosoms, it would speedily transform the race into other men, and their country into another
land. But with Romanism it is not so. A man may lie
sunk in mental darkness and in physical wretchedness, and
be every whit as good a Papist as if, instead of standing at
the bottom of the scale, he stood at the top of it. Nay, it is
not only safe, it is actually profitable, to the Church, to leave

that race in this deplorable condition. By a well-understood physical law, this very degradation and wretchedness is the most favourable condition for the rapid increase of the species; and just as in the fifth century swarm upon swarm poured down from the populous north upon the Roman empire, overwhelming both its Christianity and its civilization, so do we now see shoal after shoal issuing from the teeming land of Ireland, endangering the Protestantism of Britain and the Christianity of the world. But as all the rivers run into the sea, and the sea is not full, so, despite all the living streams that flow so continuously from Ireland, Ireland is not empty. So much the better for the Roman Church. If her harvest is great, she has no reason to complain that the labourers are few. What a happy missionary school is that over which she presides! She needs no funds to carry it on. Irish destitution supports itself. It needs only to be let alone to grow; and so there is no end of the missionaries which Rome can send forth.

These missionaries, too, are sent forth in that very condition in which they are best fitted for doing her work. All the blood she shed in the dark ages by the hands of judges and executioners was as nothing compared with the blood she shed by the hands of the rabble. It was by the rabble, sometimes in the shape of mobs, sometimes in the shape of regular armies, that she carried on her crusades and massacres from the thirteenth to the sixteenth century. And when blood shall again begin to flow in this country, the first shedding of it will be by the hands of the rabble.

But the main use and service, meanwhile, of the Irish race is to form a foothold for the Popish hierarchy all over the Protestant world. What is the key by which that Church has succeeded in opening the British Exchequer, and drawing from it some three hundred thousand pounds year by year? That key is the poor Irish. This is the open sesame

before which the golden doors of the Treasury fall back, and
the riches of Britain are poured at the Church's feet.   What
is it that has enabled her to place her chaplains in the army
and in our convict prisons?   Still it is the Irish,—the Irish
soldier, the Irish criminal.   On what pretext does she demand paid chaplains in all our prisons?   It is still the Irish.
I have given you, she says, so many criminals : in return for
these I demand so many gold guineas.   With these I will
manufacture more criminals, which will bring me more gold
guineas.   And thus the two kinds of manufacture go on
most prosperously together.   What is it that has given to
her reformatories with their ample endowments, grants of
land and money in the colonies, and schools from which the
Bible is excluded in Western Canada?   What is it that is
feeding the already great mass of Popery in the valley of the
Mississippi, as well as in Australia?   It is the Irish.   Verily,
in Irish destitution she has found a mine of exhaustless
wealth and of boundless power.

The proposed Poor Law Removal Bill of 1863 strikingly
shows what a valuable instrument is Ireland in the hands of
the priests, and how easy it were by its means to outflank
the Protestantism of Great Britain, and submerge the country
in a flood of Romanism.   The object of that bill was to enable the Irish pauper to obtain a legal settlement on a six
months' residence in any parish of England and Scotland.
As the law at present stands, the Irish immigrant has no
claim to permanent parochial relief till he has lived five years
in the country, occupied in some industrial employment ;
but the new law would have entitled him to parochial support at the end of six months, even although during that
time he had lived as a mendicant, and done not a hand's
turn.   The bill, in fact, invited the paupers of Ireland to
free quarters in Great Britain.   It placed the good of the
land before them.   In the richest of its pastures and in the

fairest of its cities might they come and pitch their tent. Had it passed, the taxes of the landlords and rate-payers would have been suddenly quadrupled; our native population would have been extruded; a Popish race would have been planted in their room; and thus a very effectual basis would have been laid, not only for additional chaplains and priests at the nation's expense, but for the establishment of the Popish Church in the country. This particular danger has been averted meanwhile, but some similar surprise may await us.

The old prophet, speaking of the invasion of Egypt by Nebuchadnezzar, describes that renowned warrior as arraying himself with the land of Egypt, as a shepherd putteth on his garment. What the priesthood really proposed was to array themselves with the land of England and Scotland, as a shepherd putteth on his cloak; and we were to sit still, like the Egyptians, and see the priests go forth in peace, laden with the entire spoils of the country. It is not the Pope in Rome that we dread; it is not the Pope even at the head of the armies of France or of Spain that we dread. It is the Pope in Ireland; it is the Pope at the head of the Irish. Here is that Church, like a second Benedict, leading forth armies of missionaries; or rather like a second Attila, at the head of new hordes advancing against the civilization and Christianity of the world. With a slumbering nation, a patronizing Government, an apologetic press, and too often a dumb pulpit, we see Rome on the high road, unless God shall prevent, to a second dominion.

PART THIRD.

ILLUSTRATIONS FROM RECENT EUROPEAN HISTORY.

PROJECTED DEVELOPMENT OF THE PAPAL AGGRESSION.

On the 19th of August 1851, a monster meeting of the Romanists of the three kingdoms was held in the Rotundo, Dublin, for the purpose of forming a Catholic Defence Association. This assemblage was a memorable one on a variety of grounds. It was sanctioned by the Romish hierarchy of both islands; it was approved by the majority of the Romish laity; it banded together in one mass the Roman Catholic population against their Protestant fellow-countrymen; and it resolved on a line of assault upon the Protestant Constitution of Great Britain, which has ever since been perseveringly, skilfully, and most successfully carried out. Few things will better show us how steadily the Papal aggression has advanced, and how surely it approaches its natural goal.

On a gilt throne sat the President of the Assembly, Dr Paul Cullen,—a man equally distinguished as a theologian and philosopher, seeing in the one character he believes that Pius IX. is infallible, and in the other that the earth stands still, while the sun, which is two metres in diameter, performs a daily journey round it. On a lower level, running right and left of the central chair, were inferior seats for the minor divinities. We use the term in its literal sense, for all are parts of infallibility. On one of these inferior thrones sat the "illustrious and eloquent prelate from Scotland," the

late Dr Gillis of Edinburgh, who, not to be outdone in rho-
domontade by the Irish speakers, who had declared the Ecclesiastical Titles Bill an infraction of the treaty of union with
Ireland, pronounced it not less an infraction of the treaty
with Scotland.   In the background of a crowded platform
were the assembled parish priests, who had come, as President Cullen remarked, from the bogs and glens of Ireland to
defend their religion, as the anchorites and hermits of Egypt
had left their caves on a like occasion in early times.

Dr Cullen came forward bemoaning the hard necessity
which had driven him upon such a demonstration.   The
good man was in utter astonishment at the persecution which
had befallen his Church, and which was as unprovoked as it
was fearful.   The Catholics of the empire were living in
peace and amity with all men when this tempest of Protestant wrath had gathered and burst.   What, exclaimed the
astonished Primate,—what have we done ?   There was no
one present to remind him of the bull of a foreign potentate,
ignoring directly the *ecclesiastical*, and virtually the *temporal*
supremacy of the British Crown and the nation's independence, and so the Primate had to reply to his own question.
" I say the Catholics of this empire have done nothing to
bring about the present state of things : they have been forced
into the attitude which they have assumed.   They never
imagined that they were committing any aggression, or invading any one's right : they were violating no law, injuring
no one."   The Catholics aimed simply at ruling Britain by
canon law,—a most innocent and lawful object, they would
have us believe, and as necessary as it is innocent, seeing it
is " the complete code of the Church," and rules all her members in *temporals* as well as *spirituals*.   This law, it is true,
declares Protestantism to be heresy, and its just and cus-
tomary punishment death by burning ; and to administer
this law, two little adjuncts may be required, in the shape of

the Confessional and the Inquisition, to extort Protestant secrets and rack Protestant joints. But then, as Dr Cullen held, the power to carry out their pet law in their own peculiar way is simple toleration, and this toleration the British nation, to his astonishment and grief, had refused; for the Ecclesiastical Titles Bill was, he averred, a hindrance in the way of the Church exercising her whole discipline, which extends to every act of the Romanist as a citizen as well as a Church member; and so the hard necessity had been put upon them of forming a Catholic Defence Association.

The principles held by the hierarchy on the toleration due to them, and the course of aggression to be followed till their Church's rights shall have been fully attained, will be most succinctly learned from the resolutions of the Assembly, which were as follow:—

" It is first declared, ' that an act lately passed by the Imperial Parliament, commonly called the Ecclesiastical Titles Act, is a violation of the principle contained in the Catholic Relief Act of 1829, and subversive of the great principle of religious liberty established in this empire.' It is next declared,—and this time unhesitatingly,—' that the present Ministers have betrayed the cause of civil and religious freedom, and forfeited the confidence of the Catholics of the united kingdom.' It is then resolved, ' that we hereby solemnly pledge ourselves to use every legitimate means within the Constitution to obtain a total repeal of that act, and every other statute which imposes upon the Catholics of this empire any civil or religious disability whatsoever, or precludes them from the enjoyment of a perfect equality with every class of their fellow-subjects;' and, finally, it is declared, ' that for the above objects we deem it necessary to establish a Catholic Defence Association, and that the same be, and is hereby, established.' "

Let it first be noted, that they hold that the Ecclesiastical Titles Bill is a flagrant violation of the great principle of toleration. It forbids them, they tell us, the free exercise of their religion. Now, we are unable to form the most distant guess what rite or dogma it is, of all those which make up their religion, which the act prohibits. May they not build a cathedral in every street of every city in the empire? May

they not sing mass in it all day long? May they not observe all the festivals and pray to all the saints in the ca-
lendar? Has their person been stript of a single gewgaw,
or their altars of a single candle? Has the discipline of their
Church, so far as it is spiritual, been meddled with? May
they not prescribe to offending members as severe and pro-
tracted a penance as they please? May they not compel
them by spiritual terrors to wear a hair-shirt, or to walk
twenty miles with peas in their shoes, or to repeat *Ave Marias*
and *pater nosters ad infinitum?* May they not shut up whom
they please in purgatory, and keep them there for a year, or
a thousand years, with perfect impunity as regards the law?
Were the priests of Edinburgh to set up on the Calton Hill,
or were those of London to exhibit in Trafalgar Square
(which we trow they will not), a winking Madonna, would
any one interfere with this foolery provided the peace were
kept? And, what is more to the point, are the taxes which
they impose upon their people a penny less since the passing of this act? It has not lowered the price of chrism or
of absolution. Christenings and confirmations still bear the
same marketable value. Crucifixes and holy candles are as
lucrative a trade as ever. Yes; the priest can gather his
dues where the landlord cannot gather his; he can gather
his dues where the lawful creditor cannot gather his; he can
glean plentifully at the heels of famine even, and gather among
graves and corpses, compelling the ghastly arm of the dead
man to contribute towards filling his purse. All this the
priests assembled in the Rotundo can do; and yet they cla-
morously demand the full and free exercise of their religion,
and grievously complain that they are lying under intolerable
persecution.

We might be suspected of exaggerating, but the meeting
itself, surely, can lie under no such suspicion. Therefore we
shall permit it to state in its own words the objects it bound

itself to pursue.   Let the reader mark that the concessions
which follow, and which were to be fought for and carried,
are styled the "temporal" rights of the Romanist :—

"As citizens, therefore," say the meeting, "and on the temporal side
of the question only, we can conceive but one object for a Catholic Defence Society, and that is, to root out every law and every administra-
tive practice which interferes with the perfect freedom of the Church,
and our perfect equality before the law.   What are these laws, and what
are these practices ?

"Of course the Ecclesiastical Titles Act is one of them.   Upon that
item of the account we need not enlarge.

"Another is the existence of the Established Church, not in its religious character, but as a favoured corporation ; its unjust possession of
titles and glebes, acquired by robbery, and retained by fraud and bloodshed ; the legislative and political authority conferred on its—so-called—
bishops ; and whatever else belongs to its temporal character as an Establishment.

"Another set of cases is the penal laws directed against the Jesuits
and other religious orders,—those odious enactments which make ' the
greatest benefactors to religion and humanity' felons, for rendering the
truest services to God and to their neighbour.

"Another is the exceptions in the Emancipation Act, which debar
Catholics from the highest offices in the legal profession ; the existing
Regency Act (3 and 4 Vict., c. 52), which, in the event of the Queen
dying while her heir is under eighteen years of age, requires the Regent
to be a Protestant, compels Prince Albert to take the oath of supremacy,
or to forfeit his claim to the regency, and forbids him either to become a
Catholic or marry a Catholic ; and, finally, the Coronation Oath and the
Act of Settlement, which limit the possession of the Crown to Protestants,
and make the conversion to genuine Christianity a forfeiture of title."

Other points are enumerated, such as chaplains in the
workhouses, and chaplains in the army and navy.   War was
also proclaimed against the Government colleges in Ireland,
and the manifesto was concluded with the intimation that
the meeting would not rest satisfied until their Church had
obtained "the free exercise and *development* of its power, its
faith, and its morals."   That is, the priests will account that
they have obtained their "temporal rights" only when, released from the laws of the country, they are permitted to

wield over their followers the whole disciplinary powers of canon law. The document ends thus :—

" Such are a few of the objects to which the Catholic Defence Society must direct its attention and its best energies ; and we repeat that, in our judgment as laymen, the Catholic Defence Society must include among its objects everything which is included in the perfect independence of the Church, the free exercise and development of its powers, its faith, and its morals, and the perfect equality before the law of all the members of the Church with the members of every other community. With nothing less than this are we, in our character of citizens, disposed to be content."

In the absence of anything like argument in the speeches delivered in the meeting, we turn to the *Tablet* of that day. The *Tablet* lays it down as an axiom, that a man's temporal rights and the rights of his Church are identical, or at least co-extensive. "The rights of my Church," says he,—"let me be of what religion I please, and apart altogether from their Divine sanction,—are as much my temporal rights as the enjoyment of my franchise or the possession of my house." This is a definition of temporal rights which will carry the Romanist very far indeed. The commonly received doctrine of mankind has hitherto been, that a man's temporal rights are limited by the just prerogatives of the Government under which he lives, and by the rights of his fellow-subjects. The members of the Church of Rome utterly ignore this doctrine. Their rights, they hold, can be limited by no powers of the British Constitution and no claims of their Protestant fellow-subjects. The Romanist knows no limits to his temporal rights but those which the decrees of his Church have set. Every claim which his Church has at any time put forth is as indisputably his temporal right as is his franchise or his house. And he holds, moreover, that he is bound as a church member, and entitled as a citizen, to agitate in every way, till he shall obtain every particle of these rights.

Where, then, can one learn the rights of their Church, and

so know when this controversy may be expected to end, and
what extent of concession Romanists will be pleased to accept
as toleration ?   Whatever the canon law teaches is part of
the rights of the Church, and, by consequence, part of the
temporal rights of the Romanist ; and when he has succeeded, at the expense of the annihilation of the rights of
all other men, in securing the privileges with which the
canon law invests at once the corporate body and the individual Papist, then, and then only, he will grant that he is
tolerated.   Well, then, the canon law teaches that a Papal
rescript is of superior force to either an act of Parliament or
a royal edict, and that when the spiritual sovereign of Christendom speaks through his legate, or through his missive, it
becomes kings and parliaments to be dumb in his presence.
Laws made against that will are not *laws,* but *lies:* they are
not to be obeyed ; they are to be spit upon.   This is the sum
of the Church's rights on the head of authority, which the
Romanists of Britain conceive they are entitled to demand
as part of their temporal rights, and to obtain which, they
have, ever since 1829, been carrying on a system of agitation and clamour.

   But, again, the canon law teaches that lands and possessions once the property of the Church are the Church's property for ever.   No length of time, no authority on earth,
not even that of the Pontiff, can alienate them, or render
them other than sacred.   Here is another part of the Papist's
temporal rights.   The enormity of the law may be supposed
to have repealed it ; but it is not so.   Every inch of land in
Great Britain and Ireland which at any former period may
have belonged to the Roman Church is her property still.
The administration of all revenues and lands devoted to
ecclesiastical uses the canon law hands over to the ecclesiastical tribunals ; and it permits the same tribunals only to
try ecclesiastical persons, be the misdemeanours of which

they are guilty what they may. This is another constituent element in the Romanist's rights, and in the toleration of his Church.

But, not to multiply instances, the canon law teaches that there is but one religion in the world,—the Roman ; that all opinions and practices contrary to it are heretical, and lie under anathema ; and that the just punishment of those who refuse to renounce heresy is DEATH. This is what the Romanist understands by his rights. Give him all this, and you have given him toleration. Erase every law which is opposed to the dominancy of his Church, restore to the priesthood half the lands of the kingdom, declare the Romish clergy exempt from all lay tribunals, and confess that theirs is the only true Church, that you are but a poor heretic, and that the Romanist has a perfect right to lock you up in his Inquisition, and to make a public *auto da fe* of you, and he will then acknowledge that you have tolerated him. Toleration, in the vocabulary of the Romanist, just means power to ignore all laws contrary to those of the Romish Church, and liberty to imprison and burn all who do not believe as the Church believes.

To obtain this equality of temporal rights, this religious toleration, the *Tablet* threatened renewed, determined, and ceaseless agitation, and specified the various objects which the Catholic Defence Society must bend its whole power to carry. First, the Ecclesiastical Titles Act must be erased from the statute-book. A Romanist orator present could find no deed which equalled in atrocity the passing of this act, save one that took place eighteen hundred years ago in the capital of Judea, and no tribunal which rivalled in infamy and guilt the Parliament which passed it, save that over which Pilate presided. "This is a law," said the orator, "to drive fresh nails into the Cross of Christ, to fetter his sacred limbs with new ropes, and to put over his head a new galling inscrip-

tion, namely, 'The sacrifice on this Cross is illegal by the
third clause of the Russell bill.'   Oh, what a resemblance !"
continued the orator, "between the present Premier, with
his Parliamentary majorities, and Pilate with the Jewish
rabble.   The Jews cried out, 'Away with him, away with
him :' the Whigs worship no God in England."

The next object to be aimed at was the overthrow of the
Irish Establishment.   With an excess of moderation, that
Establishment was to be suffered to exist in its religious capacity, but it was to be unsparingly extirpated in its character as a "favoured corporation."   The meeting did not issue
an order as yet to Romanists to pull down chapels, or dis-
perse congregations by force, or imprison, or maltreat in yet
worse fashion, men for reading the Bible ; but it proclaimed
exterminating warfare against the Irish Church in "its unjust possession of titles and glebes acquired by robbery and
retained by fraud and bloodshed, the legislative and political
authority conferred on its so-called bishops, and whatever else
belongs to its temporal character as an Establishment."

Another piece of work chalked out for the Catholic Defence Society was the abolition of all penal laws affecting
Jesuits and other religious orders.   The *Tablet* could speak
of these men but with rapture as "the greatest benefactors
to religion and humanity ;" and it loudly accused those
"odious enactments" which made these men "felons for the
crime of rendering the truest services to God and to their
neighbour."   The "services" which the Jesuits have rendered to "God and their neighbour" are now well known
to both, and doubtless from both they will in due time receive their reward.   On this point it is not necessary we
should speak : history speaks very plainly.   A modest proposal, truly ! that we should open our gates, and give a
pressing welcome and free quarters, to men whom every
Papal Court in Europe has been compelled to banish from

its dominions, and whom the very Pope himself found it necessary to put down.

The amendment of the Emancipation Act was also to be undertaken by the Catholic Defence Society. The way to the woolsack, it declared, must be opened to Romanists. Nor must Prince Albert, the meeting said, be prevented becoming a Papist if so inclined, or marrying a Papist in the event of the demise of the Crown while the heir is under eighteen years of age; and for this purpose the law which requires the Regent to be a Protestant must be abolished. And, finally, the coronation oath, which declares that no Papist shall ever sway the sceptre of Britain, must, the meeting held, be altered. An attempt was also to be made, though it is hinted at rather than stated in the plan of political aggression sketched in the *Tablet*, to erect convents, under pretence that the poor are ill cared for, and "treated worse than dogs," in the workhouses. An effort was likewise to be made to introduce Popish chaplains into the army and navy. Cases may occur in which it is the duty of the Catholic soldier to sheathe his sword when his commander bids him draw it; and it is convenient to have a priest at hand to decide the case of conscience, so that the soldier may obey his spiritual, not his temporal, leader. In fine, the vested rights of ignorance in Ireland were to be cared for. Every penny voted for the Queen's Colleges, the meeting declared, must be given to the Catholic University, or returned to the Exchequer. At all events, it must not be employed in educational purposes · the light must be kept out of Ireland.

The reader can thus look along the whole line of the Papal aggression, from its starting to its close. Commencing with the "Edict from the Flaminian Gate," or rather with the Emancipation Act of 1829, it ends with Popery upon the throne. Such is the course decreed for it by the assembled Romanists, lay and cleric, in the Rotundo; and such is its course as more minutely sketched by the *Tablet*.   The first step was to admit men who had sworn allegiance to a foreign potentate to sit in Parliament, and legislate for an independent and Protestant nation.   The second was to repeal the statute forbidding the importation of the Pontiff's bulls into Britain.   The third was the erection of the entire machinery of the Papal jurisdiction in the country,—territorial bishops, synods, and canon law.   The fourth was to root out every vestige of Protestant instruction in Ireland, by corrupting or overthrowing the national scheme, and covering the country with Popish schools and Jesuit schoolmasters.   The fifth was to draft, in large numbers, Irish Romanists into the poor-houses, the army, and the navy, and, by compelling the appointment of Popish chaplains in all these establishments, to secure a virtual endowment for their Church.   These five measures have now been very fully achieved : there remain but two ; and when these two shall have been attained, their scheme will be completed.   The first is the confiscation of the revenues of the Established Church in Ireland, and the appropriation of the lion's share to themselves ; and the second is the throwing open of the woolsack and the throne to Romanists.   These are as sure to come, unless Providence shall interpose, as to-morrow is sure to come ; and when this happens, then will come civil war.

There is not a man living on the British soil who has not a stake in this controversy, and who ought not willingly to lend his aid towards its right settlement. the patriot, who would not see his country made a fief of Rome, and the throne, in which he takes a just pride, trampled on by a foreign priest; the philosopher, who would not see science invaded in her own halls, and driven thence to make way for mediæval absurdities ; the literary man, who would not see the press subjected to an odious censorship; the friend of the poor, who would not see the fruits of the earth and the labours of the industrious consumed by a swarm of idle and dissolute monks; the father, who would not see the sanctity and purity of his family blighted by the questionings and promptings of a lecherous priest; in short, the friend of progress, who would not see the world's liberties overwhelmed and crushed by the great armed re-action which now embraces western Europe, and of which the aggression in England forms a part.

THE SYNOD OF THURLES; OR, LET THE LIGHT BE ANATHEMA.

WE could scarce imagine a better illustration of the principles we have already enunciated than is furnished in the proceedings of the "National Council of Thurles," as it was styled, which was holden in the September of 1850. The Synod was presided over by "Paul, Archbishop of Armagh, Primate of all Ireland, and Delegate of the Apostolic See;" and its object was to condemn the system of instruction adopted in the Queen's colleges, and to take measures for the erection of a Roman Catholic university in Ireland, on the model of the one founded by the Belgian bishops at Louvain.   The bishops, in Synod assembled, condemned the Government colleges, forbade the attendance in them of the youth of Ireland, and wound up by sending their decrees to Rome to be ratified by the Pope, deferring their publication till the return of the Papal sanction.   We are here shown "synodical action" at work; and we appeal to our readers whether all we have affirmed as to the uses to which "synodical action" is sure to be turned is not here verified.   We behold it inaugurating its working by proscribing the light, and championing the good old cause of ignorance.   We see it making itself the vehicle for importing the Pope's jurisdiction into Great Britain, and pitting that jurisdiction right against the Queen's.   The Government builds colleges; the Pontiff proscribes them: the Government invites the youth of Ireland to make use of these colleges; the Pontiff thunders an anathema against any one who shall dare to cross their threshold. Is not this to claim a power in the country superior to that of the throne, and to wield that power for the destruction of every measure, no matter how necessary for the wellbeing of Ireland, which has not received the sanction of the Pontifical See?

To feel how flagrant an interference this was with the right of Parliament to legislate for the subjects of the Queen, it is necessary that we take into account the real character and aim of the colleg s which provoked the sweeping condemnation of the Synod of Thurles. The object of the Government was to provide only secular education in these colleges.

Viewing ignorance as the curse of Ireland, Government sought to teach her natives letters, and indoctrinate her youth in arts and science. To make inroads on her superstition formed no part of their plan; indeed, they seem to regard the integrity of Roman Catholicism in the sister island as quite compatible with the introduction of colleges and schools. The Government had gone to the extremest length which the nature of the case admitted of, to conciliate the Romish priesthood. If that priesthood could toleiate knowledge in any form, they would have tolerated it in the form in which it was now offered them. The Bible was to be as much unknown within the walls of these colleges as if no such book existed. The lips of every professor were to be sealed on all religious subjects. The truths of physical and mental science exclusively were to be taught from their chairs. Yet the Irish priesthood emphatically and bitterly condemned these colleges, and stringently prohibited all over whom they possessed the smallest power from entering them. Should any of the youth of Ireland cross their threshold, he does it at the peril of incurring the highest displeasure of Rome. One is tempted to think that surely some heretical taint must pollute that fountain at which the youth of Ireland are so stringently forbidden to drink.   But no; it is mere secular knowledge, pure scientific truth, which the Synod at Thurles has placed under quarantine.   Ireland is a preserve of ignorance, so kept for the special benefit of the Irish priests, and must so continue for ages, lest the dominion of Rome should be shaken in it.

It is not the doctrines of the New Testament only which the Church of Rome dreads.   She feels scarce less horror at the truths of natural philosophy.   To teach the sublime discoveries of Newton and Laplace the Synod declare to be "opposed to the purity and integrity of our faith,"—"an evil of a formidable kind," say they to the Irish people, "against which it is our imperative duty to warn you with all the energy of our zeal and all the weight of our authority."   Nor is this sweeping condemnation of all knowledge and science the act of the Synod alone: it is that of their Church, as represented by her infallible head; for, say the fathers, "in pointing out the dangers of such a system, we only repeat the instructions that have been given to us by the Vicar of Jesus Christ."   And, employing a strange kind of prosopopœia, they go on to speak of the collegiate institutions as "a wolf in sheep's clothing."   Such seminaries as the Dublin University the fathers at Thurles regard as "wolves," but wolves in their natural covering.   The new wolves about to be let loose by Government on the Catholic lambs of Ireland are trebly dangerous, inasmuch as their shaggy hide and ferocious dispositions are concealed under a borrowed garment.   And severely do the fathers reprimand the Government for their excess of charity, in believing that the priests would ever tolerate any attempt to enlighten Ireland, and brand the statesmen who have erected these colleges as "not acquainted with the inflexible nature of our doctrines."

It was not surprising, surely, that our Government should
bethink them of letting in the light on Ireland.   They find
that the land is dark,—all dark,—darkness that may be felt.
Here, say the Government, is a nation of blind men.   We
have been giving them alms to the amount of millions without bettering their condition in the least; and now we shall
try the simple expedient of opening their eyes, and letting
them do for themselves.   Duly as the winter comes, this big
beggar comes to our door.   The clothes and food we gave him
last season are all used up; and now, in a half-whining, half-
threatening tone, he demands to be clothed and fed over again.
He has hands as well as ourselves, and would use them, doubtless; but here is a bandage which some mischievously-dis-
posed party has put over his eyes.   We shall undo the knot,
and watch the result.   But no; you shall not touch that bandage, say certain parties.   Ireland is ours; we have a right
to keep her blindfolded; and if you presume to restore her
eyesight, we shall denounce you as wilful, tyrannical, and
impious meddlers.   It is for our interests that Ireland should
be kept in darkness; and if you refuse to feed her, we shall
brand you as murderers.   Such, in brief, is the manifesto of
the Roman Catholic Convocation which held its sittings at
Thurles.

The question, we repeat, was one touching the admission
of light, and a synod of owls was holden to debate it.   The
doors were closed, and the public shut out; otherwise the dis-
cussions would have yielded, we doubt not, unwonted enter-
tainment.   Those ingenious arguments, those lengthy and
elaborate reasonings, by which it was conclusively demonstrated that, of all pernicious and hateful things, light is the
most pernicious and hateful,—those syllogisms by which it
was shown that a man could not take a more certain course
to ensure his destruction than to use his eyesight,—that the
only prudent and safe method is to distrust, or rather to

extinguish, his senses, and commit himself implicitly to the infallible guides which Rome has provided,—would, we are sure, have been highly prized by the public; but, alas! the doors were shut, the window-curtains let fall, every avenue closed; and behind these deep veils this assembly sat, and poured forth in its darkened cell that extraordinary wisdom which the initiated only were able to hear, leaving the world outside deeply but vainly to grieve for its irreparable loss. "I hate the light," screeches out the presiding owl, "for there has been no living in the world since it entered." "Yes," screams another; "we cannot fly abroad, as we were wont: we are driven by the garish sunlight to old ruins and gloomy caves; and if matters go on as they are doing, there will not be a shady retreat in all the world where we can enjoy the darkness which is so congenial to us." "Let the light," cry they all, joining in one frightful scream,—"let the light be anathema."

In the pastoral address issued by the Synod, it would appear as if the fathers contemplated a general crusade against knowledge. It is not in Ireland only that the light is beginning to shine, but all over the earth; and in the following passage of their manifesto they proclaim their intention of hunting it out, and banishing it from every land, and resting not till they have restored the reign of universal night. "The alarming spectacle," says the Synod, "which the Christian world exhibits at the present day, the novel but formidable forms in which error presents itself, and the manifold evils and perils by which the Church is encompassed, must be evident to the most superficial observer. It is no longer a single heresy, or an eccentric fanaticism, the denial of some revealed truth, or the excesses of some extravagant error, but a comprehensive, all-pervading, well-digested system of unbelief, suited to every capacity, and reaching every intellect, that corrupts and desolates the moral world. Is not

I

such the calamitous spectacle which the Continent of Europe offers to us at this moment ?"

When the Caliph Omar ordered the famous library at Alexandria to be destroyed, he is said to have accompanied the sentence adjudging those monuments of the learning, the arts, and the genius of antiquity to the flames, with the sapient remark,—"If these writings of the Greeks agree with the Koran, they are useless, and need not be preserved. If they disagree, they are pernicious, and ought to be destroyed." So says the Church of Rome, when erecting a funeral pile for the learning, the arts, and the genius of both ancients and moderns. If these sciences agree with the doctrine of the Church, they are useless, and need not be preserved. If they disagree, they are pernicious, and ought to be destroyed. Is not the Papal Infallibility the sum of all wisdom, human and divine ? What need is there that a man should know more ! If he knows that, he knows enough. If he knows anything beyond that, he knows more than he ought. So reason the fathers at Thurles. In truth, the denunciations of Rome threaten to be more sweeping than the brand of Omar. The Papal bull will be more exterminating than the Caliph's brand. Vast as the Alexandrian shipwreck was, something survived. The walls of the doomed edifice did not enclose all the mental treasures of the ancient world, and therefore all did not perish in the conflagration. But not so much as a line or a thought which genius ever bequeathed to mankind would possibly escape the devastation which the modern Omar now threatens to inflict on the world. When before did literature and knowledge encounter such a destroyer ? The Moslem, the Vandal, the Goth, are all outstripped by the Monk.

When the scholar takes into account the mischances of accident, the waste of time, and the revolutions of war, the number of his treasures, rather than of his losses, will be the object of his surprise. But what neither accident, nor time, nor barbarism, nor war, has been able to destroy, Rome has now the will, if not the power, to annihilate. Singly she threatens to be more destructive to the treasures which mind has accumulated, than all the calamities which, in combination or succession, have ravaged the earth. It is a total loss of its mental wealth which awaits the world if Rome has her way ; and one, too, that will be final, for there will be no need that it should ever be followed by a second. When the treasures of learning in former times perished by the rage of barbarism or of war, the thinking faculty itself survived, and, like the bee when its cells are rifled, it speedily set to work to repair the loss. But the destructive rage of the priesthood will not spare mind itself : it is the thinking faculty which it aims at destroying ; so that the night which it has decreed for the world may be unbroken by so much as one solitary ray. If it rests with Rome, there awaits the human race an eternity of ignorance.

THE "ASCOT FATHERS ;" OR, LET THERE BE DARKNESS.

IN the August of 1852, there was holden a Provincial Synod at St. Mary's, Ascot, by which the Papal aggression was advanced a stage. Immediately on the breaking up of the Synod, the fathers issued, not their decrees,—for these they had sent to Rome to be ratified by the Pope,—but a Synodical Letter to the "Faithful under their jurisdiction." This document was a curiosity in its way ; being a farrago of pious phrases, Scripture quotations, ejaculatory prayers, high-sounding self-laudations, a few quiet anathemas on Protestants, some compliments to education, which, like the "amens" of Macbeth, stuck in the throat of the writer ; the whole ending with most fervent exhortations to the cultivation of peace, of brotherly love, and the forgiveness of injuries. The paper looked as if it had been written in a foreign tongue, and perhaps in a foreign city, and done into tolerable English, and published, not so much for the sake of Romanists, as for the sake of Protestants, whom it is meant to hoodwink and deceive.

The document bore on its forehead a flagrant violation of the law of the land. "We the Archbishop and Bishops of the province of Westminster." So ran its preamble. Let the reader mark the cool effrontery of the terms "province of Westminster." How quietly did the document ignore the divisions of the kingdom by the Queen and Parliament, and recognise those only which were made by the "edict from the Flaminian Gate!"

In the document, moreover, the bishops claimed "jurisdiction,"—a term implying the possession of lawful powers, and therefore, in a case where no such powers exist, asserting a right in the Pope to intermeddle at his pleasure with the laws and institutions of this country, and to interpolate among them institutions and laws having a compulsory and obligatory force. And farther, the assembled bishops addressed only "the faithful" under their jurisdiction, which clearly implied that they have jurisdiction over the unfaithful, that is, over her Majesty's Protestant subjects, and that if that jurisdiction be not enforced, it is from a defect of power, and not of right. In this Synod we have the first instance since the Reformation of a body of Popish ecclesiastics meeting together in Great Britain, to make laws which, when they have received the assent of a foreign prince, are to be binding, are to possess authority, and are to be enforced. Here, in short, we have a Parliament framing laws, claiming jurisdiction over *all* her Majesty's subjects, and exercising that jurisdiction over a large body of them, by enforcing obedience to its laws.

The main drift of the document was to propound and enjoin upon their flocks a scheme for *minimising*, in the first
instance, and ultimately extinguishing, the knowledge of Roman Catholics, and for effecting the further object of isolating
them from their Protestant fellow-citizens, in order that they
may be brought up to fear, distrust, and hate them.

No man now-a-days, in this country at least, dare openly
avow himself the champion of ignorance. Such being the
case, the Church of Rome is reduced to the necessity of
fighting the battle of darkness under the banners of light.
Knowledge she can no more permit than before; but knowledge is breaking in upon her people in this country; and
nothing must be left undone which it is in the power of the
Church to do, to rescue her people, or more properly herself,
from this imminent peril. Her plan is one by which, under
pretence of improving education, she substitutes in its room
a thorough and unmitigated training in her dogmas. The
education of the poor, the fathers remark, is one of the most
important duties confided to the Church. This duty, they
tell us, "the Church has discharged in all ages." Indeed! If
the Church has been so painstaking and exemplary an educationist, how comes it that nations educated and enlightened
under Pagan Rome have lost all knowledge of arts and letters
under the tuition of the Church? But, the fathers observe,
while the obligation has been faithfully discharged in all ages,
the manner of doing it must vary with the circumstances of
time and place. "When faith is undisturbed," that is, when
the authority of the Church is unchallenged, and her most
monstrous doctrines accepted as truths, "then the training
of the child in the way wherein he has to walk is a simple
task;" so simple, that it may be all but left to itself. His
education has been completed when he has been baptized,
taught to repeat his Ave Maria, and handed over to his confessor. "But where on every side aggression has to be en-

countered," that is, where the light may flash upon his mind
from every book he opens, and every school and church he
enters, "endless precautions" and "multiplied safeguards"
must be employed. Such, the fathers assure us, is the case
now. And it is only through a "laborious education" that
they can guarantee to the "little ones a single sound principle, one saving truth." Accordingly, the Council goes on
to recommend an institution which has recently been erected,
and which is known by the name of the "Poor School Committee." This Committee is composed of priests and laymen
selected from all the Romanist dioceses. Its work is to
provide funds, and to regulate the working of their institution. That institution, we are told, has already been exten-
sively useful; and it is proposed still farther to extend its
utility, by adopting the suggestions of the Committee to appoint in the various dioceses ecclesiastical inspectors, "whose
duty it will be to examine the scholars in the religious portion of their education, to grant certificates, and award prizes
for proficiency in it,"—that is, in the religious branch,—and
to give any one who may aspire to the office of teacher, the
means of proving himself *morally fitted*, and to prevent the
unworthy from obtaining so important an office.

The above is a plan professedly for extending the blessings
of education, but really for guarding against its dangers. It
contemplates two objects. The first is the children of the
poor, to whom our ragged schools and our charities are now
open, and who have begun to frequent them, and to acquire
in them the elements of at least an ordinary education. But
even this small portion of light the Church finds to be frequently fatal to the "faith and piety" of the child. These
other schools, then, must be opened, and the Romanist youth
locked up in them, along with as many Protestant children
as can be induced to attend. Their religious training is to be
made the main business of the school; and we all know what

that means.   It is a contrivance brought to perfection by the Jesuits, not for strengthening, but for emasculating, the mind, —not for communicating knowledge, but for shutting it out. We can study this curious art as it is in operation on a large scale abroad.   Italy has been enjoying for ages the blessings of this kind of education, and has profited so vastly under it, that she now knows not how to read.   The only schooling which the youth of her common people now enjoy is to learn, under sacerdotal pedagogues, their catechism, filled only with questions touching the mystery of transubstantiation, the glory of Mary, and the benefits of confession.   They are never permitted, if their priests can help it, to endanger their souls by meddling with knowledge of a mere terrestrial kind.   The peculiar merits of this system of tuition have been pretty well developed in those schools in our own country which are entirely under the control of the priests.   A dozen years ago we had a few specimens of mental progress from "St. Mary's Catholic School" in Edinburgh.   These were truly of no ordinary kind.   In five years the pupil could tell his letters, in seven he was able to put them together, in twelve he had mastered the art of reading, and in twenty or so he might be ready to begin the science of arithmetic.   This is a specimen of an education "up to the mark of modern demand, and yet solid in faith and in piety."

We do not wonder that the Church is exceedingly enamoured of this mode of tuition.   It is the true way of training subjects of canon law.   To every congregation a school must be attached.   "Indeed," say the fathers, "wherever there may seem to be an opening for a new mission, we should prefer the erection of a school so arranged as to serve temporarily for a chapel, to that of a church without one."   The fathers know very well what they are about.   They wish to be beforehand with a national system of education.   They wish to have their schools built,—to have them filled with the youth of their own communion, and of others also, if they can lure them thither,—to have their own inspectors appointed, and so an excuse for shutting out the Government inspector, and for being left at liberty to manage or mismanage the business of education in any way they please.

If the Church of Rome is now sincerely set on educating the masses, let her begin at home. There is room in Italy for all her money, and for all her efforts. Let her discard the catechisms which are there her text-books, and introduce something like rational knowledge. Or if, leaving Italy and other countries to barbarism, she must play the educationist in Britain, let her do so in schools open to the inspection of the public, that so we may know that she is not teaching anti-national and demoralizing doctrines in them, and making them the mere nurseries of a Church whose dominion has all along been as fatal to the knowledge as to the liberty of mankind.

FRANZONI AND SANTA ROSA; OR, ROME'S SPIRITUAL DISCIPLINE.

In the autumn of 1850, a conflict broke out in Piedmont between the civil and ecclesiastical authorities, or, we should rather say, between the Courts of Turin and Rome, which is well worth the attention and study of intelligent men. It presents us with a nice manageable plot, not so large as to distract the attention, and yet large enough to permit a proper display of the character of Popery. We here behold that system with saucy impudence and unbearable arrogance advancing pretensions which in countries like ours it affects to explain away, or altogether to disavow. In short, there is here exhibited on a small scale, what, when transacted on the scale of other days, convulsed Europe to its centre, and prostrated its most puissant kings before the power of the mitre.

This conflict, intelligently viewed, reads most emphatically the lesson, that in every condition and in all ages Popery is the same restless, intriguing, and malignant principle. No reverse can subdue, as no concession can mollify, its intolerant and tyrannical spirit. Though humbled in the dust one moment, and seemingly a poor, pitiful, cringing thing, it is the next as ready as ever to set its foot upon the neck of kings, and to strangle in its grasp the liberties of nations. You cannot break its pride, do to it what you will, nor satisfy its ambition by any amount of power and dominion whatsoever. Chase it to dungeons,—strip it of all its possessions,—still, with the poverty of Lazarus it will combine the pride of Lucifer. Thrust sceptres into its hand,—heap diadems upon its head,—it will clamour for more power, and strive avariciously to grasp more wealth. Leave it to itself, and not a vestige of liberty will it suffer to exist. While a single right of a single human being remains uninvaded, it will not cease to plot. Such a principle you cannot regulate, —you cannot reform,—you cannot restrain,—you can only destroy it; and destroy it you must, if you would save society, or give peace to the world. And beyond doubt it is the duty of all to unite for the overthrow of what is equally the foe of the rights of all and the liberties of all,—a system which would tread out every spark of intelligence, and stifle every aspiration for freedom, and which would entomb the world in the dense shadow of a univeral and colossal despotism.

We may be permitted to bestow a momentary glance on the interest attaching to the country which was the scene of this conflict. It is no ordinary land. It is at once rich in natural beauty, and in historic remembrances of a stirring and sacred kind. There stands, in grandeur unapproachable, "Sovran Blanc." There is spread out the quiet beauty of Chamouni. There the sublimity of Sallenches opens to the eye of the astonished and delighted spectator. There, set

round with glistening pinnacles of eternal snow, reposes, in
almost more than earthly loveliness, the Val d'Aosta. But
in this beauteous land we cannot travel a mile without meeting the hideous scars which the superstition and tyranny of
ages have left upon it. Flowing with corn, and oil, and
wine, it is yet trodden by beggars. What hideous spectacles
of disease and idiotcy,—what scenes of misery and degradation,—start up at every short distance amid its loveliness
and grandeur! And what a history belongs to this land!
It is the land of the confessor as well as of the persecutor.
Here burned the "Waldensian candlestick," which shed its
heavenly light upon a small cluster of lovely valleys, while
all Europe besides lay buried in deepest night. Retribution
there surely is in the reverses which the Popish party in
Piedmont are now called to sustain. The same arm which
in other days they employed to crush the confessors of their
valleys is now touching themselves,—gently, indeed, compared with the iron weight with which it smote the Wal-
denses; yet what an outcry! The priests of Piedmont
already claim the honour of martyrs.

This little drama of priestly pretension and arrogance grew
out of a measure passed by the Government of Piedmont on
the 9th of April 1850, whereby the privilege which the clergy
had long enjoyed of being tried only by the ecclesiastical tribunals, and of withdrawing from the civil courts all causes
whatever which might appear to them to involve ecclesiastical
interests, were abolished. These were most necessary and
wholesome changes, surely. By the same measure the right
of sanctuary in churches was abrogated. This, as well as the
former, had been felt to be a grievous oppression. The country
swarmed with vagabonds and criminals, who had no sooner
been guilty of a crime than they made the best of their way
to the nearest church, and defied justice. These oppressive
privileges had been altogether abolished, or greatly mitigated,

in most of the countries of Europe, by the first French Revolution ; but they were suffered to remain in the dominions of the house of Savoy. The sanction of a modern ratification had been added to them in the shape of a concordat established between CHARLES ALBERT and the POPE. But the Cabinet of Turin, disregarding alike the antiquity of these alleged rights and the force of the recent concordat, resolved that these atrocious privileges should be swept away. In adopting this resolution, the Sardinian Government made a great stride in the path of real reform.

The clerical spirit now awoke. The clergy could not brook the idea of being amenable to the laws, like other men, or of surrendering the power which they wielded over the persons and property of their fellow-subjects, by dragging into their own courts all suits whatever in which they were pleased to hold that ecclesiastical matters were involved. Sharp and angry disputes arose, on the one hand, between the Government, with the whole body of the laity, who rejoiced in their emancipation from priestly rule, and the ecclesiastics on the other. The wise and salutary law of the Government was denounced by the priests as a sacrilegious innovation. Resistance was resolved on. A circular, which emanated from the head of the Sardinian clergy, enjoined the monks to disregard the law. A case soon occurred which tested the firmness and sincerity of both parties. Backed by the commands and the promises of Rome, the clergy attempted illegally to restore the jurisdiction which the decree of the Chambers had abolished. FRANZONI, the Archbishop of Turin, by whose mandate the clergy had acted, was summoned to answer for his conduct before the civil tribunals. He treated the summons with silent contempt. The haughty prelate was apprehended and conveyed to prison. And thus ended the first act of this singular drama.

FRANZONI's captivity lasted only fourteen days, and his re-

turn from prison was the signal for a renewal of the agitation.
The Holy Catholic Church had been outraged in the person
of her faithful son, and it became her to wipe off the affront,
and vindicate her insulted dignity.   The entire priesthood
of Savoy, from the Archbishop downwards, burned with the
desire of revenge ; but for some time no suitable occasion
presented itself.   The Vatican was consulted, but the Oracle
of the Quirinal counselled forbearance meanwhile.   At length
an opportunity of vengeance offered,—not such as sacerdotal
maliguancy could have wished, but much too good to be
let pass.   SANTA ROSA, who had made himself conspicuous
as a member of the Cabinet which introduced the "sacrilegious" law,—that law which made the monk and the layman
equal before the tribunals, which allocated civil causes to
civil judges, and which decreed that the doors of the sanctuary should no longer shut out justice in her pursuit of the
robber and the murderer,—Santa Rosa, we say, fell sick.   In
a few days his physicians pronounced his case hopeless   The
dying Minister besought the parochial clergy to administer
to him the "last offices of the Church."   He was for some
days put off with excuses.   Time pressed, and the importu-
nities of the sick man and his friends were renewed.   But
when did Rome forgive an injury which she was able to avenge?
and when did she spare an offender who was fully in her
power ?   Santa Rosa was told, that on one condition only
could the "last rites" be administered, namely, that he should
express his penitence for his guilty share in the sacrilegious
law.   The dying man courageously replied, that "he knew how
to reconcile his duty to his country with his duty to God."
Other Cabinet Ministers interposed their influence, but in vain;
and the Minister breathed his last "unhousel'd, unanel'd."

The Minister of War applied to the Archbishop to know
if it was by his orders that the viaticum had been refused to
M. Santa Rosa, and received an answer in the affirmative.

The excitement was intense in the city of Turin when the intelligence was published ; and the popular indignation against priestly intolerance was raised to its utmost pitch when it became known that the vengeance of the monks was not yet appeased, and that, not content with the virtual excommunication of the Minister for the crime of curtailing their privileges, they had resolved to deny the rites of sepulture to his body. The exasperated crowd, uttering threats of vengeance, proceeded to the convent of the order of *Servites* (servants of God), where, laying hands on a monk who was too obese to make his escape with the rest, and too frightened not to do whatever he was bidden, the populace soon made arrangements with the captured priest for the performance of the offices of sepulture. The body of the unshriven Minister was followed to the grave by all the members of Government, the army, the national guard, and all classes of the citizens ; and the decorum was undisturbed, save when the chance appearance of a priest provoked some sally of the popular hate. The Archbishop, Franzoni, was requested by the Government to resign his see ; and on his refusal, he was apprehended in his palace, and sent, under a strong escort, to the distant fortress of Fenestralla. "During the journey," wrote the correspondent of the *Opinione*, "he supported with the indifference of a Stoic the hisses with which he was greeted as he passed through the different villages."

This is the old battle of the supremacy.   It is strange that at this moment, when the idea of Rome claiming jurisdiction over temporal affairs and civil rulers is generally scouted,— though only by those who do not know her,—Rome herself should so openly and so audaciously advance that claim.   That such was the claim involved in the Piedmontese quarrel, appears undeniably from the following extract, taken from the correspondence to which this matter has given rise between the Courts of Turin and Rome, which is interesting, as being a recent deliverance of the Rome See on the famous question of the supremacy. We pray our readers to mark well its import. "He"—[Cardinal Antonelli, Prime Minister of the Pope]—briefly alludes to the concordats solemnly concluded with Piedmont, and then proposes the question, 'whether a State, particularly a Catholic one, may, on changing its political organization, disregard the disciplinary rights of the Church without the consent of the Holy See?'—a question which he answers negatively, on the ground that the Church is to be perfectly independent of the civil power, as, not having territorial limits, she is everywhere the sole arbiter of her discipline, and being by divine institution a true and perfect society, of a superior order to that of civil societies."

Now, here no claim is advanced to an immediate and direct jurisdiction over temporal affairs and temporal rulers; but practically the jurisdiction asserted is tautamount to this. Three positions are laid down: First, that the authority of the Church of Rome "has no territorial limits," that is, that her jurisdiction extends over all Christendom, and beyond it. Second, that "she is everywhere the sole arbiter of her discipline," which means, that she claims the right of saying what causes affect the interests of religion, that is, the Church of Rome. There is no matter which may not be made to appear to have a bearing more or less direct upon the interests of the Church, and therefore there is no matter over which the Church may not claim jurisdiction. She may excommunicate any minister or prince; she may abrogate laws or forbid their enactment, as we have seen her do in Piedmont, on the ground, of which she is the sole judge, that these laws interfere with the interests of religion. This is merely the temporal supremacy in another shape. The third position is more subtle, and not less dangerous, than the preceding two, namely, that the Church is "by divine insti-

tution a true and perfect society, of a superior order to that
of civil societies." In a sense this is true; but the design
of asserting it here is, not to vindicate the independence of
the Church, but to annihilate the independence of the State.
It is not the doctrine of independent co-ordinate jurisdiction
which is here affirmed, but the dogma of uncontrolled, unlimited spiritual jurisdiction. Every one who is familiar
with the history of the supremacy knows that on this very
plea Rome raised herself to dominion over States and princes
in former times. In her struggles, first with the Frank kings,
and next with the German emperors, the Church of Rome
talked of the *superiority* of the ecclesiastical over the civil,
and thus gradually but steadily advanced her pretensions
from a claim of respect to a claim of obedience,—from a
power to counsel to a power to govern.

Let this fact, then, be borne in mind,—for a fact it is,—
that the Church of Rome is advancing claims in Piedmont
which carry as full and supreme a measure of jurisdiction
over temporal affairs,—over princes and States,—as ever were
advanced by Hildebrand in the eleventh century. And let
this other deliverance of the Pontifical Court be borne in
mind, that no State can change its political organization without the consent of the Roman See. This doctrine would stereotype Europe. Not one of its States dare introduce a single
reform, or take one step in the path of political and social
amelioration, lest thereby the interests of the Church of Rome
should suffer. Nor are these doctrines confined to the Continent. Hundreds of zealous teachers are now sedulously pro-
pagating them in England and the colonies; and there, alas!
they are experiencing a reception denied them elsewhere.

LIBERALISM AND POPERY; OR, ROME'S RECIPROCITY IN
TOLERATION.

THERE were two parties to whom the Papal aggression occasioned an equal surprise: these were the Liberals on the one side, and the Roman Catholics on the other.   The Liberals were amazed that the Romanists should advance such claims as were implied in the Papal aggression; and not less amazed were the Romanists that the Liberals should for one moment oppose these claims.   In the ranks of either party there reigned blank astonishment and mortifying disappointment. It is by no means difficult to account for this.

The Liberals of Great Britain had taken the Romanists to be what they professed to be, and had espoused their quarrel, as against the Protestantism of the country, in the belief that Protestantism had done them a wrong.   They never doubted that the Church of Rome had shared in the progress of all around her, and that she was willing, perhaps a little more so even than some Protestants, to reciprocate toleration with the other Churches of the land.   The Liberals had fought the battle of Catholic emancipation entertaining these views. Their argument required that Romanists should be viewed as really liberal men : they had striven to represent them as such, in many instances, we doubt not, in the honest conviction that they actually were such.   They had repeated their argument so often as to have become at last the dupes of their own statements and reasonings ; and great was their astonishment when they beheld the Church of Pius IX. put on the features of the Church of Hildebrand, and the champions of freedom, as they had taken them to be, suddenly exhibit themselves as the astute maintainers of despotism.

The Romanists, on their side, were equally astonished.

Not conscious of any change in themselves, and feeling that change was impossible,—for to renounce the infallibility were to renounce Catholicism,—they had not realized the misconception entertained of them by the Liberals. They believed that men who had stood so long on the same platform with them, who had said so many fine things of them, and who had fought for well-nigh a quarter of a century to effect for them a release from the restrictions under which they lay, were prepared for the use which they intended to make of their new freedom, and which they did make of it in the Papal aggression. Great, therefore, was their surprise, and still greater their rage, when they found that their old friends had turned suddenly round, and become their assailants. There was an egregious misconception on both sides.

We take it for granted that the great traditionary maxims of the Liberal party are still held by the Liberals of our day. They would not, we presume, disavow the great principles taught by Milton and Locke on the subject of toleration. They would grant that there is, and must be, a line beyond which toleration cannot be carried ; that we cannot tolerate intolerance, for in that case one's self would be intolerant. Even under the government of Cromwell, which tolerated the Jews,—a rare stretch of liberality in those times,—toleration, as Macaulay informs us, was refused to Papists. And the sentiments of the Protector were those of his Latin secretary. " If all cannot be of one mind," says Milton, " as who looks they should be ? this, doubtless, is more prudent, more wholesome, and more Christian, that many be tolerated rather than all compelled. I mean not tolerated Popery and open superstition, which, as it extirpates all *religious and civil supremacies,* so itself should be extirpate, provided, first, that all charitable and compassionate means be used to win and regain the weak and the misled." And we presume also, that no liberal statesman of the present day would challenge the

x

maxim of Locke on this subject. "That Church," says the
philosopher, "can have no right to be tolerated by the magistrate which is constituted on such a bottom, that all those
who enter into it do thereby, *ipso facto*, deliver themselves
up to the protection and service of another prince. For by
this means the magistrate," he adds, "would give way to the
settling of a foreign jurisdiction in his own country, and suffer
his own people to be listed, as it were, for soldiers against
his own Government." The sentiments embodied in the following pregnant passage from the same great writer must
carry with them the assent of all real friends of liberty:—

"Another more secret evil, but more dangerous to the commonwealth,
is, when men arrogate to themselves, and to those of their own sect, some
peculiar prerogative, covered over with a specious show of deceitful words,
but in effect opposite to the civil rights of the community. For example,
we cannot find any sect that teaches expressly and openly that men are
not obliged to keep their promise ; that princes may be dethroned by
those that differ from them in religion ; or that the dominion of all things
belongs only to themselves. For these things, proposed thus nakedly and
plainly, would soon draw upon them the eye and hand of the magistrate,
and awaken all the care of the commonwealth to a watchfulness against
the spreading of so dangerous an evil. But nevertheless, we find those
who say the same things in other words. What else do they mean who
teach that ' faith is not to be kept with heretics ?' Their meaning, forsooth, is, that the privilege of breaking faith belongs unto themselves ;
for they declare all that are not of their communion to be heretics, or at
least may declare them so whensoever they think fit. What can be the
meaning of their asserting that ' kings excommunicated forfeit their
crowns and kingdoms ?' It is evident that they thereby arrogate unto
themselves the power of deposing kings ; because they challenge the
power of excommunication as the peculiar right of their hierarchy. ' That
dominion is founded in grace,' is also an assertion by which those that
maintain it do plainly lay claim to the possession of all things. For they
are not so wanting to themselves as not to believe, or at least as not to
profess, themselves to be the truly pious and faithful. These, therefore,
and the like, who attribute unto the faithful, religious, and orthodox,—
that is, in plain terms, unto themselves,—any peculiar privilege or power
about other mortals, in civil concernments, or who, upon pretence of religion, do challenge any manner of authority over such as are not associated with them in their ecclesiastical communion,—*I say, these have no*

right to be tolerated by the magistrate; as neither those that will not own and teach the duty of tolerating all men in matters of mere religion. For what do all these and the like doctrines signify, but that they may and are ready, upon any occasion, to seize the Government, and possess themselves of the estates and fortunes of their fellow-subjects ; *and that they only ask leave to be tolerated by the magistrate so long, until they find themselves strong enough to effect it.*"

With these propositions in the abstract, we doubt not, the Liberals of our day would agree. But if, nevertheless, we find them lending themselves to the propagation of a scheme of intolerance, it cannot be that they do so knowingly and of purpose, but from some lamentable mistake regarding the nature of the particular scheme. They do propagate intolerance when they further Romanism. We are compelled, therefore, to conclude that the old delusion has come back, and that, from viewing Popery as intolerant, they have begun again to view it as liberal. On no other supposition can we account for the fact, that whereas the Liberals loudly condemned the Papal aggression on the ground that it was a virtual excommunication of all the Protestant Churches, and a planting of a foreign jurisdiction in the kingdom, they have since been the strenuous supporters of that whole scheme which the priests drafted in the Rotundo, for the development of that very Papal aggression, and the diffusion of that same foreign jurisdiction over the country.

There might, prior to the Papal aggression, have been some small excuse for holding that Popery had changed its character, and yielded to modern influences ; but certainly there can be no excuse for holding such an idea now. Popery has started up from its slumber of more than a century, changed in no one iota. Infallibility is still its claim, the canon law is still its code, and its logic is still "anathema." In every country of Europe, and in ours not less, it has shown itself by great and unmistakeable facts, as haughty and intolerant as in the days of Innocent III., and no more disposed to respect, or even to recognise, right or religion in anything, save in itself, now than it was then. But we shall take a particular case. In the summer of 1851, a movement was commenced in this country to obtain from the Pontiff a little reciprocity in religion. Our demand was the *minimum* of what we were entitled to expect. The Pope had built some thousands of churches in our country : we asked leave to build but one in Rome. The Pope had sent his Cardinal to Britain, claiming our whole land : we asked but a few roods in the Eternal City whereon to worship God. Before we had time to present our request formally, the Church of Rome had given her negative through her organ the *Tablet*. No, she said ; chapel you cannot build, worship you shall not offer, within the walls of Rome. But the grounds on which she rested this refusal were even more extraordinary than the refusal itself, and well merit the study of those, if such there be, who really believe that Rome is liberal.

The reasons assigned by the *Tablet* why Romanists should have toleration and something more in Britain, but Britons no toleration whatever in the Roman States, are, in brief, as follows. First, the essence of the Roman Government is religion ; and by introducing diversity of religious belief, we are undermining and destroying the Government. Second, toleration is the law of Britain, but it is not the law of the Roman States. Third, those who are urging the Papal claims in England are, though Papists, British subjects ; whereas those who now demand toleration at Rome are not Roman subjects, but foreign heretics. The last reason, like the postscript of a lady's letter, is the real reason, and says all in a single word. British Protestants can have no toleration at Rome, because, while the religion of Romanists is the only true religion, the religion of Protestants is HERESY.

That Rome should put forth, in the face of the world, such reasons as these, betokens no common hardihood, and is an offence against the common sense of mankind. Her justification needs to be justified. It may be assumed with tolerable certainty, that when Rome thus tears in shreds, and tramples under foot, the mask of conciliation which she has worn for a century, she is prepared, not in word only, but also in deed, to show the world what she is. Protestant worship, then, cannot be tolerated in Rome, because the very essence of the Roman Government is religion. "Rome," says the Popish organ, "is a State peculiarly constituted, inasmuch as the very essence of the Government is religion. Take away the Catholic religion from the people, and, humanly speaking, you take away the very basis on which, in Rome, rests, and always has rested, the temporal dominion of the Holy See. Apart, then, from all questions affecting the souls of the people, the very form of the Government renders it necessary to exclude as much as possible a diversity of creeds, which, if it prevailed, would be fatal to the very existence of the Government." This statement contains a great truth, and one which cannot be too deeply pondered by the British nation. The essence of the Pontifical Government is religion : it is all built upon the dogma that the Pope is Christ's Vicar and God's Vicegerent. Well, then, in admitting the Popish hierarchy into this country, we were admitting not merely a religious system, but what essentially is a form of government, and a government claiming divine right, which knows not how to tolerate, and which ignores all authority and jurisdiction opposed to its own. The hierarchy is but the framework for developing the dogma that the Pope is God's Vicar,—a dogma which makes the Pope as really the Lord Paramount of Britain, of America, and of China, as of Peter's patrimony. The two things are inseparable at Rome, and just as inseparable in Britain.

But, argues the organ of the Romanists, toleration is the law of Britain, and we members of the Church of Rome can

claim the benefit of the law ; but as no such law exists in
the Roman States, it is unreasonable, impertinent, and stupid,
to demand such a thing there : no one could do so but "a
self-sufficient Anglican heretic."

Such a defence strongly reminds us of what might be supposed to pass between an honest man and a rogue. You
profess to act upon the principles of equity and fair dealing,
might the latter say. You recognise the rights of others,
and have avowed your resolution to be scrupulously guided by
them in all your transactions, and hitherto you have honour-
ably supported your character: therefore I make bold to claim
my rights from you. But you are very far from being entitled to urge the same claim in return. I do not profess
to be an honest man. I recognise no rights on the part of
"others." It is known to the whole world that I cheat, and
tyrannise, and take the advantage, wherever I have the opportunity ; and were you not self-sufficient, impertinent, and
a blockhead to boot, you would never come to me with so
unreasonable a demand. Not one whit less preposterous is
the defence of the *Tablet.*

But, argues the Romanist print, "you are no subjects of the
Roman Government who present these claims." We acknowledge with profound gratitude that we are not. Alas ! had
we the misfortune to be so, our choice would be a very plain
one,—either to worship the virgin, or occupy a subterranean
vault in the Inquisition. But what has this to do with the
matter ? Were it a demand for civil rights, citizenship might
relevantly be deemed indispensable ; but this is a demand,
not for a civil right, but a natural one,—permission to worship our Creator ; and to entitle every creature to this right,
it is enough that he wear the human form, and possess a human conscience. Under the government of Heaven this right
is possessed by all ; but under the government of Heaven's
Vicar it is not so. But if citizenship is to be the basis of

the matter, alas for the validity of the rights of Romanists! Can they be subjects of Britain? They have of late been declaring, in the most plain and unmistakeable terms, that they cannot. With a frankness that lays us under obligations, they say they will no longer be " mealy-mouthed,"—that a "divided allegiance they cannot render,"—" that the command of the Pope is the command of God,"—" that the laws of the British Parliament are not laws, but lies,—that they are not to be obeyed, but spit upon,"—" that they are to be rigorously violated,"—and that "the Queen is the enemy of ten millions of her subjects." Most affectionate, most loyal, most patriotic subjects! If the right to toleration rest on the fact of being subjects, verily the right of the Romanist to toleration is somewhat ambiguous.

But one strong reason is as good as twenty, and sometimes better; and the *Tablet* might have settled the question conclusively on his last proposition, which is, that our religion cannot be tolerated, because it is not a religion, but heresy. We poor heretics, who wish to set up,—as the *Tablet*, in diction as elegant as the spirit is charitable, affirms we intend doing,—" the abomination of desolation within the city of God," with the "avowed object of damning the souls of the Romans," instead of taking offence because the "Holy Father" refuses to take part in our impious design by granting us toleration, ought rather to be profoundly thankful that he does not repeat the experiment of the Babylonian monarch on the plain of Dura,—build a vast furnace in the Campagna, heat it sevenfold, and, assembling all the British Protestants of his dominions, compel them to fall down and worship, or do penance in his furnace. This was the only toleration granted to Protestantism anciently; and it is the only toleration, say Romanists, which they will grant to Prostestantism whenever they have the power of doing as they list.

Religious toleration, then, Rome is most willing to reci-

procate with all the world , but how is the thing to be done ?
It is a plain and manifest impossibility.   No one has any religion but herself ; and how can she reciprocate religious freedom with those who have no religion at all ?   This is like
asking one to exchange good money for counterfeit.   The
blame, then, is not hers.   Let the world grow religious, that
is, let it embrace the religion of Rome, and she will reciprocate toleration with all the earth.   That we should enjoy at
Rome the same religious rights which Romanists enjoy in
Britain, plain and equitable as the thing may appear to us,
is a truly monstrous idea ; and the fact that we should entertain it for a moment can be accounted for only, the *Tablet*
assures us, on the supposition that our Protestantism and our
self-conceit have so disordered our reason, that we are incapable of distinguishing betwixt things that differ.

THE MADIAI; OR, THE INQUISITION IN THE NINETEENTH CENTURY.

THE buildings of the "Holy Office" at Rome were closed by
the French; but wherever the Church of Rome is dominant,
there is the "Holy Office."   As an illustration of its working in our own day, we select the case of the Madiai.   There
was an atrocious coolness, a wanton and impolitic cruelty,
about this transaction, which will make it memorable when
some of the blacker and guiltier deeds of the Papacy shall
have been forgotten.

   The demeanour of the accused, so beautifully quiet and un-
obtrusive "till persecution dragged them into fame,"—their
unimpeachable and blameless conduct in all matters touching
the laws of man,—and the notoriety of the fact that they
were apprehended, arraigned, and condemned, solely on matters appertaining to "the law of their God,"—give a special

character to this crime, and make it one of the truest illustrations which even our times have produced of the spirit of Romanism. It has most unceremoniously given the lie to all the fine apologies and fair excuses its friends were framing for its past excesses. Popery had become, they assured us, very repentant, and had made "a long, last, irrevocable vow of reformation." It had laid aside that dreadful apparatus of racks and screws by which it enlightened the consciences and tore the bodies of men in past ages. The tiger's heart had been plucked out of it, and a man's heart had been given to it. No doubt of it, exclaimed the public, who, imposed upon by the "sheep's clothing," had begun to fondle the monster, and to call it a "harmless lamb," and to rate history soundly for having lied so foully upon it. These credulous persons Popery has done its best to undeceive.

It befits it to preach charity in the pulpit of Westminster: it is, too, a well-dressed and well-behaved thing on the streets of London and Edinburgh. It knows full well, that as yet, whatever may be the case twenty years hence, British law is superior to canon law, and that simpletons must be hoodwinked, and their suspicions laid at rest, till Popery is in circumstances to deal more decidedly by them. But look at it in its Tuscan lair, where it is neither muffled nor muzzled. There, as of old, its foot-prints are tracked in blood; there it knows not to show pity to any who come within its power; there it has not recanted so much as one of those tyrannical and bloody dogmas which stand written in eternal characters on the infallible pages of the canon law. To all Rome's loudly-vaunted professions, which simpletons believe, and knaves affect to believe, we oppose the plain unvarnished story of the Madiai.

In 1848 light broke in upon the capital of Tuscany; the political troubles were followed by a religious revival; and the priesthood began to adopt severe measures to prevent the

circulation of tracts and Bibles, which now began to be inquired after by the Florentines.   Our readers will remember
the apprehension and banishment of Count Guicciardini.   The
arm of the Church fell next upon Madiai and his wife.   On
the 17th of August 1851, they were surprised by the sbirri
in what the Church forbids as a crime,—the reading of the
Bible.   The house was searched; other Bibles and Prayer-
books were discovered in it; and the family was instantly
hurried off to prison, where they were condemned to the ordinary treatment, if so good, of the common inmates of a
Tuscan jail.   Rose Madiai was immured in a small unhealthy
cell in the Bargello.   She was separated from her husband,
whom she was not permitted to see, even for a few minutes.
Her health quickly gave way.   Her physician could make
no representation of her condition, nor do anything for her
relief, his visits being forbidden.   The representative of the
British Embassy, Mr Scarlet, in vain petitioned for her release, offering bail in her behalf.   The doors of the Tuscan
Bargello could be opened, no, not even for the temporary re-
spite of so great a malefactor; and poor Rose Madiai was
kept pining in confinement month after month.   At the end
of nine long months,—and nine mouths in a dungeon is a
long period,—Rose Madiai and her husband were brought up.
There sat the Judges in their robes; and there stood the prisoners in their chains.   Their crime, what is it?   Have they
plotted conspiracy against the Government?   Have they joined
in the revolution, or been guilty of robbery and murder,—that
nine dreary months of solitary confinement have already been
endured by them, and yet, after all, they must abide their
trial amid these dread forms of justice?   No; they stand ac-
quitted of all these crimes.   The very tribunal that condemns
them is careful to proclaim that they have committed no
political offence, no civil wrong,—that they are not even suspected of such things.   What, then, is their crime?   It is

this : they have dared to open and to read that blessed Book in which is written Heaven's message of salvation to a lost world. That it is so, we appeal to their Judges themselves. The words of the indictment are as follows :—

"On the evening of the 17th August 1851, the public force surprised three individuals, who, along with a girl of twelve years of age, whom the Madiai had received into their house for a short time, were occupied in the reading of the Bible translated by Diodati, having each a copy before them ; that in the house of the said Madiai were lodged not only different copies of the said Bible, and others in English, and Prayer-books for the use of the heterodox, but various works besides, of the same kind, and several copies of the same work."

And again,—

"That on the third female, who was little more than twelve years of age, and unfurnished with religious instruction, they produced the effect of her abandoning her own religion, and adopting that of her employers. This latter person the Madini took the trouble to teach to read, and thus rendered her capable of understanding the books which they supplied, viz., the Bible by Diodati, and another, entitled 'The Book of Common Prayer,' printed in London in 1848, by the Society for the Promotion of Christian Knowledge, in which were found recorded the same maxims and doctrines condemned by the Catholic Church,—doctrines which expressly assert that the existence of purgatory and the worship of images are foolish inventions ; that in the sacrament of the Eucharist there is no real transubstantiation ; and similar notorious heretical pravity indicated above."

Assassination and reading the Bible Rome ranks in the same category. For no sooner did conviction take place,—indeed, the Madiai boldly confessed the charge,—than the sentence usually passed on assassins and similar malefactors was pronounced upon them. Francis Madiai was condemned to fifty-six months at Volterra, the Cayenne of Italy, and his wife to forty-five months in the Argastolo, the hulks for females !! To this punishment were added the costs of process. Rose Madiai heard with undaunted mind a sentence which the voice of the Judge trembled to pronounce ; and when it was ended, she erected her feeble frame, weakened by long confinement ; and turning to her husband, who rose at the same instant, the two smiled sadly on one another, and tenderly embraced in presence of the court. An appeal was made to the Court of Cassation ; and a petition was at the same time presented to the Grand Duke in behalf of the prisoners. The sentence pronounced by the Corte Regia was confirmed ; and the Grand Duke, who had just made a concordat with Rome, and had really no power in the matter, returned for answer to the prisoners' petition, that it was a matter of conscience, and that the sentence behoved to be carried out.

In the February following (1853), while the Madiai were dragging out their imprisonment in the company of felons, the one in the Argastolo at Lucca, and the other in the Casa di Forza, amid the poisonous air of Volterra, the matter was discussed in the British House of Commons. The Honourable Arthur Kinnaird introduced the subject in an able speech, in which the facts of the case were clearly, concisely, and temperately stated, and was replied to by Messrs Lucas and Bower. Even these men found such a case, in such a place as the British Senate, difficult to handle. The matter was so clear, as a case of persecution simply and solely for reading the Bible, that their sophistry failed to mystify it, and their courage did not enable them openly to defend their principle of persecution for conscience' sake ; and so nothing was left them but to fall back on the " burning of Servetus" and the " persecutions of Elizabeth,"—the Papist's stock-in-trade in all such cases, although a rather disproportionate set-off, one should think, against five centuries of systematic and continuous *autos da fe.*

A single word, first of all, on this point. Granting that all the cases cited by the friends of persecution are true, and true to all the extent alleged,—What of that ? Granting that they were a hundred times more numerous than they are,—for the recorded cases of Protestant persecution can all be told in a single speech, and can all be cited in a single debate, and, when used, they are laid aside carefully, to be brought forward on the next occasion,—granting, we say, that they were a hundred times more numerous than they are, we still ask,—What of that? All these crimes are chargeable against the *men*, not against the *system*. Herein lies the grand point of difference between Protestantism and Romanism. These acts of Protestant persecution were committed by men, some of whom were only pretended Protestants, while others owed the prejudice and intolerance which led them into these errors to that very Romanism which now brings these charges against them. Every Protestant who has persecuted has, to the extent to which he *has* persecuted, violated the fundamental principle of his system, which recognises the right of private judgment ; and Protestantism, so far from sanctioning these as acts done in her service, condemns them as crimes committed against her most sacred principles.

Protestants may have persecuted ;—it would have been a miracle almost if, after ages during which the right of burning men for opinion was held and acted upon as a most sacred duty, they had not fallen into the crime of their opponents : but whatever Protestants may have done, Protestantism never persecuted. We challenge our opponents to show a single principle included in the acknowledged and fundamental doctrines of Protestantism, which, either directly or indirectly, teaches persecution for conscience' sake. Protestantism never yet shed a single drop of blood, or robbed of an hour's liberty a single human being. But how different is it as regards Romanism ! Here it is not the *men*, so much as the *system*, that has been the persecutor. The terrible persecutions which have deluged the world with blood, and shed a sackcloth gloom over the successive ages of history, are to be laid at the door of the system. The creed of the Church of Rome on this point is a compendious one : the punishment of heresy is death.   On this dogma the Crusades were founded ; on this dogma the Inquisition, with its fourteen modes of torture, was built ; and to the defence of this terrible dogma Rome is inevitably committed.   The Koran or the sword was the cry of the Mahomet of the East : Believe or burn is the cry of the Mahomet of the Seven Hills.   To cite cases of oppression committed by Protestants, or acts of toleration done by Romanists, is a mere waste of time.   These, though true, neither inculpate Protestantism nor justify Romanism.   We defend not *Protestants*, but *Protestantism*.   In like manner, we arraign not *Romanists*, but *Romanism.*   We say that it is essentially a system of persecution, and, as such, has ever persecuted, and ever will persecute ; and the difference between it and Protestantism just lies here, that the Protestant violates the fundamental principle of his creed when he persecutes, whereas the Romanist violates the fundamental principle of *his* creed when he tolerates.

And as is the creed, so is the practice, of that Church, wherever she has the power.   DEATH stands as the unrepealed penalty in the canon law against heresy ; and DEATH the Church of Rome is in our day inflicting on those whom she calls heretics.   Does the Romanist ask "Where?"   We reply, in Italy and Spain.   "The Grand Duke of Tuscany still hesitates on the subject of the Madiai," observed Lord John Russell ; "but," he justly added, "this is a matter on which hesitation implies capital punishment."   Yes, Rome has not changed the punishment ; she has only slightly changed the mode of inflicting it.   The sharp despatch of the torture, or the still sharper despatch of the stake, she no longer employs.   These are old-fashioned methods of killing, which that Church has learned to do without.   She has invented slower processes, which have the twofold recommendation of prolonging the agonies of the victim, and screening from public odium the infamy of the persecutor. The flames that licked up the limbs of Savonarola in the square of Florence were merciful, compared with those heavy leaden sufferings' which a delicate woman has been compelled to endure, in our own times, in the Bargello of the same city. In the one case the spirit is not killed, and it nobly triumphs over the sufferings of the body. It can look undauntedly upon its doom ; it knows the worst ; it sees before it one half-hour's thrilling agony, and then the triumph and the palm for ever. But it requires yet greater courage firmly to contemplate and unshrinkingly to endure the slow, corroding, ever-recurring and never-ending misery of a solitary imprisonment for life, or what is equivalent thereto. To walk through an avenue of horrors to the grave,—who can tell what suffering is in that ? There is the silence that grows from day to day and from hour to hour, till it becomes at last terrible and insupportable. Sad and strange thoughts, which the mind has no power to banish, begin to intrude themselves. The felon's dress and the felon's chain perpetually suggest the idea of the felon's character. Health gives way ; the spirits sink ; a fearful gloom begins to encompass the soul. The world of the living is gone ; it has cast the sufferer out ; yet the other has not opened its gates as a shelter from his sorrows. He inhabits a void beyond the confines of earth. Reason begins to totter : first comes imbecility, then idiotcy, and then death. Ah! it were easy to pass at once to the scaffold ; but to walk to one's grave through a crowd of terrors, each more awful than the scaffold,—who can .tell the agony that there is in a doom like this! It was this fearful doom which Rome publicly inflicted,—for we must hold the intention equivalent to the deed,—in the middle of the nineteenth century, upon the Madiai, for the crime of reading the Scriptures.

PART FOURTH.

MAYNOOTH, CONVENTS, CHAPLAINCIES, &c

MAYNOOTH.

MAYNOOTH is the central, and in some respects the most formidable, part of the Papal organization in Great Britain. It is so on several grounds. It is a fountain-head of Popery, and a fountain-head kept open by a Protestant State. Its professors are salaried, and its students are lodged, fed, clothed, and educated, for some seven or eight years, at the nation's expense. At the yearly cost of thirty thousand pounds we provide priests for teaching all over Great Britain and her colonies that very Popery which, as Protestants, we testify against as idolatry.

But farther, so long as Maynooth remains on its present footing, the endowment of the Church of Rome in Great Britain hangs over our heads. The same logic by which we justify ourselves for educating the priests of Rome would seem to demand that we should pay these men when engaged in educating others. The endowment of Maynooth is valued by the priesthood on this among other grounds, that it is a promise of something better. In the document issued by the "Defence Association," we find the priests asserting that "the Roman Catholic Church in Ireland" accepted the endowment of that seminary "as a small instalment of justice from a Legislature which had robbed her of millions." Many years ago, Sydney Smith, in his " Peter Plymley's Letters," strongly urged the payment of the Popish priesthood, shrewdly suspecting that, although they were then professed Voluntaries, they would be but too glad to receive the money. " The first thing to be done," said this quaint but brilliant writer, " is to pay the priests, and after a little time they will take the money. One man wants to repair his cottage ; another wants a buggy ; another cannot shut his eyes to the dilapidations of a cassock. The draft is payable at sight in Dublin, or by agents in the next market-town dependent upon the commissioner in Dublin. The housekeeper of the holy man is importunate for money ; and if it be not procured by drawing for the salary, it must be extorted by curses and comminations from the ragged worshippers, slowly, sorrowfully, and sadly. There will be some opposition at first ; but the facility of getting the salary without the violence they are now forced to use, and the difficulties to which they are exposed in procuring the payment of those emoluments to which they are fairly entitled, will in the end overcome all obstacles."

Our statesmen, too, it is well known, look with special favour upon the scheme of endowing the priesthood. The changes which they made upon the form of the grant were intended as the preliminaries to the accomplishment of their design. For half a century the money was voted yearly as a sort of educational grant. In 1845, the late Sir Robert Peel changed the grant into a permanent endowment, by transferring it to the Consolidated Fund. The farther progress of the matter was checked, for the time at least, by the Papal aggression ; but despite this untoward event, as our statesmen deemed it, and despite the fact, as confessed by the present Sir Robert Peel in Parliament, that the late Sir Robert, his father, had been disappointed in every one of the hopes he entertained from the endowment of Maynooth, the

L

idea has not yet been relinquished. Nor, should they attempt seriously to carry out the scheme, would they, we fear, meet with any very decided opposition from either side of the Protestant camp, the Established or the Voluntary. Not from the Established Protestants, who might deem their own endowments a little more secure in consequence; and not from Voluntaries, who reason, not very logically as it appears to us, that the addition of another Established Church to those already existing, and the increase, by some five millions, of the number of persons interested in upholding endowments, would weaken the cause of national Establishments.

Of all the anomalies with which the history of Governments abounds, there is perhaps no greater anomaly than Maynooth. Were Government to affect a lively desire for the construction and use of machinery, and yet forbid the manufacture of iron,—were it to extend in a conspicuous manner its patronage to agriculture, and yet interdict the process of ploughing,—were it to profess unwonted zeal for the extension of commerce, and yet declare illegal the art of shipbuilding,—were it to interest itself in the promotion of letters and science, and yet prohibit the erection of schools and the printing of books,—or, to come nearer the point, were it to burn witches, and yet found and endow colleges for the teaching of witchcraft,—it would act undoubtedly a most contradictory and incomprehensible part, but a part not a whit more contradictory and incomprehensible than when it takes measures to repel the Pope, and at the same time erects in the heart of Ireland a manufactory of Popery. If the thing be good, why repel it in the person of the Pope? and if it be evil, why create and encourage it in the schools of Maynooth? If the policy of the Ecclesiastical Titles Bill be right, is it possible that the Maynooth policy can be other than wrong? The policy of the Ecclesiastical Titles Bill is

manifestly founded on the principle that the priests of Rome
are a dangerous class, seeking, under a religious mask, to
seize upon political power; that they are the abettors of a
foreign prince, with whose domination their own interests
are bound up; and that therefore their proceedings cannot
be too jealously watched, or their arrogance too firmly
checked. But the policy of the Maynooth grant undeniably
imports that these same men are a public good; that the
more of them the better; that the more thoroughly they are
trained in priestcraft, the more firmly will British rule be
established in Ireland; and, in short, that they are so necessary and useful a class, that it is right to spend annually
thirty thousand pounds of the public money in educating
them.   It is impossible that both these propositions can be
true.

Since the Maynooth College was endowed, experience has
demonstrated the fallacy of every one of the reasons urged in
its behalf.   It was argued first of all, that if the Irish priesthood were educated at home, they would escape those anti-
national feelings and prejudices which they were apt to contract while undergoing their training abroad. We should thus,
it was believed, have a body of men more deeply attached to
the Constitution of their native country, and pursuing a national and patriotic policy.   In the second place, it was said
that if we are to have priests at all, it is better to have a
highly educated rather than an unlettered priesthood; and
that, could we only get gentlemen and scholars, their influence with the people would be all on the side of civilization
and order. Accordingly, Maynooth was founded and endowed
from the exchequer of a Protestant people, that the aspirants
to the Roman priesthood might be saved a journey to France,
and that, being educated and civilized themselves, they might
begin to educate and civilize their countrymen. Not only
have the anticipated results not been realized, but the exact

opposites of these results have been wrought out.   The Irish
priesthood, instead of being more national, are less national,
and to a man are now animated by a spirit of deep and bitter
hostility to Britain; and the people, so far from standing
higher in intelligence and comfort, are now sunk to a lower
depth of ignorance and barbarism.   This decadence dates from
the erection of Maynooth.   Sixty years under an institution
which was to give Ireland an enlightened and national clergy,
and a civilized and peaceful people, have sufficed to reduce
that country to the last stage of anti-national antipathy and
exasperation.   Who has not been stunned by the loud and
fearful curses which have come rolling across the channel,
fulminated from the altars of the priesthood, mingled with
the wrathful howls of a priest-ridden and maddened people?
These are your Maynooth scholars and gentlemen!   These
are the flocks tended and fed by the pious and lettered priests
of Maynooth!   Better far we had flung our gold into the
channel, than sent it across the sea, to be a curse in the first
place to Ireland, and a curse in the second place to ourselves,
by the demoralizing dogmas and the anti-national sentiments
it was there employed to propagate.

Previous to the erection of Maynooth, the Irish priests were
educated in France.   In no country in Europe were more
liberal opinions entertained on the subject of the supremacy;
and it was impossible to be educated in that country and not
to catch a very considerable portion of the liberal, the national, and the patriotic spirit of the defenders of the "Gallican liberties."   The priests educated in France were, accordingly, a superior race to the present priesthood of Ireland.
They were less the subjects of the Pope, and very much more
the subjects of Britain.   But no sooner was Maynooth erected than the high ultramontane theology began to be taught
in it.   Its professors acknowledged before the Royal Commission of 1853 that they do not receive the articles of the Gal-

lican liberties, with the exception of the first, which, we shall
afterwards show, they no more receive than they do the rest.
Maynooth, then, is a thoroughly Italian school; and from the
day it was set up, a change for the worse began to be visible
upon the clergy and laity; and now there is not a country on
the face of the earth where the Pope has more devoted and
abject slaves than in Ireland. It could not be but that Maynooth should work this sad transformation upon the national
character. The text-books employed in that institution all
teach the highest existing theories of the infallibility and
supremacy,—the superiority of the ecclesiastical power,—the
complete subordination of the secular,—the immunity of the
clergy from the civil tribunals,—the atrocities of the canon
law,—the blasphemies of the Pope's dispensing power,—the
infernal logic of Escobar, and the disloyal and anti-national
doctrines of Hildebrand; in short, doctrines are daily taught
there which would deluge both islands with blood were there
now a strong army in the country. And it is to endow an
institution which has covered Ireland with anti-national and
demoralizing doctrines, and which is sowing the same malignant principles broadcast in our colonies, that Government
devotes the money of a Protestant people.

But how have these Maynooth gentlemen done their part
as educators of the people? Their friends in Parliament
took the liberty of promising great things from them in this
capacity. But, alas! those who so promised grievously mistook the men in whose behalf they pledged themselves so
deeply. The Romish priest will not, and dare not, educate.
His dominion is founded on ignorance; and the grosser that
ignorance, the more firmly rooted is his dominion. Are we
to expect the priest to raze the foundations of his own power?
If Rome cast out Rome, how shall her kingdom stand? Has
not Government encountered the combined opposition of
that very priesthood which it has fed and reared, in its

benevolent attempts to extend a system of national education to the Irish?   And, as regards the Queen's Colleges,
no sooner had the Government erected them than the priests
of Maynooth virtually closed them, by forbidding every Roman Catholic parent, under peril of his salvation, to permit
his son to cross their threshold.   It was a singular hallucination into which the Government fell, that the better a priest,
the better a citizen.   An exactly opposite conclusion would
have been much nearer the truth.   An invasion by men
trained in all the modes and equipped with all the appliances
of modern warfare, would be a very different thing indeed
from an invasion by painted barbarians, with their rude weapons.   The College of Maynooth has effected a like change
in the Pope's invading troops.   We have exchanged the
French-bred priest, ill read in Dens, with low notions of the
supremacy, and proportionally high notions of the British
Crown, for a race of crafty, insidious, intriguing, thorough-
trained priests of the ultramontane school, who recognise but
one power in the world,—the ecclesiastical supremacy,—and
ignore all authority inconsistent with it.   Such is the priesthood which Maynooth has given us.   Ireland convulsed with
plots and barbarized by ignorance is their handiwork.

MAYNOOTH : THE NEW WAY OF DEPOSING MONARCHS.

In the year 1853, the Earl of Aberdeen being Prime Minister, a Royal Commission was appointed for "inquiring into
the management and government of the College of Maynooth,
the dicipline and the course of studies pursued therein."   In
March 1855, the Commission laid the result of its labours
upon the table of the House of Commons, in the shape of
two ponderous volumes folio.

    This "Commission of Inquiry" was issued eight years after

the college had been endowed ; and it did seem a strange
order of proceeding, to *endow* first, and *inquire* afterwards.
It may be doubted, moreover, whether inquiry was necessary,
either before or after endowing.   Why, what is it that we
endow at Maynooth ?   Is it not Popery ? And is it necessary at this time of day that we should issue a Royal Commission to investigate the character of Popery, and to inquire
whether it is compatible with the independence of nations
and the purity of society ?   Why, here is HISTORY at our
door with her report.   She has had her "Commision of Inquiry" on Popery sitting these twelve centuries.   She has
neither hastily nor partially investigated the matter.   Patiently has she sat during the long weary ages, silent, but not
unobservant, her eye ranging over every country of Europe,
her pen noting down every occurrence of moment ; and now
she throws down her ponderous volume for the inspection of
all.   Let us open it, and read for ourselves.

There is no mistaking what Popery has been, and is.   National treaties disregarded and trampled upon ; covenants and
oaths violated ; opinion put down by the rack and the exe-
cutioner ; the fountains of knowledge and morality sealed
up ; monarchs dethroned ; nations robbed of their liberty ;—
such are the blessings, as history testifies, which the world
owes to Popery.   Is there any other system on which the
experience of mankind has been so ample and so uniform ?

In all ages and in every country it is the same.   When
did Popery preach loyalty to Protestant sovereigns, save by
excommunication ?   When did it cherish freedom of conscience, save by the dungeon and the stake ?   When did it
live in peace with Protestantism, unless when it found it
necessary to circumvent by fraud that it might destroy by
violence ?   Did it not solemnly assure Huss of the validity
of his safe conduct, till it was ready to light the faggots around
his naked limbs ?   Did it not swear eternal amity to the Pro-

testants of France, till the moment had come to strike the
St. Bartholomew blow ?   And scarce had it cleared the Seine
of corpses, or cleansed the streets of Paris from Huguenot
blood, till it recommenced the same course of combined per-
fidy and cruelty, making covenants and treaties with the
Protestants, confirming them by the most awful oaths, and
in one hour sweeping away treaties, covenants, oaths, with
all the hopes that the credulous Huguenots had built upon
them by the revocation of the edict of Nantes.   Really one
knows not whether to be more indignant at the treachery
of Romanists, or more astonished at the simplicity of Protestants.

The same game has been played in our country, although
not as yet with the same tragical effects.   Before the passing of the Emancipation Act, did not Roman Catholic
bishops deny on oath some of the fundamental doctrines of
their Church, and, amongst others, the doctrine regulating
the allegiance due by a Papist to a Protestant sovereign ?
What has been the conduct pursued by the Romish dignitaries in our country since ?   Was not the Papal aggression a palpable ignoring of the Queen's jurisdiction ?   Is not
the bull *Cœna Domini*, in which she is cursed as a heretic,
annually fulminated at Rome ?   In the public meetings of
the Romanists, is not the first place given to the Pope, and
the second to the Queen ?   And have not the laws of the
British Parliament been pronounced, not laws, but lies, and
to be rigorously disobeyed ?   And yet, disregarding the in-
evitable conclusions from all these acts, and shutting his
eyes, too, to the teachings of an experience extending over
ten centuries, Lord Aberdeen came forward demanding a
Commission of Inquiry into the principles and tendencies
of Popery at Maynooth.   As well might he have appointed
a Commission to inquire whether there is light at noon-day,
or darkness at midnight ; whether ice exists at the poles ;

whether heat liquefies or congeals bodies ; whether stones fly
upwards, or fall to the ground ? Our experience on these
points is scarce more uniform and decisive than it is on the
point which Lord Aberdeen's Commission was empowered
to try.

The Commissioners summoned before them the professors,
and in some instances the students, and interrogated them
touching the doctrines taught at Maynooth. We submit,
that if the aim was to bring out fully and truthfully the
character and tendencies of the Maynooth teaching, this was
not exactly the best way of reaching such a result. May
nooth proper is neither the buildings, nor the professors, nor
the students, but the text-books. The text-books it is which
contain the system which Maynooth was built and endowed
to teach, and which, in point of fact, is being taught there,
and, through the priests, is being inculcated on their flocks
in Ireland and throughout the empire. To these text-books
must all have recourse who wish to know what Maynooth
really teaches on the important questions of the Pope's deposing power, and the relation of a subject to a non-Papal
sovereign. 'The Commissioners, instead of sitting in judgment on Maynooth, permitted Maynooth to sit in judgment
upon itself,—to appear at the bar, and enter an elaborate and
ingenious piece of special pleading in its own behalf.

That special pleading is, however, a total failure as a defence of Maynooth. The true doctrines of that seminary will
not be hid. To one who has eyes to see and a heart to understand, they shine through the sophisms so artfully and
abundantly employed to veil them. Let us first hear Maynooth on the Pope's temporal power : and certainly our meed
of admiration is due to the ingenious and conscientious, yet
very efficient, way in which Rome now goes about the business
of deposing sovereigns, and which is so great an improve-
ment on the ruder methods of former days. We find the

Rev. Henry Neville, the professor of the first year's theology at Maynooth, before the Commission. Mr Neville is asked, —"What doctrine is taught at Maynooth respecting the civil or temporal power of the Pope or of the Church?" He answers,—" The opinion of the college, as far as I could learn, has always been, that no such power, direct or indirect, belongs to the Church or to the Pope."—(Report, &c. vol. ii., p. 56.) Equally explicit is the evidence of Professor Furlong. "Is the teaching of Maynooth," he is asked, "distinct upon this point, that the Pope has no power to interfere, directly or indirectly, in the affairs of temporal kingdoms, and no power of dissolving the oath of allegiance?" He answers,—" Yes."—(Vol. ii., p. 91.) We find the same witness saying,—"The Pope has no right to interfere in purely political affairs,—none whatever : he can decide an abstract question, whether a certain course of conduct on any occasion would conflict with the laws of morality, or be in accordance with them, in the same way that any moralist could, but with a higher sanction and authority ; but we do not allow, nor does the Pope claim, any authority such as a superior exercises over a subject in any political matter." "He could give no general power of direction as to any political matter, could he ?—He could give no general power of direction, only inasmuch as he is the supreme authority from which we receive the exposition of the natural and divine law." "He could only interfere with politics so far as they come within the province of morals ?—Yes."—(Vol. ii., p. 101.)

The careless or uninstructed reader of these answers would certainly carry away with him the impression that the Church of Rome has now revoked all her former teachings on the head of the temporal power of the Pope. The professors at Maynooth most distinctly deny that the Pope has any temporal jurisdiction. They most distinctly say that he has no power to depose sovereigns, and no power to release subjects from their oaths of allegiance. And no doubt the statement, although in point of fact utterly untrue, is yet in point of form in strict agreement with the present phase of Catholic dogmas; for, according to these, the prerogative wielded by the Pope at this day is not infallible *jurisdiction*, but infallible *direction*. Her Majesty's Commissioners, not knowing this distinction, were completely misled and deluded by the above averments; for in the preface to their blue books they say,— "We see no reason to believe that there has been any disloyalty in the teaching of the college, or any disposition to impair the obligations of an unreserved allegiance to your Majesty." We should think that the professors at Maynooth were somewhat astonished at their own success in making it be believed that the doctrine of their Church was changed, and that they no longer taught a *divided* allegiance, and no longer placed in the Pope's hands a deposing power. How do we reconcile the averments of the Maynooth professors with the known and unalterable law of Rome? They are very easily reconciled.

Direction is but another name for temporal supremacy. That supremacy is not now wielded in the same direct and formal way as in mediæval times, but by a mode that is somewhat circuitous and inferential. The Pontiff sits upon the Seven Hills, not now as the magistrate of Christendom, begirt with the sword of the temporal power, but as the lawgiver of Christendom, with the great statute-book of his kingdom, the canon law, open before him. He tries questions of morality, and pronounces upon points of duty; and duty, in his view, enters into all political and temporal affairs. His advice is not merely advice that *may* be followed: it is advice that *must* be followed, and *will* be followed. It is the divine and infallible judgment of God's Vicar, binding, under the highest sanctions, on the conscience of every Romanist ; and the man who dares disobey becomes an eternal anathema.

But let us pursue the Maynooth evidence a little farther, and we shall soon see that the professors, while they affect to deny that the Pope has any temporal power, or any right to depose sovereigns, do actually admit that nevertheless, and indirectly, he has such power and authority.   Let the reader ponder the following interrogatories and replies.   The Rev. Dr Moriarty is before the Commissioners, and is being examined on the subject of the Pope's temporal power.

" What was the doctrine taught at Maynooth when you were there as a student, respecting the distinction between the spiritual power of the Pope and the temporal power of the sovereign ? We were taught upon that matter what we swore in the oath of allegiance, that the Pope has no temporal power, direct or indirect, in these realms."

This seems very plain.   It would appear an out-and-out denial of all power, direct or indirect, for temporal effects, in the Pope, and would seem to place him on the same level, as regards temporal jurisdiction, with any Protestant minister in the world.   But the examination continues :—

" Can he enforce a temporal matter by spiritual sanction in foreign countries ? He cannot enforce a temporal matter *as such ;* but he can enforce by spiritual sanction the obligations of conscience, which regard or affect temporal matters."

To this answer Dr Moriarty appends an explanation, to the effect that he views power as *subjective,* not *objective ;* and he illustrates his meaning by saying,—" When, as confessor, I direct the restitution of stolen property, or the rescinding of an unlawful contract, the object is a temporal matter, but the power is purely spiritual."   He might have added with equal truth,—When the Pope, as Vicar of Christ, directs the deposition of a sovereign, or the rescinding of a subject's allegiance, the object is a temporal matter, but the power is purely spiritual.   This is confirmed by the interrogatory and reply that immediately follow.

" Would the Pope have a directing authority with regard to the exercise of temporal rights or temporal privileges ?—So far as they may become questions of morality or cases of conscience, the direction concern-
ing them appertains to the Church, which is the authorized exponent of
the law of God upon earth, and therefore to the Pope, who is the supreme
pastor and teacher of the Church."—(Vol. ii., p. 128.)   " The question
whether or not, according to the principles of the English constitution,
a case may arise in which a subject (there being a violation of the correlative duties of the sovereign and the subjects) may rebel, is a question,
not of law, but either of constitutional propriety or general prudence.
Are not both these matters entirely of a temporal nature ?—They are
temporal matters."   " If they are purely temporal, are they not out of the
jurisdiction of the Pope ?—Though temporal, they are not purely temporal.   Every deliberate act which man performs is moral or immoral,
and has therefore its spiritual relation."—(Vol. ii., p. 130.)   " If a man
were disposed to transfer his allegiance, or to give it up, that decision of
the Pope would enable him to give it up with a safe conscience, would it
not ?—Yes ; for a Catholic should feel his conscience at rest when acting
in accordance with a decision of the Pope."—(Vol. ii., p. 131.)

So at last the truth comes out, and very clearly too.   The
Pope has no direct temporal authority ; he has no indirect
temporal authority ; but he has a *spiritual* power which he
exercises over temporal matters for temporal effects.   He
has the power of direction in all matters in which duty is
involved ; and in what matter is duty not involved ?   This
direction is authoritative and infallible.   To the Romanist
it is the command of God.   He dare not oppose to it the
conclusions of reason ; he dare not confront it with the rights
of conscience.   He has but one course : he must obey, or—
dreadful alternative !—be damned eternally   A spiritual consideration is this eternal damnation, doubtless ; but it is a
spiritual consideration which carries with it to the poor
Papist a coercive power so overwhelmingly irresistible, that
the prisons and scaffolds of kings are, in comparison, impo-
tent and futile.

The Pope, then,—Pius IX. as really as Innocent III.,—
retains the right and the power to depose sovereigns ; but
he exercises that power, not by an act of *jurisdiction*, but by

an act of *direction*.   As the infallible director of consciences,
it belongs to him to say, simply as a question of morals, and
for the purpose of directing the faithful in a point of duty,
whether kings have a valid title to their throne.   But what
in his mouth is a piece of purely spiritual direction, speedily
becomes in the hands of those to whom it is addressed an
act of purely physical force.   Verily it appears to us to matter wonderfully little to the sovereign who loses his throne,
whether it be by temporal jurisdiction or by spiritual direction.   Either way the result is the same,—his throne is lost.

MAYNOOTH: A SURE AND INGENIOUS WAY OF RELEASING
SUBJECTS FROM THEIR ALLEGIANCE.

WE advance to another branch of our subject.   The right of
the monarch to reign has its correlative in the duty of the
subject to obey; and the power that claims authority over
the one must of necessity claim an equal authority over the
other.   We have just shown that the Pontiff exercises the
right of saying when the monarch's title is valid : we now
proceed to show that, on the admission of the Maynooth professors, he exercises the right of saying when the subject's
allegiance is binding.

Let it be here once for all observed, in order to meet the
ignorant objections sometimes urged in behalf of the Pontiff's
"direction" or "advice," to the effect that, after all, it is
much on a level with the direction and advice which a Protestant minister may address to the members of his flock,
that so far is this from being true, there is all the difference
in the world betwixt these two things.   The Pope's advice,
simply as the Pope's advice, binds the conscience of the Papist.   The Protestant pastor's advice, simply as the Protestant pastor's advice, has no binding power whatever.   The

Protestant exercises his right of private judgment: he tests the "direction" of his pastor by the Bible,—the infallible director of conscience, and the supreme standard of duty. If he finds the course enjoined at variance with the Word of God, he holds it to be of no force whatever; for it is a first principle of Protestantism, that the man who gives and the man who receives this direction are both alike bound to bow to the supreme authority of revelation.   But with the Papist it is not so.   He has no right of private judgment.   He has no standard by which he can or dare try the Pope's direction. There is no higher authority to which he can carry his appeal.   The Pope's direction is final, is infallible, is divine. The man who resists it sins mortally; and, continuing to resist, perishes everlastingly.   In short, there is all the difference betwixt these two cases which there is betwixt a rational being, whom you influence by reason, and a machine, which you move by main force.

We return to the question of the allegiance of the subject. Dr Moriarty is still before the Commissioners. He is asked,—

" Are there no circumstances under which the Pope could release a citizen from his oath of allegiance?—Most emphatically I say, none."— (Vol. ii., p. 128.)

This seems a most unqualified denial of all releasing power on the part of the Pontiff.   It was meant, doubtless, that it should be taken as such.   But let us mark the sophistry of the reply.   Dr Moriarty continues:—

" But as our greatest constitutional lawyers, and, as I think, our best theologians, hold that there are cases when the allegiance of the subject ceases, and when the Government of a country may be justly overthrown, I consider that the Pope is the fittest authority to decide, in many cases, whether such circumstances have arisen.   In many cases he could not decide ; and I firmly believe that in such cases he would not undertake to do so.   In no case can he cause the allegiance of a subject to cease, his power in such a matter being simply declaratory, not enabling."— (Vol. ii., p. 129.)

We wish the reader to mark the latter part of the answer,

and tell us, if he can, what is the difference, in their practical
results, betwixt these two methods of annulling the allegiance
of the subject. The Pope's power in such a matter, Dr
Moriarty informs us, is not *enabling;* it is declaratory. The
Pope cannot *make* a monarch's title invalid; he can only
declare it invalid: he cannot annul the allegiance of the subject; he can only declare that it is already annulled. That
he means this, and simply this, Dr Moriarty makes, if possible, still more undoubted and clear by his answer to the
following interrogatory:—

"Then it [the decision of the Holy See] would have the effect of releasing the conscience of a subject from an obligation which the oath of
allegiance had imposed upon him before, would it not?—It cannot," replies Dr Moriarty, "effect a release: it can simply inform the conscience
that a release is already effected."—(Vol. ii., p. 129.)

So, then, when Romanists affirm that the Pope has no
releasing power, they mean that he has no such releasing
power as is *enabling,* but that he has a releasing power which
is *declaratory.* He cannot, say they, *make* the allegiance of
a subject non-existent: he can only *declare* that it is already
non-existent. This is a very nice distinction, or rather, we
ought to say, it is a very contemptible quibble. So long as
it pleases the Pope to hold a sovereign as a lawful sovereign,
he has no power, say Romanists, and, we may add, he has
no motive, to release his subjects from their allegiance; but
whenever it suits the Pope's infallibility or policy to hold
that the sovereign has ceased to be a lawful sovereign, then
his subjects are told that their oaths of allegiance no longer
exist. The Pope, let us mark, does not say,—"I release
you from your oaths:" he is careful to tell us that he has no
power to do that: he possesses only the power of declaring,
authoritatively and infallibly, that they are already released.
Yet we must not say that the Pope has a deposing power,
or wishes to have it: none but very wicked people say so,

and these will, in time convenient, receive from canon law the due reward of their sayings. The Pope possesses no power in the matter, except the poor right of saying that a sovereign has ceased to be a sovereign, and that his subjects have ceased to be his subjects, and so quietly opening the door, or rather permitting the door to open itself, for all that may follow.

It is hard to determine whether we ought to be more astonished at the impudence of the men who can juggle in this way, or at the simplicity of the men who are deceived by such juggling. Suppose, instead of the despoiling a monarch of his crown, it were a case of common robbery. The accused is put upon his trial; and he defends himself by saying,—I never touched a penny of that man's property; in fact, I never saw him in the face before: I simply expressed my honest opinion to these men, my followers, that I had a better right to his possessions than he had; and straightway, by some means or other, for which I disclaim all responsibility, his goods were transferred from him to me. Or let us suppose that it is a charge of murder, and that the person accused says,—"I protest that I never spilled a drop of that man's blood, or injured a hair of his head: in truth, I carry no sword wherewith I could do injury to any one: I simply chalked a death's-head and cross-bones upon his door, and soon thereafter he became *non-existent*. I take nothing to do with the practical interpretation given to my well understood sign by my hired and sworn assistants. If they mistook the counsels of spiritual direction for the commands of temporal jurisdiction, that is no affair of mine." The defences supposed would be every whit as good as those which the Romish theologians are accustomed to make of the Pope's very clever and ingenious method of deposing sovereigns.

SHOWING HOW REBELLION MAY BE PREACHED ACCORDING TO
MAYNOOTH.

POPERY, age after age, retires deeper and deeper into the
darkness. In proportion as the light increases, the Papacy
drops thicker and yet thicker veils betwixt itself and the
world. Whenever its designs are in danger of being discovered, it folds over them the skirts of its sable mantle. If
still they shine through, it doubles the folds. It would appear thus to quit the scene of human affairs; but in reality
it is all the while, in virtue of its invisibility, going deeper
into the very heart of them. The Papacy is neither a less
influential nor a less meddlesome thing at this day than it
was centuries ago: but it is a far subtler and a more invisible
thing than it was then. Innocent III. sat openly upon his
throne; and whatever he did he did boldly and defiantly,
neither disguising his acts by pretexts, nor excusing them
by apologies. He governed with a bold truculence, which
inspired respect after a fashion, while it awakened universal
dread, and extorted universal worship, making kings bow
as low before his footstool as the poorest peasant in all their
dominions.

But the Papacy of our times has transformed itself into a
spirit of darkness. It no longer permits to the world a sight
of its proper visage. It maintains, no doubt, the shadow of
its former pomp; it places upon the Seven Hills a piece of
imbecility as its representative, the senility of which helps to
persuade men that itself has become senile: but the Papacy,
immortal in its malignities, and gathering increased strength
from increased experience, has retired behind the scenes, that
it may the more completely govern a world which it affects
to have forsaken. It sits in all consciences; it prompts, in-

stigates, and compels all to serve it; and, working by others' hands, it disavows the strifes, revolutions, and bloodshed which are its handiwork. Its newest contrivance is to substitute past time for present time, and to refuse all responsibility for its proper actions, by pleading, when they become actions *de facto*, that they were done *de jure* a year, or a dozen years, ago. Is a country convulsed, and a sovereign deposed by violence?—that is no rebellion; for in the judgment of Rome, the sovereign who has now been deposed *de facto* was already deposed *de jure*. His subjects who have taken part in his overthrow have not violated their allegiance in the least; for how could they violate what had long before become *non-existent?* This is the doctrine which we give thirty thousand pounds annually to have taught to the students at Maynooth, in order that they may teach it to their followers all over Great Britain and her colonies. And should that doctrine come to be acted upon some of these years,—as why should it not?—what reply should we be able to give, when told,—" You sanctioned that doctrine when you endowed an institution to teach it; and why should you object to our carrying out what you yourselves were at such pains to have taught?"

How adroitly Maynooth teaches men the proper time and circumstances in which to rebel, may be seen from the following interrogatories and replies. The same witness, the Rev. Dr Moriarty, is still before the Commissioners.

" Suppose the case of a conflict arising in this country between the subjects and the Crown upon a question warmly agitated, and with respect to which some persons were inclined to overstep the limits of allegiance, and plunge into rebellion. In such a case, would the Pope, if not appealed to, have the power of declaring that such a state of things had arisen that the Irish people professing the Roman Catholic religion might rebel against the English Sovereign?—Supposing the Pope in full possession of the circumstances, he has power to declare to us what the natural and divine law prescribe as our conscientious duty.

" Has he authority to issue a declaration, without being appealed to, which would terminate the obligation of the oath of allegiance ?—The appeal adds nothing substantially to his right or power. It merely puts him in possession of facts. His declaration cannot terminate the oath of allegiance if it has not been already terminated by the force of circumstances. He can merely make known the fact to those who were ignorant of it, or who doubted it.

" Would his declaration in any manner augment the right to rebel, or in any manner relax the duty of obedience ?—Certainly not. But he can teach men when they should obey, and, by a necessary consequence, when they may rebel."

The Pope, then, possesses the power of giving judgment in the supposed case, although no appeal may have been made to him by the parties ; and his judgment, when adverse to the sovereign *de facto*, has this exact amount of power in it, that it does not command men to rebel : it only teaches " men when they should obey, and, by a necessary consequence, when they may rebel."

The Romanist body in Great Britain still continue to submit to, although they can scarce be said to obey, the law. Are we therefore, it may be asked, entitled to conclude that their allegiance remains unaffected and entire, and that it is resting upon them as a positive duty ? And are we to infer that in the eye of Rome and of Roman jurists the Queen is regarded as the Sovereign of Great Britain *de jure*, and not simply as Sovereign *de facto ?* By no means. In the Maynooth examination the release of English Papists in the days of Queen Elizabeth was touched upon, and the principles which regulate Romanists in all such cases were brought into view. " A release from obedience," said Dr Moriarty, " does not imply an obligation to disobey. There might be," he added, " prudential reasons for continuing to obey, even though not bound to do so." Dr Moriarty was farther asked, —" At the same time, if a man were disposed to transfer his allegiance, or give it up, that decision of the Pope would enable him to give it up with a safe conscience, would it not ? —Yes," he replies ; " for a Catholic should feel his conscience

at rest when acting in accordance with a decision of the
Pope." Taking these statements into account, the likelihood, indeed the almost certainty, is, that the Romanists of
Great Britain are at this hour released from their allegiance,
if not by a formal sentence of the Pope, yet by the understood interpretation of the Roman law applicable to their
position, although, for "prudential reasons," as Dr Moriarty
says, they continue "to obey, even though not bound to do
so." It is material to observe, in fine, that the "Maynooth
Evidence" was supervised at Rome before being published
in our country, and consequently it expresses the opinion not
merely of the Maynooth professors, but of the Pope and the
sacred college.

We see against what a subtle foe the nations of Europe,
now fighting for their independence, have to contend. Truly
it may be said of them, and of our own nation among the rest,
that they "wrestle not against flesh and blood, but against
principalities, against powers, against the rulers of the darkness of this world, against spiritual wickedness in high places."
The Papacy has gone deep indeed into the darkness; thick
clouds encompass it, through which mortals cannot gaze; but
from the midst of the gloom and silence in which it sits it
launches its bolts upon the world. Its hand is not seen; but
the stroke is all the more sudden and sure. If the bolt is
invisible, not so the destruction which it inflicts. Kings are
tumbled from their seats; the ties that bind nations are dis-
rupted; and the furies of revolution and war, obedient to the
summons of this invisible demon, start up, to scourge mankind and desolate the earth.

"SPIRITUAL DIRECTION" AT THE HUSTINGS.

It only remains that we glance at the manner in which
Popery, as it limns its own likeness in the "Maynooth
Report," conducts itself on the hustings, and at the "spiritual
direction" which it there tenders to those whose consciences
it has entirely in its keeping. It is the priest, and the priest
alone, that votes in Ireland. No doubt his flock go to the
poll, doubly armed,—with the franchise, which Government
has provided them with, and the shillelagh, with which they
have provided themselves; but both franchise and shillelagh
are at the service of the priest; and, as regards any really
independent and intelligent exercise of the right of election,
the ostensible voters might as well be absent, and the matter
left exclusively in the hands of the priest, the real voter.
Such an arrangement would make not a particle of difference in
the result, and would greatly benefit the cause of public order.

If there is no temporal matter that is *purely* so, surely a
matter that so nearly touches the emoluments, and more
especially the prospective emoluments, of the "Church," as
the Parliamentary franchise does, must involve in a large
degree the question of sin and duty. Maynooth takes this
view decidedly of the matter. We find the Rev. Dr O'Hanlon,
librarian of the college, and prefect before the Dunboyne
establishment, before the Commissioners. He is asked whether voting at elections be a temporal or a spiritual matter,
and answers thus :—

" A vote for a member of Parliament may become a spiritual matter,
because its direct and immediate effect may sometimes be the commission or avoidance of sin. In the case supposed, I should think no Catholic priest or laymen would hesitate to vote for the man who is disposed
to favour and protect Catholic interests in Parliament.

" If the electors require information or instruction, as they do frequently in many parts of Ireland, I think the priest, as such, is not only justified, but bound, to teach and explain their duty.

" What do you mean by their duty ?—To select the parties whom they conscientiously believe to be the fittest to represent them in the House of Commons, and to discharge the duties of a Member of Parliament.

" Would he (the priest) be warranted in withholding any sacraments of the Church from a man by reason of his preferring one candidate to another ?—Absolutely speaking, he would ; because a priest is not only warranted, but bound, to withhold the sacraments from a man who is disposed to commit a mortal sin ; and as the case may absolutely arise in which a person, by preferring one candidate to another, would exhibit that disposition, a case may consequently arise in which the priest would be not only warranted, but bound, to withhold the sacraments from a man by reason of his preferring one candidate to another."

When the superior fitness of a certain candidate is "undeniable," and the judgment of the priest is clearly expressed in his favour, it would be "mortal sin," according to Dr O'Hanlon, to vote for another candidate ; and the voter who is suspected of meditating the commission of so great a crime is to be deterred by the threat of "withholding the sacraments," that is, by the threat of damnation. If you do not choose to obey the priest, he has no power, he says, to compel you. He cannot coerce the body ; he can only *direct* the conscience : he cannot hang you in this world ; he can only burn you eternally in the other. The dominion of the Roman Father is confined to the domain of conscience, and his rod of rule is *eminently* and *purely* spiritual : but behind the *spiritual direction* of the mitre, and at no great distance, is ever the *physical force* of the mob. To return to Father O'Hanlon, we might extract much more of the same nature from his evidence ; but we content ourselves with only one other passage :—

" Whether it would be a sin or not in a particular case, the elector himself is the judge, according to his own conscience ?—Of course, he is ultimately the sole judge ; but his judgment must be grounded on rational motives ; otherwise it would be rash and imprudent, and might be erroneous, *as it would undoubtedly if it stood in opposition to the morally certain opinion of the priest.*"

These principles received an ample illustration at the first
general election in Ireland after the Papal aggression,—that
of 1852.   The Catholic Defence Association, intent on
creating a powerful Romanist party in Parliament, framed
beforehand a list of candidates, and set a-working the whole
machinery of their Church to force these candidates upon
the constituencies.   Electors were taken from their beds at
midnight, and sworn upon crucifixes : whole congregations
were driven to church, and had their voting-tickets dealt out
to them from the altar.   The confessional was employed to
discover who had pledged themselves to independent candidates, and released from their promises, in virtue of the dispensing power.   Electors were taught that paradise was to
be earned, or damnation incurred, at the hustings.   If any
should dare to vote otherwise than in the Church's behalf,
for them there were in reserve the most terrible penalties.
In vain should they implore at the hands of the priest the
baptism of their child, or the last sacrament for themselves
at the hour of death.   They would be banished from society
here ; their future lot would be assigned them with Judas ;
and their eternal companions would be devils.   That an
ignorant and superstitious people, who believe in the reality
of these tremendous threatenings as firmly as they believe in
their own existence, should be able to exercise, in the face
of a tyranny like this, the rights with which the British
Constitution has clothed them, is utterly incredible.

This consideration may suffice to show how utterly beyond
human power it is to enfranchise a people situated as are the
Irish Romanists.   We defy you to make them free and independent citizens, do for them what you may, or give to
them what you will. Load them with immunities and votes ;
enact measure after measure for their political enfranchise-
ment ; the whole of that power passes wholesale and at once
into the hands of the priest : you have but augmented the

power of the Church, and deepened the slavery of the people. What strange delusion was it, future ages will ask, which led the men of the nineteenth century to strive so earnestly to extend political rights to the Irish, and pay so dearly for the rearing of a class of men to rob them of them?

Nothing could be plainer or simpler than the rule laid down for Popish representatives in Parliament. They are taught, in all their speeches and votes, to have regard to but one thing.—the interests of "Catholicism." They are free to act according to their fealty to the Queen, only when the prior claims of the Pontiff are satisfied. With them it ever must be Rome first, England next. The account of their stewardship is to be rendered in the confessional. In fact, it is not to their constituents, but to the priest, that they are accountable. One man sits for Father this, another for Father that, and not for the borough or county in which the hustings may have been set up simply as make-believes of popular representation. Popish Ireland would be as effectually represented in Parliament by a single priest as it is at present by forty or fifty Members, all acting under priestly direction, and all speaking and voting as one man. It is recommendatory, moreover, of this simpler but equally real representation, that it would be an immense saving of the time and temper of the House.

NOT TWO ROMANISMS IN THE WORLD.

PARLIAMENT, when it appointed its Commission, challenged the Maynooth divines, in effect, to a defence of their system. In that defence we never doubted that all the resources of Jesuitism would be brought into play. Nay, we were even prepared to find, in a case in which Romanism stood on its trial before the world, that counsel would be taken with the best Catholic intellects in Europe. This was done; for, as we have already said, the "Evidence" was rised and purged at Rome before being published in Britain. But even after its friends have done their best for it, Romanism may still be convicted as utterly corrupt in morals, and thoroughly anti-national and treasonable in politics. The passages we have adduced from the " Evidence," when stripped of the veil which has been cast over them, make this, we think, very plain. It is the old visage that looks out upon us from behind the mask. It is the paint only that is new. Such as the world saw it in the twelfth century, when liberty fell before it, and kings quailed at its look, such are its iron features still. The Popery of the canon law and the Popery of the "Maynooth Evidence" is one and the same Popery. The latter document, equally with the former, makes the head of the Roman Church the infallible judge of morals, and the supreme director of consciences; and what more is needed to enable the Pontiff, when opportunity suits, to plant his foot upon the necks of kings, and loose the obligations and oaths of nations? The "Maynooth Evidence," equally with the canon law, visits heresy with temporal punishment; and what is wanting in that case, save the power, to renew in the cities of Britain those fearful tragedies which were enacted of old on the plains of Languedoc and in the valleys of Savoy? If the priest has power to withhold absolution from the man who refuses to vote as he bids at an election, which the "Maynooth Evidence" says he has, has he not power to withhold it from the Prime Minister, the Monarch, the nation, that refuses to subordinate its political power to the interests of the Church? The question of prerogative can in nowise be affected by the number of persons concerned. If the power of the priest is good as against one man, it is good as against a million. If he can cut off from the communion of the faithful, and adjudge to eternal flames, the poor franchise-holder in

Ireland, why may he not wrap the entire realm of Britain in the gloomy terrors of excommunication and interdict, discrown our Queen, suspend our tribunals, close our churches, silence our bells, and deny graves to our dead,—in short, cover the whole land with the dire tokens of the dreadful wrath of the Pontiff? Fair and plausible as it looks, the root of all these pretensions is in the Maynooth document. In its quiet bosom sleep all these elements of destruction; and time and opportunity only are wanting to develop that document into a second canon law.   If any one were beginning to dream that there were two Romanisms in the world, —one on the south of the Alps, arrogant, ambitious, and peculiarly dangerous to monarchs, and another on the north of the Alps, meek, self-denied, spiritual, and perfectly harmless as regards national right and kingly prerogative,—he must by this time, if he has thought over the "Maynooth Evidence," have begun to discover his mistake.   Whatever facts that Report may have striven to conceal, it has made one truth at least very apparent,—even that there is but one Popery in the world.   There is not an Ultramontanism and a Maynoothism, as was beginning to be thought. The Popery of Maynooth is the Popery of Rome; and the principles taught in the Collegio Romano are not a whit more ultramontane than those taught in the Hibernian seminary.   Indeed, we are not without our suspicions that the Maynooth Popery is the more ultramontane of the two, inasmuch as it was deemed prudent, before permitting it to appear before the world, to make it undergo a certain amount of excision and modification at the hands of Italian Popery.

CONVENTS; OR, HOW TO STEAL A COUNTRY AND ITS PEOPLE
PIECEMEAL.

WE turn to yet another very formidable phase of the Papal
aggression: we refer to the rapid multiplication of conventual
establishments in Great Britain.   The Reformation cleansed
our soil from these abodes of lawlessness and lewdness, of
licensed beggary and sanctified vagabondism; but the locust
brood have again returned.   Along with them, we may be
sure, will return the same moral and physical devastation
which marked their course in other days.   We cannot ima
gine a more effectual way of inoculating society with the
most virulent vice than by permitting the erection within its
bosom of such establishments uncontrolled by law.   That
confraternities of men and women should abandon all the
relations and all the duties of society,—that they should hold
themselves exempt from the obligation of contributing in the
smallest degree to either the material or the mental wealth
of the nation, and, while living on the fat of the land, share
with their fellow-creatures in neither the labours of peace nor
the perils of war,—is unnatural and monstrous.   But that
they should be at liberty to withdraw themselves, with their
property and their deeds, beyond the sphere of the law, and,
while converting their abodes into castles inviolably fortified,
whence they issue forth to prey upon others, that no one should
be at liberty to follow them into their retreats, and to inquire how they spend their time, to what uses they devote
their spoil, and what deeds it pleases them to commit in their
well-guarded seclusion and security, is more unnatural and
monstrous still.

In Papal countries conventual establishments have proved
a terrible scourge.   They have contributed largely to the

dissolution of morals, to the prostration of law, and to the ruin of industry. Scarce had Piedmont awoke to her new life, till she began to grapple with this terrible abuse. She felt it to be a hindrance in the path to liberty, which it behoved her at any cost to get rid of. Beginning with the most useless of the monkish orders, and proceeding to a total dismantling of the whole organization, she broke up their fraternities, sold their houses, and confiscated their lands, being convinced that she could be safe only when the last of these establishments had been razed from her soil. Spain has been following in the wake of Piedmont, though not to the same extent. Last of all, the Italian Government in 1863 suppressed all the Monastic orders in the kingdom, with the exception of those in Sicily. It appropriated to State purposes the property and revenues of these establishments, broke up the male houses, turned adrift the monks, giving a small pension to each, and hung the death-sentence over the Capuchins and the nuns, by forbidding them to receive new members. It is one of the strange anomalies of our times, that what "Catholic" Governments are labouring to root out, we are at pains to plant.

The Monastic orders are increasing in our country at a rate which is truly marvellous. In 1829 there was not a single nunnery or monastery in either England or Scotland. In 1865, as any one may see by consulting the *Catholic Directory*, there are not fewer than two hundred and one monasteries, male and female. This is an increase which has seldom been equalled, and which, perhaps, never was surpassed, even in a Popish country. On the return of the Bourbons to France, the conventual system began rapidly to recover from the blow which the revolution had dealt it: still it required forty-three years under "Catholic sovereigns" to add ninety-five new foundations to the existing ones. In a period of time eight years shorter, we have seen more than

double this number spring up upon the soil of Britain. Two
hundred convents in the brief space of half a lifetime, and
in a Protestant country! With such rapid strides does the
monastic system return among us.

In many points this system comes into conflict with the
laws of the country and the subjects of the Queen.   In every
such instance it violates and sets at nought the former, and
enslaves the latter.   The act of 1829 forbids the establishment in this country of the male monastic orders of Rome.
This prohibition was renewed in the act of 1860, which provides for the due administration of Roman Catholic charities,
Despite the law, of the two hundred and one "Religious
Houses" mentioned above, fifty-eight are monasteries. These
are clearly illegal.   Every new monastery is a new violation
of the law.   This the Government know perfectly well, but
the power to uphold the law against the Popish faction has
passed from them.

In another point do these establishments set at nought
the statutes of the realm.   The law of 1860 forbids the acquisition of property by the Monastic orders of Rome. This
enactment is evaded by the monks living together in community; not as an order under a common vow, and holding
their property in common, but as so many individuals volun-
tarily associating together, each holding his property, with
power to dispose of it as he pleases.   Such is the constitution of the Oratorians at Brompton.

The act of 1864 requires that all burials taking place
within the precincts of these conventual establishments shall
be registered.   It has been proved by undeniable facts that
this law is disregarded ; that burials take place in the ceme-
teries of these places which are not registered ; that sometimes the dead are interred under false names, and the marks
by which they might be traced are obliterated.   We find Mr
Newdegate, when moving in the House of Commons, the 3d

March 1865, for a Select Committee "to enquire into the existence, character, and increase of monastic or conventual establishments or societies in Great Britain," saying, "it was proved that there were more burials within the precincts of the convent (Colwich) than appeared in the register of deaths. It was proved that coffins were seldom made outside the convent ; but that rough carpenters were employed within the establishment to make packing cases, without any of the usual appurtenances, in which the bodies were committed to the grave."

Other outrages upon the liberties of the subject are becoming common on the part of these establishments. It is their occasional practice to entice persons of weak mind, or under age, within their precincts, to baptize them after a residence of a few hours or a few days, and then to retain them in defiance of the authority of their parents and guardians. From several others we select the cases of Miss M'Dermot and Miss Ryan, which are well known to the public. The latter was taken from a convent in London, and transferred to a lunatic asylum in Belgium. "She screamed, she struggled, she implored assistance from every passer-by ;" notwithstanding, the priests were permitted to violate the law with impunity, and carry off their victim. The case was brought under the notice of Government, who referred it to the law-officers of the Crown. The opinion of the latter was that the law had been violated, but not with a bad intention ; and there the matter rests. To seize the subjects of the Queen, drag them by violence from the country, and consign them to a foreign madhouse,—the most terrible of all prisons,—is, say the law-officers of the Crown, "a violation of the law ;" but then it is done for the good of the "Church," and so not with "a bad intention," and therefore it may be done with impunity ! Could there be a more manifest token that a judgment lies upon the nation,

than that the constituted guardians of its liberties should be
left to so stultify themselves?

Conventual establishments are a double theft: they are a
theft of the subjects of the Queen, and they are a theft of tho
soil of the country.   They are, in the first place, a theft of the
subjects of the Queen.   The community that inhabits the convent, whether great or small, is a community reft from the
Crown of Great Britain; for within its walls that Crown has
no power.   The members of that community are no more
amenable to the rule of our Queen than if they lived in
another country or in another planet.   Within the convent
walls another king and another law bear sway, and the conventual members are the subjects exclusively of that king
and that law, not *in theory* only, but *in actual fact*, inasmuch
as recent legislation has guaranteed to British convents perfect
exemption from all inspection or intrusion on the part of the
law.   In doing so, our Parliament has sanctioned not merely
the *religion* of the Pope, but the *authority* of the Pope.   They
have thrown the shield of British power around intolerance
and illegality.   The inmates of our conventual establishments
are a distinct and independent nation encamped on our soil,
and quite as much an irresponsible and foreign community
as if they lived in Russia, or in Italy, or in China.

True, outside the walls of the convent the nun or the monk
is amenable to British law; for abuses which the law knows
it will correct, and crimes which the law sees it will punish.
But inside these walls,—and the majority of their inmates
permanently live inside,—the law is absolutely without the
slightest control over monk or nun: it is alike powerless to
punish or to protect.   The law may follow them to the
threshold of their convent; but there it is arrested; it dare
not enter.   It is denied the usual means of knowing the
crimes that may be there committed, and is forbidden the
facilities given it in other cases to discharge its functions as

the guardian of the person and the liberty of the subject. No doubt, if complaint should reach it from the interior of these places, the law has power to open the convent-door; but, alas! a lofty wall with iron gate encloses the nun. She is watched day and night. She is forbidden all intercourse with her relatives, unless once a year, in the presence of others. She has gone too deeply down into slavery for cry or groan to be heard from her. There is an awful gulf betwixt her and the law, which she cannot pass. We can no more expect petition or complaint from the interior of convent or monastery, although on British soil, than from the heart of Siberia, or the bottom of a French bastile or a Roman inquisition. In fact, every such establishment is a little Siberia, a veritable bastile,—the opprobrium of our liberty, which it affronts, and of our soil, which it pollutes.

But, in the second place, convents and monasteries are a theft of our very soil. It is stolen very ingeniously, no doubt, but still it is stolen. Every square rood which the convent walls enclose is so much territory lost to British law and British liberty. It is completely disjoined and dissevered from the rest of the country. It is, in fact, a portion of foreign soil pieced into the free earth of Britain. It is to every practical purpose quite as much a piece of Italy or of Spain as if it lay beyond the Alps or the Pyrenees; for within its limits no law is known save canon law, and no king is obeyed save the monarch of the Vatican. That portion of our country's soil lies as far beyond the sceptre of Victoria as if it formed part of the Papal States. Every inch or acre of conventual territory is so much abstracted from the domain of the Queen, and so much added to the territorial kingdom of Pius IX. in Great Britain. And if one acre may be so abstracted, why not a thousand? Why not the whole country?

No reasoning is needed to show the dangerous and into-

lerable character of such acquisitions. They are utterly in-
compatible with the peace and the loyalty, as well as the
industry, of our country. Every acre added to these establishments is so much of our soil annihilated. Nay, better
were it that it were annihilated than that it should remain
to feed, to clothe, and to lodge a body of men who hold of a
foreign head,—who are, within their convents and monasteries, entirely independent of our authority and law,—who
contribute not an iota to the nation's wealth or wellbeing,—
and who keep no terms or connection with the country, save
to prey upon it always, and to foment treason and sedition
now and then.

CONVENTS VERSUS HABEAS CORPUS.

On the 10th of May 1853, Mr T. Chambers moved in Parliament for leave to bring in a bill for opening both monasteries and convents to the inspection of the authorities. The
motion was opposed by the Minister of the day, Lord John
Russell; but, though carried against Government, it was never
passed into law. On such a question one might suppose an
assembly of Englishmen could come to but one conclusion.
Had the question come up as one touching the liberty of the
subject, which was its true character, and not as a question
involving the prerogatives of a Church, there would have been
found no difference of sentiment respecting it. The Commons of Great Britain would have united as one man in proclaiming the great principle conceded so early as the days of
King John in Magna Charta, afterwards confirmed in the
reign of Charles II. in the famous act of Habeas Corpus, and
held by all statesmen who have flourished since, to be one of
the main foundations of British liberty, namely, the inviola-
bility of the subject save by the authority of law.

But unfortunately the question did not come up in this form : it came up as a question affecting the discipline of the Roman Catholic Church. Thus the element of Romanism was imported into it ; and wherever that element enters, farewell to all rational and constitutional views on any question that may chance to be discussed.   On the approach of that element there gathers straightway around great principles a thick opaque atmosphere, impassable to the clearest eye ; the heads and hearts of statesmen give way ; and the great axioms of civil and religious liberty,—all, in fine, which at other times and in other circumstances is most surely believed amongst men,—are first questioned, and then denied. Under the bewildering influence of this element, men seem to forget all they ever learned, and to lose sight of all the acts and pledges of their public life. They sink at once into political dotage and political inconsistency, and advocate views which would go to raze the whole fabric of British liberty.   There is not one of our leading statesmen who would not manfully resist the Crown, were it to encroach but by a hair's-breadth upon the liberty of the subject ; and yet an encroachment which they would oppose to the uttermost if made by any of the constituted authorities of the land, they tolerate, nay, they defend, when it is made by the Roman Catholic Church.

The question touching conventual establishments is exceedingly plain.   It is simply this,—whether British law shall cover the entire area of the British territory, or whether there shall be persons and places to which the jurisdiction and protection of the law shall not extend ? This is the question.   Stated in this its true form, it is one on which the Constitution has pronounced so distinctly,—on which all the great interpreters of the Constitution have pronounced so distinctly,—and on which that innate love of liberty which is a second nature in every Briton pronounces so distinctly,—that

it will not bear to be discussed. It is so obviously just and
right that the power and protection of the law should extend
to all the subjects of the Queen, and that there should not
be a foot's-breadth of her soil under the dominion of a foreign
code, that the question is admitted even before the discussion begins. There was not one of the opponents of Mr T.
Chambers' motion who dared to grapple with, or even to
look at, the question in this form. They insisted pertina-
ciously,—and some few, we fear, against their better light
and convictions,—that the motion would lead to restrictions
on religious liberty. There never was a grosser misrepre-
sentation of any question. The question has nothing whatever to do with religion. It refers, and refers exclusively,
to personal liberty. The law finds the door of a convent
closed against its authority ; and it says, " Every door in the
realm must be open to me, in order that my functions, as
the custodier of the liberty of every man and woman in the
kingdom, may be discharged. The door of every jail is open
to me ; the door of every lunatic asylum is open to me ; the
door of every factory, and of every castle and palace in the
kingdom, is open to me ; and this door, which alone of all
the dwellings of the realm is closed against me, must be
opened too." And the law is right. Like death, with im-
partial foot it must cross every threshold, else civil equality
and universal personal security cannot exist. The law cannot sustain as an excuse that, this being a convent, a Papal
anathema, like another flaming sword, guards the entrance.
It must prosecute its mission of giving personal liberty to all.

But, observe, the law does not interfere in the slightest with
any of the ecclesiastical arrangements of the convent. It does
not render penal the belief of any Papal dogma. It does not
abrogate the ghostly authority of the Lady Abbess. It does
not prohibit the taking of the veil, or cancel the vows of the
nun. It does not interfere with penances even, provided the

submission thereunto be voluntary. Tho nun may lick tho dust at the feet of the Lady Abbess a hundred times a-day, if so it please her. She may pass whole days in social seclusion and confinement, and wear sackcloth for weeks together, if she do it with her own free will She may repeat, within her grated chamber, as many Ave Marias and pater nosters as she may deem to be for the good of her soul. High-born and delicately-bred, she may, if she choose, charge herself with the drudgery of tho whole establishment. She may be as happy as she pleases, or as wretched as she pleases: the law will pass by, and leave her in the undisturbed possession of her self-sought happiness or her self-inflicted misery. But if she wishes to reclaim her rights as an Englishwoman, the law says, "You shall have them. I know nothing of your vow never to leave these walls alive; I know nothing of the canon law, which has barred your egress with a fearful anathema; I recognise in you a subject of the British Crown; and I protect you in your right of personal liberty inherent in every British subject. You wish to be free: the door is open; go forth." If this be not a matter appertaining to civil liberty exclusively, and having no reference to religious matters whatever, we confess to having lived all our days in utter ignorance of what constitutes liberty, civil or religious.

We are content to rest our case against conventual establishments on this one undeniable fact, that both the law and the practice of these establishments are in violation of personal liberty, and come into collision with the most fundamental rights of the British Constitution. Something like an attempt was made to deny this in the course of the discussion in Parliament; but the thing could not be denied. "Private liberty," says De Lolme, "according to the decision of the English lawyers, consists, first, of the right of *property;* secondly, of the right of *personal security;* thirdly, of the *locomotive faculty.*" A woman, when she takes the veil, loses all three. She becomes as one dead and in the grave. Body and soul—"property," "person," and "locomotion"—are under the dominion and at the disposal of an absolute and irresponsible authority. But, it may be said, it is in her power to surrender all her rights if so she please. This we grant. It is in the ulterior results that the grievance lies. The nun may discover that she has been entrapped into her vow, or she may come to regard it as unlawful, and so wish to recover her rights. British law says she has the power to do so at any moment. But canon law says No; she cannot recover them. There is a gulf between her and the outer world, over which the law cannot pass to help her, and over which she cannot pass to obtain the help of the law; for among the rights of which she was denuded when the black veil descended on her unhappy head, was the "locomotive faculty." Whatever the mental or bodily torture she may be enduring, she cannot make known her case. Nor is there any power in Britain to compel a Lady Abbess to produce her for the satisfaction of her friends. They may suspect that all is not right, and wish to have their fears set at rest by a personal interview; but no; they are met at the door of the nunnery by a message from the Lady Superioress, that their relative has no wish to see them, and no desire to leave her present abode. Thus the law stands paralyzed at the convent-door. The domain within is under the exclusive jurisdiction of canon law; and, let the oppression practised be what it may,—let fetters be employed to coerce the will, —fasts, penances, darkness, to tame the spirit,—let deportation, or death itself, crown the whole,—that convent-door cannot be opened,—that wretchedness the law can neither reach nor remedy.

Oh, said some of the defenders of this system, there is a Habeas Corpus Act. True, but of what use is it? It is stopped at the door of the convent. It is most effectually arrested and disarmed by the silvery tones of the Lady Abbess. The poor victim within has just as much consolation in thinking there is a Habeas Corpus Act outside, as the sailor on his battered deck has of knowing that there is a life-boat on shore, or the famished beggar that there is turtle-soup in the banqueting-room of the Lord Mayor. Disguise this system under whatever sanctimonious pretences you will, we say it is tyranny; and let even a Russell defend it, it is, notwithstanding, a blow at the root of British liberty.

PARADISES WITH BOLTS AND BARS.

ONE is curious to know what could be urged against so reasonable a demand as that convents should be open to the inspection of the law. Some of the objections are not a little remarkable. The interests of morality will suffer, it has been gravely maintained, should this demand be conceded. You will interfere with the conscience of the nun, and you will teach her to tamper with her oath, if you open her convent-door, and give her an opportunity of escaping. This is the substance of all that has been pleaded against the proposal that law should have free entrance into the innermost recesses of these establishments, and that nowhere on British soil should there be a human being who has not access to British justice, if he has a wrong to be redressed or a right to be recovered.

So, then, it is in the interests of morality, and of the rights of conscience, that the iron gate of the convent is to be kept locked and bolted on the nun! Morality and conscience! The greatest excesses have been committed in the name of liberty, and the greatest crimes have been done under the sanction of morality and conscience. It was never more glaringly so than in the present case. To enforce the conventual vow, and to enforce it often upon a reclaiming nun, and a reclaiming conscience, you must commit a great constitutional wrong: you must systematically outrage British liberty. Of course, there are nuns who are perfectly voluntary in taking their vow, and perfectly voluntary in abiding by it. To these the opening of the convent's door brings neither good nor evil. But it is equally well known that there is another class, who have repented of their vow, who have come to regard it as immoral, and who wish to recover their natural rights, but who cannot, because the conventual law declares their vow irrevocable and eternal. To such the convent is a prison which inflicts a double slavery,—the slavery of the body and the slavery of the soul. It strikes down both liberties,—the liberty of the person and the liberty of the conscience,—at one blow. Neither of the twain can the wretched inmate of the convent assert; for a fetter which she cannot break, and which the law cannot reach, compels her to be an unwilling inmate of a place from which she fain would flee, and an unwilling adherent of a system which her conscience abhors. British law and British toleration are both, in the person of the nun, outraged and set aside. It tends wonderfully little to mitigate the horrors of such a confinement, that it is passed amid crucifixes and relics, chantings and vespers; and that a man with a shaven crown, instead of an ordinary turnkey, keeps watch and ward. It is a real imprisonment notwithstanding; and the pretexts that are employed to conceal its true character may in certain circumstances only intensify its anguish.

If such pleadings could be dignified with the name of argument, we should say that the sophistry of the reasoning is abundantly transparent. We wish to set free the *person* of the nun from unlawful constraint; and our opponents represent this as an unjustifiable attempt to set free her *conscience* from lawful vows.   They know quite well that this is not an affair of *vows* at all.   The nun is free to take her vow, and free to keep it : that is a matter betwixt herself and her conscience solely ; and we meddle not with it.   It is not the conventual vow which we wish to dissolve ; it is the conventual bolt which we wish to draw.   Should the nun wish to release herself from her vow, and return to the enjoyment of her natural rights, we maintain that no foreign law, such as canon law, has a right to come between her and the law of Britain, which says that she is at liberty to resume these rights at pleasure ; and when Parliament legislated that the convent-door should not be opened, it just sided with the priest against the natural rights of free-born British subjects, and declared that the conventual vow shall, in point of fact, be irrevocable.   It, in truth, so framed its legislation, that canon law shall override British law, and that the jurisdiction of the Pope shall supplant the jurisdiction of the Queen. This is to us the most distressing and mortifying part of the whole affair.   That the priests of Rome should greedily grasp at all the power they can obtain, is to act as they have ever done, and ever will do.   But that the constituted guardians of British freedom, who pride themselves on their nice appreciation of liberty,—that men like Earl Russell, who charged the Grand Duke of Tuscany with murder for delaying to open the prison-doors of the Madiai,—should by express legislation enable Popish priests to do in Britain precisely what the Grand Duke did in Tuscany,—imprison unto death free-born men and women, the subjects of Britain's Crown,—is astounding and unnatural.   Have our statesmen a double conscience ? or, like the pagan sophists, have they a double faith ?

To tell us that the nuns are all very happy, and have no wish to leave their retreat, is but to employ falsehood to vindicate injustice.   There is no man with sense enough to count

the ten figures on his hands who will believe this. Human
nature is human nature, even in a convent. Passions which
ought to have been stifled for ever beneath the veil's dark
shroud will break out afresh, and burn with a vehemence to
which restraint acts but as fuel. The world will appear fairer
than ever, now that the convent-walls eternally forbid a return to it; and that vow which when first assumed was light
as the gossamer, will grow heavier day by day, till at last it
begins to bind like adamant, and press upon the soul like a
mountain. This is the real history, we are firmly persuaded,
of the majority of nuns. If there be any truth or uniformity
in the principles of human nature, this must be their history.
There are no prisons in the world whose doors enclose more
wretched captives, or a class whose misery is of a more re-
fined, agonizing, and hopeless description. If the nuns are
so very happy that not one of them would leave their abode
though the doors were set wide open, why do the advocates
of nunneries insist so strenuously on keeping these doors
barred? Why not make the experiment of opening them?
This certainly would be the shortest way of ending the controversy: it would silence, even if it did not convince, cavil-
lers and doubters. But so long as they fight so determinedly,
men will believe that they do not fight without a motive.
No Protestant has yet said anything against convents half
so severe as the assertion of their friends, that investigation
would be tantamount to suppression.

It is not on the Continent alone that these "Paradises"
seem able to retain their happiness only when hedged round
by bolt and bar. The same safeguards are employed among
ourselves; betokening a lurking suspicion that without them
the happiness of these places would take flight and be gone.
Hence the introduction of a style of subterranean architecture into these buildings, termed "grottoes." Delightfully
secluded retreats, we doubt not, are these same "grottoes."

And oh, the happiness of their inmates ! They dwell in a stillness which the voice of man never disturbs, and amidst a gloom which no ray of sun, or, it may be, no glimmer of lamp, is ever permitted to dispel. There the nun may indulge her meditations and raptures wholly without risk of the slightest intrusion from the enjoyments and temptations of a world which the stony roof and iron door of her "grotto." so effectually shut out. "There is direct and sworn evidence in existence," said Mr Newdegate, in his speech in Parliament, 3d March 1865, that "there are convents in the midland counties : there is one at Princethrope in North Warwickshire ; and under that convent are several underground cells, with very strong doors, and very good locks." And, referring to the evidence given on oath by a scholar in the convent of Benedictine Nuns at Colwich, he said, " that statement was, and it stands in the affidavits, that the greatest severities were practised in that convent,—that she had seen nuns imprisoned,—that she had known them to be kept short of food,—that she had seen one nun forced into this underground cell,—that to the best of her belief she never came out alive,—that she attended the service at her funeral, and saw her consigned to her grave in the convent buryingground."

But though we argue for the inspection of nunneries as a matter of fair and even justice, and of the equal administration of the British Constitution, that is no reason why we should not also take into account the moral effects of these establishments. Nunneries are not untried institutions: their fruits have been often tested, and are well known. History has gleaned her experience of them from a wide field, both as regards time and as regards territory ; and her verdict is, that the good they may have done has been altogether exceptional, and has flowed mainly from that very publicity and restraint which is sought to be extended to them here.

And, after all, that good weighs but as a feather in the scale
when compared with the tremendous evils to which convents
have given rise. The theory on which convents are founded
is an immoral one, inasmuch as it reflects disparagingly upon,
and is in some sort a condemnation of, an institution which
the Creator has placed as one of the grand bulwarks of social
morality. The Sabbath and marriage, as they are coeval, so
they are analogous as regards the place they occupy and the
end they fulfil. Marriage holds the same rank among social
which the Sabbath does amongst moral institutions. The
genius of Rome, as the great antagonist of purity, has been
shown in nothing more than in the way in which she has
singled out these institutions, and levelled her attacks at both.
The Sabbath of the moral law she has set aside by the holi-
days of the Church, to which she ascribes a higher sanctity
than to the day of sacred rest. Marriage she has laboured
to set aside, in like manner, by the institution of celibacy,
which, she says, is a far holier state than that of marriage.
Rome has laboured to pull down these twin pillars of the
social temple. The Sabbath she has attempted to bury under
a multitude of saints'-days and fête-days, which she rigorously
enjoins, while she more than tolerates the desecration of the
Seventh day. Marriage, in like manner, she has laboured to
bring into disrepute, and consequent disuse, by extolling the
conventual vow as a vow to God, while it speaks of the ma-
trimonial bond as but a promise to man ; and especially by
interdicting her clergy from marrying, lest they should be
defiled, while, with singular inconsistency, she places marriage in the category of a sacrament.

A powerful argument against nunneries would be the picture of their own morals, if we dared to draw it. But we
dare not. The conventual system escapes in part the condemnation it merits, from its very obnoxiousness to that
condemnation. We recommend those who believe these

establishments to be the abodes of piety,—a sort of celestial infirmaries for the cure of the weary and the heavy laden,—terrestrial paradises, where humanity becomes again unfallen, and where there is no serpent to tempt the inmates to taste forbidden fruit,—just to look into the " Life of Scipio de Ricci," Bishop of Pistoia, and ponder the facts there detailed. There they will see the kind of holiness that is cultivated in these abodes, and the sort of angels by which they are tenanted. These revelations have received recent corroboration. Since the passing of the Conventual Suppression Bill by the Italian Parliament in 1863, many discoveries have taken place of subterranean passages connecting the male and female convents of Lombardy and Tuscany.

There is another class of witnesses, whose testimony is not less condemnatory of these establishments. We refer to the Popes. The Popes, we may be sure, would do nothing to bring odium on establishments of which they have been the patrons and promoters, without necessary cause ; but how often have they interfered, not simply in the way of imposing restraint, but in the way of suppressing these establishments altogether ! The Papal edicts abolishing these establishments, all men will hold, are graver proofs of their incurable wickedness than even the startling revelations of those eye-witnesses who have lifted the veil, and shown us the lewdness of which the conventual establishments were the abodes in all the countries of Europe. It is in Italy and Spain, where convents are best known, that they are most detested ; and surely a Protestant nation may be excused for discountenancing what almost every Popish nation in Europe has been compelled to suppress. On this subject we find the Rev. Hobart Seymour speaking as follows :—

" It will be recollected that one of the measures that immediately preceded the Reformation of the Church of England was a measure for the suppression of the monasteries. That measure has been denounced by our Roman Catholic friends as a measure of robbery, and spoliation, and

sacrilege; as a measure of such a character, that none but a heretic could
have devised it, and none but a tyrant could have sanctioned it. Perhaps they are nearer the mark than they themselves are aware, for that
measure, whatever was its character, was originally devised by a Cardinal,
and sanctioned by a Pope. The facts of the case are these :—Cardinal
Morton was Papal legate in this country at the Court of Henry VII.
He found the monasteries in such a state of demoralization and disorganization, that he applied to the Pope for the requisite powers to amend
and improve them. Pope Innocent VIII., then at Rome, immediately
complied with the request, and issued his rescript or bull giving the requisite authority. But inveterate abuses take long to eradicate; and before
the work had well begun, Cardinal Morton lay in his grave, Henry VII.
was gathered to his fathers, and Pope Innocent VIII. had gone the way
of all flesh. We find next Cardinal Wolsey upon the scene as Papal legate
at the Court of Henry VIII. Cardinal Wolsey found some of the monasteries in a state of disorder,—disorder in their finances, disorder in their
morals; and he applied to the Pope for the requisite powers, not, like
his predecessor, to amend and reform, but to suppress, the monasteries.
Pope Clement VII., then at Rome, immediately complied with his request, and issued his bull or rescript to the Cardinal Legate, authorising
him, as he saw fit, to suppress all and every monastery in the whole realm
of England. So that if this measure were a measure of robbery, and
spoliation, and sacrilege,—if it were a measure that none but a heretic
could devise, and none but a tyrant could sanction,—there is no truth
more certain than that it was devised by Cardinal Wolsey, and sanctioned by Clement VII."

Every reader of history knows the state in which the Reformation found the convents. The face of Europe was bloat-
ed and blotched with these unsightly irruptions of the evil
virus of Romanism. The sloth, the gluttony, the lewdness,
of the monks became the butt against which such writers as
Erasmus and Rabelais levelled the polished shafts of their
satire. Nor was the corruption of the convents of recent
origin at the time of the Reformation. So intensely active
was their inherently vicious tendency, that their profligacy
was coeval almost with their institution. Some of their
living defenders, while admitting their present degeneracy,
speak of their former existence as eminently serviceable, and
that what we now behold is but the iron age of monachism.
But, alas! where are we to seek for its golden age? We go

back to the thirteenth century; but even then, almost under the eyes of their founders, the conventual establishments had become corrupt. Their golden age, like that of Saturn, lies, not in the land of real history, but of fable. Shall we leave so horrible a legacy as this to our children?

PIEDMONT : AN ILLUSTRATION.

ON the 8th of January 1855, a bill was introduced into the Parliament of Turin, for the suppression of the convents, and the more equal distribution of Church lands.

Sardinia did well to throw off the terrible incubus which had hitherto pressed upon all her energies, industrial and political. In that country, according to information furnished at the time to the French journal *La Presse*, there were seventy-one religious orders, divided into six hundred and four houses, composed of eight thousand five hundred and sixty-three individuals. This was a prodigious army, considering that the population of Piedmont is only four millions and a half, and that its territory, though comprising the rich basin of the Po, is mostly made up of lofty mountains, covered with the glacier or clothed with Alpine pasturages. The expense of feeding these six hundred houses, with their army of eight thousand strong, formed an item of two millions and a half of francs. This represented a capital of forty-five millions of francs, which the greatest admirer of these fraternities will scarce deny to have been a very handsome remuneration for their services. The loss of these services the kingdom bore with great equanimity. Indeed, though we have seen these monks a hundred times in this same country of Sardinia, we never could make out what their services were. They did not teach the youth; they did not pray with the aged; they had no taste for reading, and as little for labour. From morn-

ing to night they lounged in the streets, or about the wine-
shops ; and when the hour of dinner arrived, they trooped
homewards, to retail the gossip of the town and discuss their
wine.   The bill of the Sardinian Minister proposed the suppression of all these communities, with the exception of those
whose vocation it was to preach, to instruct, and to tend the
sick ; that is, it spared all which had even the appearance of
public duty to perform, and it abolished those which by the
very rules of their order were bound over to sheer downright
idleness.   The existing members of these last the bill indem-
nified with pensions ranging between two hundred and fifty
and eight hundred francs per annum.   We cannot see any
very atrocious wickedness in this proposal, at least any such
wickedness as was enough to bring down on the kingdom of
Piedmont the terrible calamities with which the Pope threatened it.

But these eight thousand five hundred and sixty-three "religious" formed but a small part of the mighty army encamped
in Piedmont.   The second part of the bill had respect to the
secular clergy, and aimed at a more equitable division of the
Church's property among them.   In Sardinia there are seven
archbishops, thirty-four bishops, forty-one chapters, with eight
hundred and sixty canons attached to the bishoprics; seventy-
three simple chapters, with four hundred and seventy canons ;
eleven hundred livings for the canons ; and, lastly, four thousand two hundred and forty-seven parishes, with some thousands of parish priests.   Black robes and brown, shovel hats
and cowls, covered the whole country ; and we can easily
conceive why the Piedmontese nation, burdened with too
much good company, should wish to reduce it a little, without
our having recourse to the charitable construction of the
Pope, that the men of Piedmont are sinners above all the
men of Italy.   The proposal of the Minister astonishes us by
its mildness.   What the Government of Sardinia proposed

was, not the sequestration, but the more equal distribution, of the Church property. The domain of the Church repre sents a capital of four hundred millions of francs, with a yearly revenue of seventeen millions and upwards. This immense sum was divided amongst the clergy in grossly unequal proportions. The higher clergy were enormously wealthy, while the curates were in state of dire indigence.

Up till 1848 the real ruler of Piedmont was the Pope. He had from twelve to twenty thousand persons stationed in it, all under oath, or under vows equivalent to an oath, that they would obey only the orders that came from Rome. These men held in possession one-fourth of the lands of the kingdom; they were exempt from the jurisdiction of the laws; they claimed the right of dictating to all the subjects of the kingdom how they should act in every matter in which duty was involved, that is, in every matter absolutely; and they had the power of compelling obedience by penalties of a peculiarly stringent and powerful kind. It is obvious at a glance that the government of the kingdom was completely in the hands of these men, and that every other authority in Sardinia was powerless in their presence. Hence the struggle which commenced in that country for self-extrication from a power which had usurped its government. One-half of its object it had already accomplished: it had succeeded in reducing under the authority of the laws the persons of these ecclesiastics. But another and most important step remained before Piedmont could be said to have wholly recovered its independence : it was necessary to subject the property of these men to the authority of the laws. That property was at once dangerous to the loyalty and fatal to the industry of the country, not mainly on the ground of its enormous amount, being, as we have said, a fourth of the kingdom, but mainly on the ground of the tenure by which it was held. It was held, not by the law of Sardinia, but by the canon law, which

o

placed the sole regulation, use, possession, and revenues of
that property in the power of the Vatican.　The law of Sardinia, as things stood, could no more touch these estates, or
dispossess their occupants, or say how a penny of their revenues should be spent, than if they were situated in Britain
or in America.　They were actually foreign soil pieced into
the country of Piedmont, garrisoned by foreign emissaries in
the service of a foreign power.

In this respect the lands of the clergy differ widely in
every Papal country from the lands of the nobility.　The
wealth of the nobles, it is true, may become enormous, their
estates may be overgrown, and they may employ their position for the purposes of oppression; but even when they
do so, they can be dealt with and chastised with comparative
ease.　Their estates remain part of the country in which they
are situated, and so are subject to the country's law.　Not
so the lands of the clergy.　In the eye of canon law they are
as much a part of "Peter's patrimony," however remote the
quarter of the world in which they are situated, as "Peter's
patrimony" itself; and if the temporal power meddles with
them in aught, it does so at the risk of arraying against itself
both the spiritual terrors and the material resources of the
Vatican.　This it is that gave its importance to the struggle
in Sardinia.　It was not a question whether there should be
a few hundred monks, more or less, in that country; or whether the revenues of its clergy should be more equally distributed; but whether Piedmontese law should be co-extensive with Piedmontese territory.　In short, it was a struggle
on the part of Sardinia to recover a whole fourth of its soil,
which had been torn from it by a foreign power, and which
was held and used by that power against the country itself.

BEGGING NUNS; OR, ALMS FOR THE POOR PRIEST.

The Papal aggression, which so many people believed would remain a mere scheme of spiritual conquest, developed on paper, but never to be translated into fact, is bit by bit extending itself over the whole kingdom, and working itself silently into the very framework of our social life. It is coming nearer and closer to us every hour, and fixing every day a tighter grasp upon our liberties and our goods. By threatening the timid, by cajoling the simple, and by impudence and falsehood where other arts fail, Rome compels us to furnish the means of our own undoing. Its dignitaries and seminary priests are revelling in the pensions which they receive from Government; and, as if all this were nothing, a comprehensive scheme for the persistent and systematic begging of the whole country has been organized, and is now being put in practice. The bishop thunders at the door of Parliament, and, in a tone not to be denied, demands new and richer grants; and the nun, with foot so soft and knock so gentle, comes to our doors to receive our charity. Rome in Britain is a vast organization for raising money and acquiring power.

In pursuance of the plan of making Popery in Britain sustain itself, a swarm of begging nuns have been turned loose, and are making themselves rather unpleasantly familiar and free in the homes of our citizens. Their plea is charity. They plead the cause of the orphan and the widow, the sick and the dying: so they say. As they stand before you with bending figure, with air so submissive and beseeching, and address you with voice so silvery and soft, you begin to feel that it is rude to say "No;" or, should you muster firmness to meet their quiet supplication for alms with that curt and

ungracious monosyllable, the meek and patient creatures to
whom it is addressed refuse to understand you. You have
but drawn upon youself a fresh torrent of solicitations, more
pressing, more insinuating, uttered in tones still more silvery
and silken, till you think that you hear the widow and the
orphan pouring their entreaties through them into your ear.
If still you are obdurate, the suppliants before you are patient as ever ; their serenity is imperturbable ; their sweet-
ness is something seraphic. Your heart begins to smite you ;
and you begin to meditate a retreat from the position you
have taken up. Your vacillation is quickly perceived, and
instantly taken advantage of. The nuns follow up their success and complete their victory by a stroke of pathos reserved
for the last,—"Will you give us nothing for the poor ?"

There is nothing more praiseworthy than charity ; but few
things are more mischievous than alms indiscriminately and
uselessly given. This sort of charity is not simply money
lost : it is industry checked, idleness rewarded, beggary and
vagabondism pampered and encouraged. To give to the
common sorner is to feed the villain and rob the orphan :
to give to the ordinary mendicant of Rome is to do all this
tenfold. In no form have alms been productive of worse
consequences. To the Christian man it is enough to say,
that he is thereby supporting a system which the Bible and
the laws of the land declare to be idolatry, and which has
uniformly proved itself the foe of our liberty and our intelligence. This single consideration will suffice to determine
his resolution ; but there are others over whom it will have
no power. To them we say, the introduction of the conventual system of Rome will be as fatal to our industry as to our
religion. Its only virtue is to fill a country with beggars.
It invests mendicancy with a religious character, and takes
away the shame of beggary, which is at least one safeguard
of the independence and honest pride of a population. That

spirit it has effectually broken down in all the countries where it prevails, so that it is no disgrace to beg ; and in Spain and Italy almost every one begs. The "good fathers" beg, say they : why should not we ?

If these nuns are animated by so great a compassion for the poor, why do they not go to Italy, rather than to London and Edinburgh ? For one unhappy object the prey of poverty or of disease in Great Britain, they must know that there are a hundred such miserable beings in Italy. The roads in some places are littered with beggared, diseased, woe-struck creatures ; the towns swarm with the maimed, the halt, the paralytic, and the lunatic. What a spectacle of disgusting filth, hideous disease, and abject misery, is exposed to the eye at the door of every Italian church ! Who cares for these unhappy beings ? Who tends these victims of disease and penury ? Who binds up their sores, or begs from door to door to purchase bread or build an hospital for them ? There are no pitying nuns in that land. The cardinal rolls past in his red chariot, and leaves these helpless creatures in their wretchedness ; and the Capuchin, with his well-filled wallet, hurries past on the other side, scarce venturing a glance at the frightful mass of festering disease and filth, of idiotcy and villany, that is so near him. This, we fearlessly affirm, is the true picture of purely Papal lands. We ask, why do not these sisters of charity bestow their attentions where they are so much needed ? If it be indeed pity for the wretched that stimulates them to their labours, why do they not hurry to Italy ? Why, especially, do they not go to the Papal States, where the objects of disease and poverty are dying untended in thousands ? Why do they come to Britain, where we have so many hospitals,—where the sight of misery and disease is comparatively so rare,—and where, of every three pounds of taxes for the poor, two at least are for the Irish Romanist ? If we need *sisters of charity*, or.

as we prefer to style them by a less monopolizing and assuming name, "nurses," let us by all means have them. But we have yet to learn that the Protestant women of England are less tender-hearted than the foreign *élèves* of Cardinal Wiseman, or that the wives and daughters of Great Britain are less fit, or are less disposed, to tend the sick, than are those dark-veiled, and yet darker-visaged, nuns who are now beginning to show themselves on our streets. Seated at the bedside, with their grim features, on which moping melancholy has stamped its unmistakeable impress, and their hollow sepulchral voices, one should think that they must seem to the dying man, not angels of mercy, but the *avant couriers* of purgatory.

But we deny that the spoils of these begging expeditions are ultimately destined for the poor, or that the poor will in the long run derive from them any benefit beyond having the alms that ought to have reached them intercepted and eaten up. The " poor" for which the nuns beg is in reality some lusty and well-fed priest, who is starving on half-a-dozen courses a-day. But even should it be that the poor of our wynds and closes are so far fed by charity, these poor will be able to give all the more for masses, for indulgences, and for the innumerable priestly dues with which they are burdened, and which the very poorest must pay; and so the "Church" it is which reaps the harvest in the long run.

The more ungracious parts of the system will be concealed and modified in our country till we have become a little more reconciled to it; but in Italy and Spain, where it dares to disclose all its grossness, and is seen as it is, the idea never enters any one's head that the poor have any interest in the matter, or are in any way the beneficiaries of the conventual system. The monks and nuns fill their own bellies, and, only when they are not able to consume all, give their leavings to the ordinary beggars. In the Italian towns it is always seen

that monkery and beggary flourish together, and that the
more numerous and wealthy the conventual establishments
in any particular city, the greater the hordes of beggars. This
is clearly shown in Mr Seymour's " Pilgrimage to Rome,"
who farther states that "the most debauched and profligate
characters of the land are amongst these inmates of the cloister."   In Rome, where the number of these establishments
exceeds all bounds, and where monks and nuns form a large
proportion of the population, and are found begging at all
hours and in all dwellings, it is necessary to raise subscriptions among the laity for the relief of the destitute ; and one
of the first acts of regenerated Piedmont was to suppress conventual beggary, as a crushing incubus upon the industry of
the State, and a barefaced robbery of the alms of the orphan.
This was one of the greatest of the many great services of
Cavour, for which his countrymen were not unthankful. Will
Protestant England and Scotland foster what Papal Piedmont
was compelled to put down ?

CHAPLAINCIES.

ONE thing only was wanting to perfect the territorial foothold of the Church of Rome in Great Britain, and to bring
the Papal aggression within sight of its destined goal : it
lacked that Popery should make itself one of the endowed
religions of the country.   It was shrewdly suspected that the
priests had begun to cast coy but eager glances towards the
status and other more substantial advantages of an endowed
Church.   It was also known that the project of pensioning
the Roman faith was favourably regarded by our statesmen,
who deemed it a sure and certain way of making the priests
their servants for ever.   The object towards which both have
been working has now been virtually accomplished.   A re-

cognised and salaried official of the Church of Rome is attached, in one capacity or another, to almost every department of the national ministration.   In the army, in the
Government prisons, in the Government hospitals, at our
naval ports, in our national schools, and, soon to be, in our
poor's-houses, is the priest, confessing and shrieving men, saying mass, and eating the bread of a Protestant State.

The Prison Ministers' Bill of 1863 was simply permissive.
It allowed the magistrates to appoint or not, as they might
see cause, a paid Popish chaplain in the prison of their re-
spective counties.   Very few such appointments were made ;
and in May 1864 the Government, in fulfilment of a pledge
given to the priests, brought in a *compulsory* bill, which gave
power to the Secretary of State to order absolutely the appointment of Popish chaplains in those prisons where circumstances appeared to him to warrant such a step.   The
bill was defeated, but it will most probably, after some time
has elapsed, be again brought forward.   The proposed measure was a very high-handed one.   It was, in short, a manifest violation of the constitutional usages of the nation.   At
present the prison-door is open to ministers of every denomination.   The Popish prisoner has only to signify his wish,
and the priest will visit him.   But the assumption by the
Secretary of State of the power of *compelling* the magistrates
to appoint and the rate-payers to pay Popish chaplains, is
a superseding of the magistracy of the kingdom in reference
to the regulation of prisons, and an arrogation of arbitrary
power of taxation over the rate-payers.   It reminds us of
the days of the Star Chamber, and shows us that there is no
part of British liberty which our Government are not prepared to sacrifice at the call of the Roman faction.

Thus has the element of Romanism been poured into every
duct and channel of our national organization, so that the
public service has become, in a sort, a ministration of Popery,

and the Romish priesthood, as a paid and sanctioned institution, is now co-extensive with the area of our empire. This is a national endowment; for Rome cares little about the name, if she can secure the thing; and an endowment she has secured, which, in money's worth, surpasses any endowment enjoyed by the Presbyterianism of the country. Her yearly revenue from the State at this moment is upwards of three hundred thousand pounds; and, large as this sum is, it will not long remain at its present limit. Having respect to the new demands of Rome, it will inevitably amount very soon to half a million. To this we must add the sums daily poured through a hundred channels into her coffers: the supplies, for instance, sent from the foreign propaganda, the gifts of wealthy perverts, the dowries of nuns, the weekly dues of members, termed "the offerings of the faithful," the spoil of death-beds, the sale of dispensations, sacraments, and pardons. Here is a pecuniary resource and strength already vast, and which, yearly increasing, will soon enable the Church of Rome in Great Britain to rival the wealthiest establishment in the land.

We have to add another source of revenue which Rome has stealthily opened in our country. She has discovered an easy and ingenious method of taxing the whole kingdom for Popish objects. Does she need fifty or a hundred thousand pounds to rear a cathedral, to build a church, to found an orphanage or a convent?—she has only to issue her fiat, and the money is forthcoming, the bulk of it being drawn from Protestant pockets. How does she proceed? She organizes a lottery for behoof of the special scheme. She prints a million of tickets, which she sells at sixpence a-piece. These she sows like snow-flakes over the country. She has the adroitness to induce Protestants to aid her in their sale. They accept her bribe of a free ticket, but forget the punishment with which God has threatened in his Word all who take part with idolatry. The few high prizes are generally the gift of wealthy persons: the rest are of small value; and when the drawing has taken place, and the proceeds are realized, a prodigious balance must remain to the "Church."

This device is capable of raising almost any amount of money. Some half-dozen such lotteries have been advertised during the course of the present winter (1865). The author has in his possession packets of tickets for four of these: one packet for "St. Peter's C. Church, Phibsboro'," the numbers of which range from 91,926 to 299,016; another packet for "St. Mary's Female Blind Asylum, Portobello, Dublin," the numbers of which range from 384,952 to 384,954; another packet for "St. Patrick's New Cathedral," the numbers of which range from 580,672 to 580,674; and a fourth packet for "St. Mary's Male and Female Orphanage, Lanark," the numbers ranging from 515,621 to 515,627. One ticket in the last-mentioned lottery, in the author's possession, is marked as high as 894,509; which leaves it noways doubtful that not fewer than a million of tickets were spread over the kingdom in behalf of this scheme. These lotteries are admitted by the authorities to be in violation of the law, but the Government stands by and sees the law broken.

Supposing that only half the issue for any one scheme is sold, the nettings must be prodigious. The whole sum realized in Great Britain and Ireland by these Popish lotteries we shall estimate very moderately if we set it down at half a million. Add to this the half-million—for it now approaches this sum—received from Government, and another half-million, at the very least, realized by the gifts and tithes of her people, and the result is seen to be a yearly revenue enjoyed by the Church of Rome in Great Britain very little, if at all, inferior to the revenues of the Pontifical Government itself.

It is in verity an ominous transition through which we

are passing. The State is separating itself more and more
from the evangelism of the land ; and just in proportion as it
divorces itself from the Christianity of the New Testament,
does it draw closer year by year towards Romanism.   At the
same moment that the State turns its face away from the light
of revelation, it bends towards the darkness of idolatry. This
is portentous indeed. It recalls the memory of those times
in France which preceded the outbreak of the great revolution, when a mocking atheism walked hand-in-hand with a
hooded superstition.   It looks like the closing of a cycle,—
like the filling up of the cup. The shadow has of late gone
down many degrees on Great Britain; and portents that cannot lie begin to warn us that we are nearing a great moral
crisis.

There is one other lesson of history which we should do
well to ponder at this hour.   When religion begins to be
fettered and oppressed, we may be sure that civil tyranny is
at no great distance.   When Asa stretched forth his hand
to imprison the Seer, "he oppressed," we are told, "some of
the people the same time."   Our secularists keep themselves
at ease touching the Papal aggression and the rapidly aug-
menting power of Romanism in the State, by saying,—or, if
they do not say, they think,—that whatever may become of
our Protestantism, our constitutional rights cannot and will
not be attacked.   They never made a greater mistake.   Our
civil liberties are at this moment in more immediate danger
than our religious ones.   The priests have no intention of
straightway setting up the stake. Nay, for some time to come
they will scrupulously abstain from all open attack on our
religious customs and rights.   They know that nothing would
be more impolitic than to begin a persecution of this sort.
They will strive to change the law, and, having effected this,
they will do all the rest at their own convenience.   They
have already lowered the tone of British legislation : they

have already led our rulers into several overt breaches of the
Constitution.   In every Papal document which is issued, the
Queen's prerogatives are ignored ; in every convent which is
erected, the personal liberty of the subject is outraged. There
are cases, besides, in which the letter of the law has been
invaded, and in which our rulers have betrayed, by their
silence, if not by their consent, the interests of British liberty.
We are coming to have one law for the Protestant and another for the Romanist.   It is so already in some points.
The right of free discussion has been attacked : it will be so
again more determinedly.   One part of liberty after another
will be singled out for assault, till the whole is overthrown.
Our rulers hoped to be the masters of the priests : they
have ended by becoming their tools.   Romish cupidity and
arrogance have not yet reached their limits ;and the men who
conceded former demands will also concede those that are
yet to be made.   It is easy to indicate the point where this
double approximation of Rome to our Government, and of
our Government to Rome, only can meet,—the grave of British liberty.

FATHER M'GURR ; OR, HOW THE POPISH ENDOWMENT SCHEME BEGAN.

It is instructive to look back to the commencement of this
affair of endowing the Romish priesthood, and to compare
the small beginnings from which it arose with the formidable
dimensions it has now reached. It was first mooted in 1853.
In that year it was whispered that the Romanists had concocted a plan to attach a salaried priest to every regiment in
which there were Popish soldiers, and a paid chaplain to
every jail, and that Lord Palmerston and Sir Charles Wood
had given their consent to the scheme.   The public were

warned at the time that this was just the planting of an endowed priesthood over the kingdom.   Ten years thereafter,
that is, in 1863, the scheme, which received general disbelief
when first announced, was carried through.   And now the
faith of Rome is one of the endowed faiths of the nation; and
the Church of Rome, in her character of a State-paid Church,
has a wider territorial basis in Great Britain than any other
Church of the country.

The matter cropped out, first of all, in the garrison at Chatham.   To that garrison a chaplain was attached, with a salary
of eighty pounds, who "administered the rites of the Church"
to the Romanist soldiers in the corps.   This priest was a quiet
sort of person,—one of a class whom Rome always employs
as a pioneer.   He went through his official routine, and seemed
to care for nothing beyond.   Any wish to proselytize or to
give annoyance, much less to dominate, appeared wholly absent from his thoughts ; and having thus, by a course of easy,
good-natured behaviour, earned a reputation for his Church
as a quiet inoffensive society, such as statesmen love, the
priest was removed, and a new man took his place.   The new
functionary, whose name was M'Gurr, was fitted for the new
times.   The Church, whose humble son and representative
he was, had rights; and these he would enforce.   He showed
his mettle first of all on the subject of his own salary.   Eighty
pounds for a "soul-priest!"   Was ever such niggardliness
heard of !   Some poor dissenting divine might be glad of it ;
but what a sum to offer to one who could sing masses to save
souls !   No; he would not work for the British Government
on these terms.   If their soldiers should depart without the
last rites of mother Church, and be shut up in purgatory here-
after, he must lay the loss of these souls at the door of Government.   And the Government having the fear of the priest
before their eyes, bargained with Father M'Gurr that, over
and above his salary of eighty pounds as chaplain, he should

have five shillings for every visit he chose to pay to each soldier in the hospital. These, we think, were fair terms. He surely might pay four visits a-day. He had no lengthened or laborious services to perform. He had only to rub a little chrism on the sick man's head, and, in extreme cases, to put a wafer into his mouth, and that was all. He had earned twenty shillings of the Queen's money. Twenty shillings a-day would quadruple the priest's salary, and convert his eighty pounds a-year into four hundred. But the nation must not grumble at giving these four hundred pounds of its money to Father M'Gurr. He sings masses to save souls.

The priests of the Church of Rome are seldom burdened with superfluous modesty; nor did Father M'Gurr meet such reception from the Government as should make him stop short in his efforts, and leave the matter but half-done. So auspicious a commencement gave token of a most prosperous issue, and to that issue the priest proceeded to push the affair. The Government had secured that M'Gurr should not sing mass for nothing; but permission to perform mass as the well-salaried chaplain of the garrison was not enough: he must have a chapel in which to perform it. A mass is no common affair, and it cannot be celebrated by the wayside, or in the open air, where the wind may blow the wafer away, and the priest may be horror-struck at seeing his god consumed by the fishes of the sea, or devoured by the fowls of the air. To prevent the occurrence of so terrible an accident, the priest must have a chapel,—a chapel provided for him by Government; and nothing less would content him than the chapel of the garrison. This was his next demand. Up till this time the Romanists at Chatham had contentedly occupied a place of worship in the neighbourhood. No complaints had been made that this building was in any respect inconvenient. But the church which was good enough for a chaplain of eighty pounds a-year was not nearly good enough for one in receipt of four hundred ; so, packing up his wafer, he demanded a nobler shrine for his god, even the garrison chapel. The request was laid before the Secretary-at-War. This high official transmitted it to the commandant of the garrison, with the interrogatory whether he knew of any " military reason" why the request should not be granted ? The commandant replied that there was no " military objection ;" and accordingly the authorities at the Horse Guards placed the garrison chapel at the service of the priest. It was to be used conjointly by the English chaplain and Father M'Gurr. It was to be a place of Protestant worship one part of the day, and a mass-house another part. The God of the Bible was to be proclaimed in it this hour, and the god which Innocent III. was the first to invent was to be adored in it the next.

If our Government supposed that now there was an end of the matter, they were not long in finding out their mistake. Scarcely had the order been issued to turn out the Protestant chaplain and his congregation, and to give the chapel during part of the day for the celebration of mass, than Father M'Gurr was heard knocking as loudly as ever at the door of the War-Office. What does he want now ? Salary he has got,—the chapel he has got ; what more does he need ? He needs an altar on which to place his wafer. The Government had not thought of this, but they were now reminded of their omission. How could they take their stand here? for of what use is a chapel to a Romanist without an altar, seeing the Church does not convert men by the ministration of doctrine, but by the application of wafers ?

Thus was the scheme fairly inaugurated; and, proceeding by easy stages, it has come in ten years to be as good as consummated.

CHAPLAINCIES: CRIMINALS IN EXCHANGE FOR GOLD GUINEAS.

A PARLIAMENTARY return of religious instruction in prisons
was obtained by Mr Lucas towards the close of 1853, and
an abstract of it was published soon after in the *Tablet*. The
total number of prisoners in the prisons in England on the
25th day of September 1852 was twenty-one thousand six
hundred and twenty-six.   Of the total criminal mass which
on the day specified filled our prisons, namely, twenty-one
thousand six hundred and twenty-six, there are set down to
the Church of England sixteen thousand and seventy-seven;
to the Presbyterian body, four hundred and ninety-six; to
Dissenters of all classes, one thousand three hundred and
ninety-one; and to the Roman Catholics, two thousand nine
hundred and fifty-five.   It thus appears that the contribution
of the Roman Catholic Church to the criminal population of
the country is one-seventh.   A seventh part of the crime
that pollutes our land, and a seventh part of the expense of
punishing it, is caused by that one sect alone.   Now, what
ought to be the number of Romanist prisoners in our jails,
supposing that Church furnished only her fair proportion, in
other words, supposing that the religion of Rome was not
less favourable to morals than Protestantism?   This it is easy
to ascertain.   We shall take the population of England at
its usual estimate, which is twenty-one millions, and the Romanist population in England also at its usual estimate,
namely, one million.   This would give a thousand as the fair
proportion of prisoners from that denomination.   Instead of
this, it is within a few units of three thousand.   The Romanist population in England is to the Protestant population
as one to twenty, while the Romanist prisoners are to the
Protestant prisoners as one to six.   Each million of the Pro-

testant population, including Jews, Infidels, and the lapsed masses generally, yields considerably below a thousand criminals. Each million of the Romanist population yields well nigh three thousand. If, instead of one million of Papists, we had twenty-one millions amongst us,—in other words, if England were a Catholic country (and our Government seem determined to afford every facility for making it such),—what would be the state of morals? Crime would be raised to four times its present amount. Where we have now but one jail, four would scarce suffice; and where we now pay one pound for the criminal police of the country, we would henceforward be compelled to pay four pounds.

Recent statistics make the ratio of Popish crime much higher. By the last Parliamentary return (Prisons, No. 150, Session 1864) it would appear, that in England, of 8070 prisoners in convict prisons, 1747 are Romanists, or nearly one-fifth; and of 27,307 in city and borough jails, 5533 are Romanists, or nearly one-fifth. Thus, in England, one out of every hundred and twenty-four of the Popish population is an inmate of either a convict prison or a city or borough jail. In other words, the crime-producing power of Romanism is sevenfold that of Protestantism.

These are palpable facts, and, we should think, sufficiently decisive in their character for the purposes of the legislator. Yet very different practical inferences are now being deduced from them. We see in them the very strongest argument why a system so destructive to the nation's welfare,—a system that contributes so largely to fill our jails, and to increase the expense of our criminal justice,—a system which undermines the morals of the country, and along with that its order and industry,—should be discouraged in every legitimate way. But our Government draw just the very opposite conclusion from them. They see in them an argument to subsidize and foster Romanism. A system whose destructive

P

influence is a palpable and acknowledged fact, established by
Government returns, and vaunted by its adherents themselves, is to be taken into pay, and employed as one of the
elements by which our country is to be ruled and civilized.
There surely must be some great and radical difference betwixt us and our rulers on the first and fundamental duties
of a Government. On no other supposition can we deem it
possible, that where the facts are admitted on both sides, and
where their moral and social bearings are so manifest and
undeniable, the practical inferences from them should be so
widely different. If it be admitted that the first and great
end of a Government is the ruin of a country, then all is
clear : the conduct of our Government becomes perfectly
intelligible: there is in it a thorough and beautiful consist-
ency. If there be a system which all experience has demonstrated to be ruinous beyond all others, and which accom-
plishes its work of destruction on the largest possible scale
and in the shortest possible time,—a system which, in every
other country where it has prevailed, has laid in the dust all
that is great, and magnanimous, and virtuous,—a system
which has covered Ireland with idleness and mendicancy,
and which, so far as it has prevailed in Great Britain, has
been the patron of crime, and the grand purveyor of the jail
and the scaffold,—if, we say, there be such a system, then
Government acts a most paternal and dutiful part when it
summons that system to its aid, and gives it every facility
for operating on the country. All this is plain, logical, and
defensible, starting from the premises that the moral and industrial ruin of a country is the first duty of its Government.
But should Government repudiate this principle, and affirm
that the prosperity, and not the destruction, of the country,
is the first end of their office, then we are totally at a loss to
comprehend their policy. It is a perplexing and confound-
ing enigma.

Why, what do they do? They publish carefully prepared tables, in which they show that Romanism is eminently demoralizing,—that we have to thank it mainly for fil'ing our jails and creating our criminals; and yet they tell us in the same breath, that this same demoralizing agent they mean to employ in the cause of the propagation of sound morals. They have the most implicit faith that the same system which fills our prisons will empty them. Though a teacher of bad morals outside the jail, they are confident that Romanism will be a teacher of good morals inside of it; and that though its tendency, when taught from the altar, is eminently to create disorderly subjects, when taught in the prison its tendency will be equally efficacious in converting disorderly subjects into peaceable and loyal citizens. This is as hard of belief as the hardest sayings of the Schoolmen. It is an absurdity nearly as great as transubstantiation itself.

The Church of Rome is not the lynx-eyed society she gets credit for if she does not quickly find out how to profit by this policy. It opens to her a sure and short road to the national exchequer. All she has to do is, to give us criminals, and get back gold guineas in return. She has extraordinary powers, exceeding seven times those of any other Church, in the matter of manufacturing criminals; and she will be greatly wanting to herself, which she never was before, if she do not find grounds on which to claim endowments in all our towns. This henceforward is the game which the priests will play. They will compel us to pay, in the first place, for making criminals; and they will compel us to pay over again for the pretence of turning these criminals into honest men. There must be more criminals to procure more endowments; and these endowments will in turn procure more criminals. The manufacture of the two will go on most prosperously together,—criminals creating endowments, and endowments creating criminals; and thus the nation will be cheated out of its money and its morality at the same time. This is modern statesmanship.

The proposed endowment of Popish chaplains in our convict-prisons is based on a principle that virtually ignores the truth of all religions. Protestantism and Popery cannot be two religions. If the one is true, the other must be false; for the one, in all its fundamental principles and leading objects, is the very opposite of the other, and therefore both cannot be divine; for a proposition and its converse cannot be true. But the proposed Government measure places both these systems on a level: it assumes that both are true, and that both are equally entitled to respect, and equally efficacious as a religion. Now, a measure which places both on a level can be fairly construed in no other light than as affirming the falsehood of both. For to say of two contradictory and opposite systems that both are equally true, is just another way of saying that both are equally false.

On this ground, then, we object to the measure. It embodies in a public act, and stamps with the sanction of Government, the prevalent philosophy of the day, which treats all religions as equally divine,—another phase of universal scepticism. It dethrones the Bible from its supremacy as a revelation, and the one infallible standard of truth,—that Bible which the British Constitution recognises, and on which its leading provisions are based. It holds that the adoration of a wafer is equally lawful with the worship of the Supreme, and that the "mummeries" of Romanism are equally profitable with the verities of revelation. This is the language of the act: it is gross, undisguised infidelity; and against that infidelity we beg, in name of the British Constitution and our common Christianity, to protest. It is an attempt to rebuild the Pantheon, and to provide a niche beneath its dome for every vagrant system that pleases to call itself a religion.

The scheme, besides wearing an aspect of impiety, is ill-timed. It is an insult to the Protestant faith of the country, which represents the fall of this system as an era of happiness to the world : it is an insult to the enslaved nations of the Continent, who are everywhere showering their maledictions on Rome as their oppressor ; and at a moment like this, when all around are seen the portents of this system's approaching destruction, the attempt to prop it up looks like an open defiance of that Power which has decreed its ruin. There is nothing in history which this policy so much resembles as the attempt of Julian, styled the Apostate, to rebuild the Temple, that he might thereby falsify the sacred oracles, and undermine Christianity. The one attempt will no more succeed than the other ; but it may over again draw down these lightnings which on the former occasion scattered both the building and its builders.

THE PRIME MINISTER AND THE TEMPTER.

EVER when the Prime Minister of Great Britain is in straits, and power seems to be departing from him, there comes the Tempter, and says,—" All these things,—votes at the hustings, votes in Parliament, a new lease of power,—will I give thee, if thou wilt fall down and worship me." " Agreed," cries the " Minister," before the Tempter has well ceased speaking. " I close with the offer. So great an amount of power for a sum so small ! I were a fool to decline so tempting a bargain." Straightway the doors of the Treasury are thrown open, and pensions and dignities are poured at the feet of the man with the shaven crown. The priest departs with a half-concealed leer brightening his face ; and the " Minister," ensconced in the privacy of his closet, rubs his hands, and chuckles over his bargain. By the grace of the Pope he finds himself and his party still in office.

A few months pass away, and it begins to be seen that for
this time at least the priest is to have the best of the bargain.   To those that fish in troubled waters there is nothing
more undesirable than a lengthened calm.   The horizon becomes suddenly overcast, and the Minister is in deeper waters than before.   There is heard the knock of some one at
his closet-door.   Again the old stealthy foot is on his threshold ; and again there appears his former friend, come to rescue him a second time.   The old terms are propounded a
little more imperiously ; pensions somewhat more liberal, and
status just a shade higher and better defined, are demanded,
or—descend from power.   The Minister has no alternative,
—he accepts ; and when left alone to ruminate over the
transaction, he rubs his hands with a little less of enthusiasm ; while the priest departs, his countenance broadening
into a leering smile of grim satisfaction.

Yet again troubles thicken round the Minister, and yet
again his ghostly deliverer stands before him in the silence of
his closet.   He shows to the tottering statesman the power
and glory from which he is about to descend : armies no
longer led by him, fleets no longer at his command, revenues
no longer at his disposal, senates no longer swayed by his
eloquence, and majorities no longer voting on his side.   "In
all these," says the cowled man, "will I reinstate thee, provided thou fall down and worship me with money and dignities."   Again the knee is bent.   Again he prostrates himself and the empire before the representative of a sacerdotal
tyranny, deeply and foully stained with its insult of the Queen,
and its anathemas of her Protestant subjects ; and again he
stoops to buy its ghostly help, to keep him a few days longer
in place and power.   But it is this time as before.   The promises of the mysterious personage with whom he traffics are
broken, and the bargains he has made prove worthless.   A
political rival outbids him in the grace of the priesthood ;

and the power he had striven to retain at the cost of his own dishonour, and the surrender of the principles of British liberty and toleration, he loses after all, and descends from place amid the reproaches and denunciations of the very men he had laboured to conciliate.

Such has been the history of British legislation, under the head of Romanism, these thirty years past. It has been a series of concessions, as manifestly useless as regards the object for which they were made, as they are undeniable violations of the Constitution. Every promise, without exception, has been falsified. Were we not solemnly assured that, would we but open the doors of Parliament to the members of the Romish Church, complaint or murmur from Ireland we should never hear more? We did as was desired; but alas for the promised era of tranquillity! Then it was that the reign, not of peace, but of monster meetings, was opened in Ireland. We next purged the statute-book of every let and hindrance to the introduction of foreign bulls, the Papists promising to be upon honour with us in this particular. Scarce had the change been made till the Edict from the Flaminian Gate was launched upon the country, and the framework of the Pope's authority was set up all over England. We framed the Ecclesiastical Titles Bill, but permitted it to remain inoperative on the assurance that synodical action would be a purely spiritual thing. The first use which Provincial Synods made of their new jurisdiction was to put down the Queen's Colleges. The presence of foreign Jesuits in the country is openly avowed, despite the act of 1829, which forbids their entrance. Monasteries are illegal, but that does not in the least prevent their spreading all over the land. Papists were taken solemnly bound not to use the power with which they might be invested to the detriment of the religious establishments of the country. They redeemed their pledge in the Papal aggression, when they ignored the validity and the

Christianity of every Church in the land ; and now the appropriation of the ecclesiastical revenues by one body of religionists they denounce as spoliation and robbery. To almost every branch of the national service there is attached a staff of priests ; but has the gold of statesmen made them the tools of statesmen, or conciliated them to the interests of a country which now to a large extent educates, feeds, and clothes them ? These persons are less its citizens than before. The country of the priest is his Church. Thus has every expectation and hope failed, and yet we persevere in our course of concession. Our Government are ever surrendering principle, but never purchasing peace : they are continually conceding without conciliating. And now, does not every man see, unless, indeed, he chooses to be blind, that the more we concede, the more we are asked to concede, and that the last concession we never shall see till the hour when there shall remain nothing more to be conceded ?

The peace of the country is at this hour in greater peril of sudden interruption than it was in 1829. The "messages of peace" which our statesmen boasted they had sent to Ireland have turned out but incentives to war. The Fenian brotherhood are drilling their bands ; and a smouldering insurrection waits the signal from abroad to start up on the soil. The murmur of discontent, the wail of misery, the howl of sedition, the altar-commination, still distract that unhappy land : blood still defiles it. The cry of the priest is still "oppression and injustice." The "Church" still says, "Give, give." From our statesmen all power and all inclination to arrest the evil have departed.

Rapid as has been the development of the Papal aggression, and formidable as are its present dimensions, we are about to have a yet further extension of it. It is understood that a Select Committee of the House of Commons, appointed to inquire into the administration of the poor-laws, are about to recommend "the appointment of Romish priests as chaplains, and the celebration of mass in union workhouses." This proposal, if adopted, which it is likely to be, will increase seriously the burdens on rate-payers, will add to the influence of the priesthood, and further,—although this is a consideration which weighs little, we fear, with the majority, —will deepen the guilt of the nation. It will, moreover, bring in its train a host of new claims, which will inflict more expense, and give rise to fresh troubles. To every workhouse in which a Romish chaplain may be placed, Papists will demand that a separate Romish chapel be added. This must needs be provided with altar, vestments, and other requisites for Popish worship. Next will come separate schools in connection with the chapel, for Romish boys and girls, and, of course, the appointment of schoolmasters and schoolmistresses with salaries, as also books, papers, and other things for the scholars. Behind these demands others still are seen looming in the distance ; among which we may mention a compulsory creed-register in all workhouses and district-schools, the farming out of pauper children in convents and monasteries, and the appointment of Popish chaplains to hospitals and lunatic asylums.

And let us mark how arrogant withal. The nation will have simply the privilege of paying these chaplains. The guardians will possess the power neither of appointing nor of dismissing them. The bishop will select the priest to be appointed; to the bishop's authority alone will he be responsible ; nor without the bishop's consent will the guardians be able to dismiss him. All this, we are told, falls within the range of the Church's discipline, with which if we interfere, we deny her toleration. In 1859 the priests withstood the Government Poor Law Commissioners on this very point. The Commissioners dismissed one chaplain, and appointed another. Bishop MacEvilly declared that "the giving and taking away of spiritual jurisdiction," as in the case of the dismissal of a chaplain and the tendering of his office to another, was an "indirect, if not a direct, invasion of episcopal authority ;" and the Government had to yield the point. In 1860 the Government were similarly defeated, Dr Cullen telling them, with reference to a priest whom they had dismissed, "You have never given, and you could not give, to the Rev. Mr Fox the power of performing such duties." And in 1864 the same thing happened at Pontefract, Yorkshire, where the magistrates fixed the salary of a newly-appointed prison-chaplain of the name of Barron, but which Mr Barron, to the astonishment of the magistrates, declined, saying that he should not be "allowed to accept the office at the salary agreed upon," and that he was bound by the ORDERS of his superiors with reference to the salary. If already the tone of the priests is so haughty, what may it be expected to become when they shall enter our prisons and workhouses, not by permission, but of right ? But a yet greater principle do these cases illustrate. They show us what Rome's understanding of her "discipline" is, and that it is her fixed determination to hold us pledged by the Catholic Emancipation Act to permit her to carry out that "discipline" to its very utmost limit. Every jot and tittle of her canon law must she be allowed to exercise, otherwise we deny her toleration. But it is as really a part of her discipline to punish heresy by the stake as it is to give or withhold spiritual functions ; and if, when we dismiss a priest whom we pay with our own money, she now tells us that we are interfering with her discipline, when we attempt to rescue some unhappy heretic around whose limbs she is piling the faggots, will she not again tell us that we are interfering with her discipline ?

THE BATTLE; OR, POPISH ORGANIZATION IN BRITAIN.

WE deem it of importance at this stage to present our readers with a concise view of the whole organization of Romanism in Great Britain. In this way we shall be able, as it were, to look over the whole field, and to see at a glance the breadth and power of the Papal aggression, the steady advance it is making, the great number of points on which we are being attacked; and, last and most melancholy of all, the fact that it is ourselves which are furnishing the means of this attempted overthrow of our faith and our liberty.

First comes Maynooth, the great arsenal of the war, where the soldiers are trained and the weapons forged.

Next is the Cardinal, the captain-in-chief of the host; and around him are his twelve suffragan bishops.

Distributed amongst these, and stationed throughout the country, are fourteen hundred priests. Their services are supplemented by the secret agency of five thousand Jesuits.

We have a large body of nuns distributed in our cities, having it as their daily vocation to forage for the Church.

We have Popish congregations daily multiplying; we have schools sending forth year by year a continually increasing body of youth trained in the highest type of Romanism.

We have reformatories, where our criminals are taught a darker craft than any to be learned in their own dens. And then, too, there are monasteries and convents, whose doors the law cannot open, and whose secrets we leave in congenial darkness.

As if this machinery, constructed by Rome, although largely upheld by British money, were not enough, we give her the use of our national organization. We admit her

priests to our army, our jails, our hospitals, and soon we
shall admit them into our workhouses, and into every one of
our national institutions.   Thus have we engrafted Romanism upon the national trunk, and made provision that it
shall grow with the development of our national life, and
expand with the extension of the national action.

But, to come to particulars : it is shown from the Romish
Directory of 1865 (we quote from the Report of the Scottish Reformation Society for 1865) that there are in England 941 Romish churches, chapels, and stations ; in Scotland,
191 ; in all, 1132 ; while in 1829 there were only 449.   It
is likewise shown that there are at the present time 58 monasteries or "communities of men" in England, none as yet
in Scotland ; while in 1829 there was not a single monastery
in England or Scotland.   There are also in England 187 convents, 14 in Scotland, making in all 201 ; while there were
none in 1829, so far as publicly announced.   There are in
England 1338 priests, including 17 bishops ; in Scotland,
183 priests, including 4 bishops ; in all, 1521 ; while in
1829 there were only 477, or about one-third of that number.
The Church of Rome has now ten colleges in England and
two in Scotland.

"Dr Wiseman, at the conference above referred to, stated
that the largely increased number of bishoprics ' were established in 1850 in accordance with geographical considerations.
One of these sees had only at first one priest, and now contains a cathedral.   The soil which had been fallow was cultivated, and produced abundant fruit.   In Wales we now have
nine missions, two colleges, and eight convents, within a comparatively narrow space.   Since the re-establishment of the
hierarchy in 1850, we have held three provincial councils.
We have chapters to take the proper ecclesiastical steps when
bishoprics become vacant.   We have also the germs of the
parochial system.   The bishops have also bound themselves

to endeavour to establish large seminaries as soon as possible. All this has the [Roman] Catholic Church accomplished in England by its own strength alone.' Dr Wiseman also referred to the organization of committees, which seem to have been appointed in each diocese 'to defend,' as he is pleased to say, 'the rights and interests of [Roman] Catholics.' 'These committees,' he further adds, 'are named by the bishop, and composed of a priest and of two laymen of zeal and rank.' 'The committees assemble in London, and divide the funds arising from collections made in all the churches and chapels of England. The Government has recognised these committees in all matters which relate to the [Roman] Catholic religion. The committee is the medium through which the complaints of religious communities are made known to the Government.' "

Of Popish schools in England and Scotland the Report says,—"The Report of the Committee of Council on Education for 1861–62," says the London Protestant Alliance, in their Address for 1863, "gives the following facts respecting Roman Catholic schools in Great Britain :—Treasury grants to Roman Catholic schools, £35,195. Total grants from 1839 to 1861, £215,868. Number of Popish schools inspected in 1861, 243. Number of teachers in 1861—male, 331 ; female, 805 ; total, 1136. Scholars at examination in 1861—boys, 11,716; girls, 13,868; total, 25,584. The following relates to expenditure :—Romish reformatory schools in Great Britain, £15,154. Maynooth grant, £26,000. National schools in Ireland (proportionate part to Romanists), £205,000. Romish chaplains in Irish prisons and workhouses, £10,000. Romish reformatory schools in Ireland, £5060. India and our colonies, £40,000 : making, with what is expended on Romish military chaplains, and Romish schools in Britain, a grand total of £344,502 paid by Government for Popish purposes during the year. The amount of public money worse than wasted in this way is likely to go on increasing till some great organic changes are effected."

" The proportion of females over males in these schools is very large," says the Report of the Scottish Reformation Society for 1864. " Take the number in average attendance. In the day-schools females form 53 per cent., and in night-schools 72 per cent.; while in schools of other denominations this proportion is only 43 and 27 per cent. respectively. This is a most striking difference. The large preponderance of females in Popish schools seems to be increasing. This peculiarity will yet have an important bearing on domestic service in Protestant families, and on mixed marriages among the population. There is another fact to which we would here call attention : 4737 females attend Popish evening-schools ; while the number of females attending evening-schools of all denominations, including Popish schools, is only 7402 ; that is to say, two-thirds of all the females at evening-schools attend Popish schools. Hence it would appear that the Church of Rome is using this class of schools most vigorously for her own purposes ; and we much fear that many females of Protestant families attend such schools."

"There are," says the *Bulwark* for February 1863, " 32 Popish Members of Parliament, 22 Popish Peers, 45 Popish Baronets. There are (including Ireland) 4475 Popish clergy, 3404 Popish chapels, &c., 172 monasteries (illegal in England and Scotland), 419 convents and nunneries, 47 Popish colleges, with numerous Jesuits. The Popish population is increasing in the rural districts and towns of England and Scotland. The Government maintains Romish priests, monks, and nuns, in schools, in prisons, in workhouses, in the army, at naval ports, as well as in the great training school for Popish priests at Maynooth. Thus annual endowments are given to Popery from the British Treasury to the amount of not less than £300,000." Since 1863 the annual grants to Popery have risen to upwards of £344,000.

We suspect that the Romanists, foreseeing troublous times on the Continent, are converting the riches laid up in their churches and monasteries into cash, and transferring their funds to this country. We suspect also that the despotic Powers, hating, as they do, Constitutionalism, are liberally subsidizing the Papists in Britain, as their best allies in the work of dividing our nation and crushing our liberty. Certain it is they could not employ their money to better purpose. But the crowning danger lies in this, that the Popish faction have now the control of Parliament. The poise of political parties is so evenly adjusted, that the Romanist vote, thrown into either scale, suffices to turn it. They can thus unseat any Ministry which may dare refuse to buy their support; and our Government, lacking the courage to throw off this vile subjection, respond to each new demand with more chaplaincies and richer pensions, bartering for place and power our blood-bought liberties. Thus all things conspire to leave us free to consummate our apostacy, and receive its punishment.

PART FIFTH.

MISCELLANEOUS.

CAN ROMANISM BE TRACED IN THE NEW TESTAMENT?

It may be a silly notion of ours, but we cannot help thinking that Romanism would be none the worse of a little support from Scripture. It is very unreasonable, no doubt, to quarrel with Popery because it does not agree with the Bible; but such unreasonable people there are, especially in lands which have been long overrun with heresy; and with all deference to an infallible Church, we think that an effort ought to be made to conciliate such persons. The Bible, somehow, has come to be much read and greatly deferred to in our country; nay, there are not a few who would rather listen to what it says than take the word of any ecclesiastic, however dignified; and so long as this prejudice retains its hold, Rome must just submit to flatter it, if she would succeed in her designs. Sad it is, doubtless, to see men so enthralled by a stiff, puritanical, inconvenient book, which is perversely silent on the "glories of Mary" and the "infallibility of Peter,"—which does not pay a single tribute to relics, or contain so much as one invocation to saint or angel,—which does not warn men of the dangerous and deadly practice of eating flesh on Friday, or of saying prayers in a tongue which the people can understand,—or, to sum up all in one word, which does not warn men against itself, by telling them that it is the most dangerous of all books, and that it is mortal sin to read it, unless one is furnished with the permission of his bishop : it is sad, we say, to see such a book, so full of grave omissions, and containing no warning against the most deadly errors, receiving implicit homage from men who contumaciously spurn the authority of a Church which "cannot err." Nevertheless, it may be doubted whether the wisest way is to fly in the face of this prejudice, and whether it would not be more advisable,—so long at least as there are Bibles in the world,—to try to make it appear that the Bible, rightly interpreted, is not the foe, but the friend, of Rome.

There is no denying that Rome has an extraordinary gift in extracting hidden meanings from the sacred text ; but she will need all her ingenuity to get successfully over the profound silence of the Scriptures on all those topics on which it was most for her interest that it should have spoken out. We do not deny (for of what value would be the denial of heretics ?) the dictum of an infallible Church, when it declares that MARY is the grand conspicuous figure from beginning to end of Revelation ; that the heavens were created for her throne, and the earth for her footstool ; that it was to her coming and work that the august prediction in paradise pointed ; that it was for Mary that the patriarchs waited, and of her that the Hebrew seers spoke ; that whether it was prophecy, or type, or song, the theme was still the same,—the immaculate purity, the divine virtues, the universal dominion, of Mary ; that she is the Redeemer of the world, and made expiation by her sufferings, "not for her own sins, but for ours ;" that she is risen from the dead, and has ascended into heaven ; that in her resides "the whole fulness of the Godhead ;" and that "no man cometh unto the Father but by Mary." When Romanists affirm all this, as they do, all we say here is, that in our case, and in the case of such as ourselves, it would greatly contribute to our confidence in

Q

the declarations of an infallible Church were we to be shown
but one solitary line in the Bible supporting this doctrine.
If Rome can trace any resemblance, however faint, on the
inspired page, to her peculiar theology and her peculiar rites,
or any agreement therewith in the teachings and forms of
the primitive Church, we will make all allowance for the
faintness of the impression, and the partial accuracy of the
agreement, on the ground that the times were early, and the
state of the Church infantile. But still we would not do
justice to ourselves, even in the eyes of Romanists, did we
not demand that we should be shown, in the beliefs and actings of these days, the rudiments at least of purgatory, of
transubstantiation, of the confessional, of image-worship, and
of the other tenets and rites of the Romish Church.

It would vastly strengthen the primacy, for instance, were
we to be shown in the *Acts*, or in any other part of the New
Testament, that after the ascension of Christ, Peter passed
as his Vicar ; that he always wore a three-storied cap ; that
the apostles formally installed him in the primacy, by seat-
ing him in his chair and carrying him on their shoulders ;
and that, having brought him to the Church on Mount Zion,
they placed him on the high altar, burned incense before him,
and, kissing his toe, addressed him as " His Holiness."   To
make the matter of primacy still clearer, it would be well to
show us the proof that all causes which arose in the primitive
Church were adjudicated upon exclusively by Peter, as they
had been before by Christ ; and that the moment his decision
was given, it was hailed with an unanimous shout,—" Peter
hath spoken : the cause is determined." Show us the seal of
the fisherman's ring at the end of his epistles, and point out
the verse in which is contained the claim of "infallibility"
or of "primacy."   Does he begin his letters,—" Peter, the
Vicar of Jesus Christ, and Head of the Universal Church,
to the strangers scattered throughout Pontus, Galatia, Cap-

padocia, Asia, and Bithynia ?" If not, why does he conceal
this "cardinal truth" of Christianity, the knowledge of which
"is necessary to salvation on the part of every human being ?"
Are we to conclude that all these strangers scattered throughout these various countries were lost because Peter neglected
to declare a full gospel to them ?—that, writing for their instruction, he dwelt on minor points, and altogether omitted
the first great cardinal doctrine of revelation ?

Did Peter go about in red stockings ? and did he use in
his devotions, as we know his successor at Rome does, a mi-
niature Madonna, a crucifix of ebony, and a small crystal
basin for holy water ? Did he possess himself of his Master's
crown—we mean the crown of thorns—when he laid claim
to his Master's power ? or did he even then evince a han-
kering after a tiara of gold ? Would it not add great force
to the doctrine of purgatory, in Protestant minds at least, to
be shown the passage in which it is recorded that, when
"they stoned Stephen," and when James "was killed with
the sword," Peter issued a decree enjoining mass to be said
in all the churches of Judæa, Samaria, and Galilee, for the
repose of their souls ? or that he advised Christians to go
on pilgrimage to their tombs, and there perform their devotions, or to possess themselves of a rag of their raiment,
or a drop of their blood, or, better still, of a finger or a toe
of the martyrs, as an infallible preservative against evil ? One
such plain fact as this would be worth a thousand of those
ingenious arguments which Romanists are in the habit of
advancing, but which they candidly tell us we cannot comprehend so long as we permit ourselves to be guided by our
understandings. Why did no evangelist of the early Church
bethink him of putting on the leathern girdle of John the
Baptist, or his raiment of camel's hair ? and why do we never
read of the early Christians repairing to his tomb to say their
ora pro nobis ? Were they deficient in veneration for the

martyr, than whom there had not arisen a greater among
those born of women ?   Luke was a painter, and, we cannot
doubt, occupied his talents in multiplying portraits of Christ
and the apostles, which were hung up in the churches, and
used as helps to devotion by the early Christians.   But it
may justly surprise us that not the slightest allusion to the
practice can be found in the New Testament, though certainly the cause of image-worship would be all the better of
some such support.

Did Paul don a scapular and light candles before preaching
his great sermon on Mars Hill ? and, having ended, did he
cross himself, and invoke the Virgin for the conversion of his
hearers ?   On descending from the Areopagus, and survey-
ing the temples, statues, and images of the crowded city, did
he say to the Athenians,—" Ye are not far from the kingdom
of heaven.   Ye have only to give Christian names to these
Pagan deities, and go on as you are doing, worshipping them
with prostration and incense.   The Lord of heaven and earth
dwelleth in temples made with hands, and is worshipped with
men's hands, and is like unto gold, or silver, or stone graven
by art and man's device ?"   Did Timothy receive the tonsure ?
Did Barnabas perambulate Asia Minor with a rope round his
middle, carrying, as his only armour, bits of the true cross,
and beads carved out of the olives of Gethsemane or the tim-
ber of the house at Nazareth ?   Was the boat in which Peter
plied his vocation on the Sea of Galilee cut up into little
pieces, and distributed among the first missionaries of the
cross ?   When Silas and Timotheus went to Macedonia, did
they carry with them a winking Madonna, hoping by her aid
to convert to the faith the rude inhabitants of this part of
Europe ? or, when Paul exhorts Timothy to approve himself
as "a workman that needeth not to be ashamed," is he to be
understood as meaning that, before setting out on his mission,
Timothy should provide himself with crucifixes, images, rosa-

ries, phials of holy water, and recipes for chrism, of which the
Romanists of our day lay in a plentiful stock when about to
set out on a missionary tour to the heathen ?   But there is
no end of such questions. We do assure our Romanist friends
that it is a great stumbling-block in our way that we cannot
find the least trace of these things in the New Testament ;
and there is no way of stopping the mouths of those who declare that Romanism is a pure invention, an impudent im-
posture, palmed by priests upon the credulity of those whom
they keep in gross ignorance, but by showing that there are
numerous and manifest traces of all these doctrines and rites
in the actings of the Church of the Apostles.

SPAIN : THE PENALTY OF BIBLE-READING.

In the autumn of 1862, two citizens of Spain appeared
before the tribunal of Grenada, charged with a certain offence.
Their names were Matamoros and Alhama ; and the offence
of which they were accused being found proven,—indeed, being
confessed,—they were sentenced, the former to eight years',
and the latter to nine years', imprisonment. In Spain this
sentence is equivalent well-nigh to death, endured, as it must
be, not within the walls of a prison, but in the galleys. Only
the more robust, and only those equally callous to moral as
to physical suffering, could survive nine years' penal servitude in Spain. Their daily task must be performed under a
burning sun. To the rigour of the sun is to be added the
weight of their chains. To their chains is to be added their
enforced companionship with the refuse of the most sunken
population of the most sunken country in Europe,—with murderers, robbers, and desperadoes of every class, who will regard themselves as less vile than the heretics Alhama and
Matamoros. What crime, we may well ask, brought down

on these men so awful a doom in a country like Spain,—a country in which laws are enacted, but no one obeys them,— in which proclamations are issued, but no one heeds them,— in which crimes are done, but no one is punished for them,— a country in which a little gold will buy pardon for the greatest crime, and even escape from the deepest dungeon? What unheard-of crime brought down on these men this punishment, than face which, many would rather mount the scaffold? That crime is soon told. In the judicial ethics of the most Christian and apostolic kingdom of Spain, it is a crime which towers high above murder, above robbery, above perjury. That crime is the reading of the Bible. Simply for reading the Word of God were these two men condemned by the Spanish Government to nine years' penal servitude.

What a proof, not only of the bigotry of the Spanish Government, but also of the unchangeable spirit and character of the Church of Rome! Wherever she is mistress she absolutely withholds and forbids the Bible to the people. That book which God has given to the race as their common heritage,—which bears on the very face of it to be addressed to every man,—whose epistles are sent, not to the Bishop of Corinth or to the Bishop of Thessalonica, but to the Corinthians and Thessalonians,—not to any chief man, but to all the members of the Church ; that book which Augustine blessed God had been translated into all the tongues of the civilized world ; that book she prohibits ; that book she burns. Her theory is, that God has imparted his will to the " Church,"—that the Church has imparted it to the priest, and that the priest alone has power to reveal it to the people, and that the people are bound to receive whatever sense or non-sense the priest is pleased to extract from the Bible. And as is her theory, so is her practice. In Spain the statutory penalty of Bible-reading is death by fire ; in Savoy, till the Revolution of 1848, to have a Bible in one's house inferred ten years' imprisonment in the Castle of Pignerol; in Italy, till the Revolution of 1859, as to this day in the Papal States, to possess a Bible is death. Thus she condemns men's souls to inhabit a desert; and when they would refresh their own souls, or awaken the heavenly life in those of others, by a draught from the fountain of life, she snatches the cup from their burning lips.

Spain has of late laid down a few railroads; she has constructed a few ships; and, raking amid the ashes of her long-extinct chivalry, she has recruited a few soldiers; and their "intrepid deeds," their generals tell the world in their despatches, have been witnessed with "tears of admiration." And, taking credit for these achievements, accomplished at the cost of incredible pangs, and trumpeted forth in magniloquent phrases, Spain lately demanded to be admitted into the council of the great Powers. The dotard and bigot that she is! With the monk's cowl darkening her intellect, the fires of a dark superstition streaming from her eyes, the crucifix and beads dangling from her nerveless fingers, the brand of the Inquisition upon her brow, a bundle of faggots under her arm, and a long train of beggars and assassins at her heels, she came recently knocking for admittance into the council chamber of the European Powers, and claiming a right to sit side by side with Britain. Side by side with Britain! The ghostly, priest-ridden, and beggared Spain,— the Spain of the twelfth century,—seeking still to rule the world by the Inquisition!—herself moping in darkness, and labouring with all her might,—which, happily for mankind, is small,—to replunge the world into the same darkness in which, with other creatures of night, she herself nestles; shutting against men the Word of God, and consigning them to a dungeon when they would attempt to revive their own spirits, and rekindle the souls of their fellow-countrymen, at that fountain of purity and power.

A worthy and competent ruler of Europe indeed! Let
Spain be told that she ranks below even the Turk in liberality
of opinion ; that she is not a kingdom of men, but a vast brotherhood of monks ; that she is the opprobrium of that Europe which she would fain rule, as Philip II. ruled it, by
hired assassins and bloody *autos da fe.* Let Spain, we do
not say administer, but create, justice in her own country.
Let her teach her people the art of honest labour, and show
them how to live by the spade, and not by the stiletto. Their
country was a paradise under the Moors,—a wide garden of
citron-groves, of corn-fields, and opulent cities ; but now, in
the hands of a people out of whom the Inquisition has burned
the soul, it has become an expanse of treeless and herbless
deserts, of burnt-up sierras and mouldering towns. Let Spain
know that a dense ignorance, styled the prop of the throne,
and certainly the safeguard of the altar, enwraps her whole
land in its dismal shadow,—that her grandees, without cul-
ture, without true nobility, without the soul of honour, have
degenerated into mere court puppets,—hereditary cringers
before the idol of royalty, which itself sits rotting in sloth
and sensuality on a throne that once ruled, but is now the
scoff, of the world,—that the scions of that nobility, sunk in
physical as well as mental decrepitude, disgrace the soil which
their ancestors defended by their valour and adorned by their
genius. Let Spain know that her kingdom is a land where
the virtues die, and only the vices live,—a house of darkness, in which thought is proscribed,—a land where the light
of knowledge dare not shine, and in which, should any one,
weary of the darkness, open his eyes in search of the sweet light
of truth, he meets only the lurid glare of persecution's torch.

It is true that Spain, not daring to carry out this atrocious
sentence in opposition to the universal condemnation of Protestant Europe, has changed it into one of perpetual exile.
This makes it none the less a true illustration of the spirit of

Rome, whose behests Spain is simply carrying into effect. The old alliance betwixt arbitrary government and an infallible Church is still maintained, and will be to the latest hour of their common existence. The covenant betwixt the two is prompted by common dangers, and cemented by reciprocal benefits. All over Papal Europe the Church wields her spiritual thunder in behalf of the State, and the State places its temporal sword at the service of the Church. To this Spain bound herself anew by recent concordat.

The *Correspondencia* of Spain attempted a vindication of this atrocious sentence. And what was that vindication? "These men," said the *Correspondencia*, "were condemned, not because they were Protestants,—seeing that nobody is punished in Spain for religious opinion,—but because they openly, with tongue and pen, excited a propaganda in favour of Protestantism, which is forbidden by the Constitution of the State." A memorable distinction, worthy of the Jesuits, from whom it came! Teva and Matamoros were condemned simply for reading the Bible and lending it to others; but then, we must not say that they were condemned for religious opinion. In Spain no one is punished for his religious opinions; but you must keep your opinion locked up in your own breast. The moment you breathe it in word or whisper, or translate it into worship, down comes the Spanish Government upon you; and you are sent to the galleys for transgressing the limits of religious freedom, and sinning against the State. You are free to think whatever you please: no power under heaven can prevent you doing this,—no, not even the Spanish Government; even the rack sometimes fails to discover thought: but the moment your opinions are found out, if these are different from those which the Constitution of Spain prescribed, then must you expiate them in the dungeon and the galleys. Perhaps the *Correspondencia* did not see that, in offering such a vindication, it added a new in-

famy to Spain. The *Correspondencia* said that the sentence
of the tribunal of Grenada is strictly legal, and is in harmony
with the Constitution of Spain. In saying so, it just affirmed
that the Government of Spain is by its very Constitution a persecutor for conscience' sake ; and that, were it as powerful as
in the days of Philip II., it would fill the world with the same
tragedies with which Philip II. covered Europe with blood
and himself with infamy.

THE REVOLUTION : ITS POLICY REVERSED.

"THEY have sown the wind, and they shall reap the whirlwind." So says an old book, whose authority, we fear, does
not stand particularly high with politicians. For some years
back we have been most industriously occupied in sowing the
wind. We have been throwing away, as worse than useless,
all the securities which the Revolution gave us for the enjoyment of our liberties. The principle established at the Revolution, and represented by the accession of the House of
Hanover, was just this, that the professors of the Roman
faith being, as their own creed expressly bore, and as their
past history had incontestibly shown, the subjects of a foreign
prince, though entitled to full and absolute toleration, and to
all the security of our laws, had no claim to share in the government of the country. This was the principle established
at the Revolution. On this basis did the great statesmen
who accomplished it intend that the Constitution should
henceforward rest. In national ethics there cannot be a principle clearer or more undeniable than that the citizens of
a country only are entitled to administer its government.
The Revolution sanctioned this principle, and said to the
members of the Roman Church, We exclude you from power,
not because your faith is wrong, but because your allegiance

is wrong.   We will tolerate your worship, but we cannot
endow it.   All the protection of person and property which
our laws can yield, with all the social and personal benefits
which flow from our Constitution, we shall most willingly
accord you ; but a right to legislate and govern is what we
cannot give.   This was an undeniably equitable adjustment
of the long-standing quarrel between the citizens of the country proper and the foreign faction who were ever aiming at
seizing its government.

This, and this alone, was the principle which the Revolution established, and which it brought into practical operation.   As a Church, we protested against the *religion* of the
Pope ; as a State, we protested against the *authority* of the
Pope ; and the Revolution was just the embodiment of that
protest.   We had no option—so our forefathers judged—
betwixt that principle and foreign serfdom.   With it came
independence and liberty ; without it were base subjection
and foreign thraldom.   But in process of time we began to
question whether the principle on which we had accomplished
the Revolution was a sound one.   By and by we went a little
farther, and admitted that it was erroneous.   We next conceded that it was a wrong done the Papist.   When we had
got this length, we had, in fact, passed a condemnation upon
the Revolution.   We in effect said, "we were all wrong in
banishing the Stuarts ; all wrong in alienating the national
endowments from the Romish Church ; and all wrong in
shutting the doors of Parliament against the members of the
Roman communion ;" and from that day, although it has
been much the fashion to applaud the Revolution as an event,
it has been not less the fashion to reprobate it as a principle.
Of course, having come to the conclusion that the Revolution was wrong,—wrong as a principle, though we still style
it glorious as an event,—we have since made all haste to
undo it ; and in the course of the few short years that have

elapsed since we got our new light, we have made really wonderful progress. Proceeding at the same ratio for a few years
to come, we will defy any one to tell that a Revolution in
the Protestant sense ever took place in Britain. History, of
course, to those who may consult her page, will make known
the fact, that a hundred and eighty years ago a change of
this sort did pass upon the country ; but of that change scarce
a trace will remain upon the face of society. We have been
dealing with the Revolution as the Jews did, who built the
tombs of their dead prophets, and erected crosses for their
living ones. We garnish the monuments of the Revolution,
and we celebrate its anniversary with all the pomp of drums,
flags, and speeches ; and we say, had we been in the days of
our fathers, we would have fought side by side with WIL-
LIAM ; whereas, by repudiating the principle of the Revolution, and by devoting our money and our legislation to restore
the institutions which the Revolution overthrew, we show
that we are the sons of the men who strove to bring the
country under the yoke of arbitrary government, and that,
had we lived in the days of our fathers, we would have been
found fighting, not beneath the banner of WILLIAM, but beneath the banner of the STUARTS.

Having so long and so industriously sowed the wind, we
are now beginning to reap the whirlwind. "It hath no stalk :
the bud thereof shall yield no meal." Our rulers have great
credit in their handiwork, certainly. Their deeds are beginning to praise them in the gates of their own land, and to
publish in foreign countries the wisdom and patriotism of their
policy. The men whom the Revolution excluded from the
government of the country because experience, as well as their
own avowed principles, proved that they could not legislate
without betraying, and could not govern without oppressing,
we have recalled. We have listened to their clamour ; we
have grown pathetic over their imaginary wrongs. With

posts, and pensions, and sums of almost fabulous amount, have we loaded them. Every avenue of the Constitution have we opened to them ; every bulwark of the country have we placed in their hands. Well, after thirty years of sowing, we are now beginning to reap the harvest ; but of what kind is that harvest ? Is the bud yielding meal ? Is it in peace,—is it amid abounding signs of order, loyalty, and concord,—that we are bringing back our sheaves ? Alas for the golden promises amid which we sowed the seed ! It is not the songs, but the howlings, of the reaper that fall upon the ear. Belfast for three days in the hands of an army of Popish wreckers, and simply because the men of Ulster had dared to meet, not to denounce the Pope, not to say one word to the discredit of the Virgin, or to drop so much as a hint impugning the truth of purgatory, but simply to petition for equality of rights and equal administration of justice in the matter of Popish and Protestant processions. There is Birkenhead, the scene of renewed rioting and bloodshed, attempted to be set on fire, that, under cover of the confusion and alarm, the citizens might be murdered and their property destroyed ; and for what ? Simply because a society, partly political, partly literary, had resolved to meet for the discussion of a strictly secular point. And there is the metropolis itself, the scene of conflict betwixt the military and the Romanists. And what led to this piece of civil war ? Simply the exercise of what Englishmen have been accustomed to regard as their birthright, and which they never dreamed any party either would or could deny them,—the right, namely, to express their opinions freely on political questions, and to give vent to their admiration of a hero who had earned not only the gratitude of Italy, but of the civilized world. Yet, as if Hyde Park were Italy or Spain in the middle ages, those who assembled there were told that they could express their sentiments only at the peril of life. These

are the harvest that is crowning our seed-time.   We have
sown the wind, and now we are reaping the whirlwind.

We were warned that we had no right to expect that the
course of the moral world would be suspended in our behalf,
or a miracle wrought in order to save us from the consequences
of our own folly.   But those from whom these warnings came
were set down as men of disordered imaginations, whose very
sleep was disturbed by imaginary terrors of the growth of
Popery.   Our rulers knew better, we were told.   They had
a secret that could transform tigers into lambs, and that could
make priests who had bound themselves by oath, soul and
body, to the priest-king of Rome, steadfast friends of Queen
Victoria ; and so a policy of surrender was adopted.   What
progress have we to show for thirty years' concession and conciliation ?   Are we not compelled to make the humiliating
confession, that things have been going on from bad to worse,
and that now the very men whom we have fed and pensioned,
and whom we have gorged with ever-growing grants from the
public Treasury, are found at the head of a conspiracy to put
down the free expression of public opinion all over the kingdom ?   So signally has our policy of concession broken down.

And, as if to make the failure of that policy still more
manifest, it is remarkable that the whole force and fury of
the Roman faction have been directed, not against our religion, but against our liberty.   "Ah !" how often has it been
said, "if you fanatical Protestants would be at peace, and
not stir up dissension by stirring up controversy, we should
have no annoyance from the Romanists !   It is you, by dis-
playing the 'red flag,' who goad to madness the Roman bull.
You are the real peace-breakers."   "Civil war !" said such ;
"we shall have no civil war, unless the old Covenanters rise
from their graves, or unless their modern descendants, sword
in hand, take to the hill-side."   The riots at Birkenhead and
Hyde Park give the lie to this theory, and ought to teach

our statesmen that the faction on whom they have lavished
all their caresses hate them not less than they hate the zealous Protestant, and include both in the category of fanatics,
and are prepared to put down, not religious liberty only, but
all liberty. And where is it that these riots have broken
out? One guessing beforehand would have indicated "Scotland," where the Protestantism is strongest, and where the
"red flag" hangs daily before the eyes of the Romanist. Yet,
no ! it is not the land of John Knox,—it is Episcopalian England,—which has been disturbed. And let us mark, that the
bishops, in their pastorals, have had the effrontery to tell us,
that if we don't give up the free speech to which we have
been accustomed, and post up in our factories and workshops
a list of interdicted topics, on which our workmen are to
be silent, peace we need not look for. They do not say to
us as yet, unless you give up your psalm-singing and your
conventicle-attending, we shall do so and so : that will come
in its own time. They say, unless you give up your free talk-
ing and your free printing, you may look for broken windows
and broken heads, and all the other et ceteras by which Romanists are wont to give practical effect to their notions of
liberty.

THE TROUBLER OF EUROPE.

In the March of 1859, just before the breaking out of the
war in Italy, a discussion took place in Parliament touching
the disquiet that prevailed in Europe, in the course of which
certain great truths were enunciated, which the world at
large, and Great Britain in particular, would do well deeply
to ponder. Providence works out its grand problems in the
slow course of a thousand years, and gives them such breadth
and prominence, that they remain lessons for the race to all

time. Of such a nature were the problems brought into view
by the discussion to which we refer.   They were the sum-
mings up of history,—the teachings of a thousand years,—
the solemn utterances of the Great Ruler, verified by the
nations of Europe, who had exemplified, some in their prosperity, and others in their ruin, the truth of the principles
proclaimed.   Often had these principles been put before the
world in the form of theological dogmas ; but now they were
presented as well-ascertained political experiences, and announced from a stage fitted to give them universal publicity. .
The discussion, indeed, was a great sermon, spoken to the
world, illustrating by great facts the principles of the Divine
government, and the essential conditions of the prosperity of
peoples.

All parties in Parliament were at one on this point.   They
found Europe ill at ease, deeply troubled,—its nations weighed
down by forebodings and political terrors.   They inquired
the cause of this political and social feverishness : they all,
one after one,—Lord Palmerston, Mr Disraeli, Lord John
Russell,—put their finger upon the same spot, and said, here
is the seat of the mischief ; here lurks the malady that torments the body politic : it is at Rome, and nowhere else,
that those fires smoulder that threaten to rend Europe in
pieces.   If in France every forge, every arsenal, every port,
rings with warlike preparations,—if cannon are being bored,
if transports are being manned,—if regiments are being put
on a war footing,—if in Austria column after column is being
marched to the Ticino, and stores, arms, and soldiers, are
being poured into the great fortresses that guard the Mincio,
the Po, and the Adriatic,—if everywhere, to the remotest
extremity of Europe, men are whetting the sword, and the
trumpet is calling to battle,—it is Rome that has awakened
all this stir, and marshalled all these armies.

It is the perpetual, incurable, unbearable misgovernment

of the Papacy that has brought on this vast danger. Had a Protestant controversialist asserted that the grand disease of Europe was the Papacy, and that unless this disease was eradicated, it would work, and that speedily, the ruin of the system, he would have been little heeded. It would have been said that his theological hatreds were distorting his views, and conjuring up before his mind imaginary terrors. But when the great statesmen of England say the same thing, their words must command attention. No theological animosities, no sectarian prejudices, have misled them. They have formed their opinions simply as statesmen. They find Europe heaving like ocean before the coming storm,—they cast anxious eyes around,—they examine every point of the horizon,—to see where it is the tempest gathers. As one man, they point to the Vatican. It is there, they all exclaim, the dark cloud, so fearfully charged with lightning, rises. The great troubler of the world is Rome.

Popery,—this purely spiritual thing, as many affect to regard it,—has within the past forty years broken the peace of Europe not fewer than a score of times. Let us recall the more prominent of these instances. In 1823, the Netherlands' Government had to step in, and dissolve two religious confederacies dangerous to the State. In 1824, the tranquillity of Bavaria, Saxo-Weimar, and Saxony was disturbed by religious commotions. In 1825, we find the Bishop of Malines in conflict with the Belgian Government. In 1827, the pretensions of the Court of Rome were too much for even the bigoted Ferdinand of Spain, and he had to bar his kingdom to the nuncio of the Pope. The same year, the Jesuits in Belgium, allying themselves with the Radicals, whom they hated, effected a revolution, and expelled a Protestant king; at the same time that their brethren in Saxony were creating disturbances by plotting in the opposite interest. In 1830, Charles X., listening to Jesuit advisers, pub-

R

lished the famous ordonnances which lost him his throne.
In 1834, we find the bishops of Spain supporting the Carlist
insurrection, and drawing down upon themselves the chas-
tisement of their Government. In 1837, the Archbishop of
Cologne was in open rebellion against his sovereign, the
King of Prussia. In 1838, the Austrian bishops prevailed
on the Government to banish the entire population of the Zel-
lerthal, who had become Protestants. In 1842, the bishops
of France made war against the Government universities, as
their brethren in Ireland did at a later period.

Their next exploit in the same country was to originate
the expedition to Tahiti to root out the Protestant missions,—
a step which had well-nigh drawn on a war betwixt the two
countries of France and Britain. In 1847, the war of the
Sonderbund, which convulsed Switzerland, grew out of the
machinations of the Jesuits. In 1850, we had the quarrel
betwixt the Archbishop Franzoni and the Court of Turin,
which we have already described. We have had since that
time several risings of the Piedmontese peasantry at the instigation of their curés. The brigandage which since 1859
has been the terror of the Neapolitan territory has been
clearly traced to the Court of the Vatican. Of late years,
Louis Napoleon has been compelled, on more than one occasion, to nip conspiracies in the bud by dissolving secret Jesuit confederacies. And, not to prolong our enumeration, it
has been suspected, on no slight grounds, that the war now
raging in Poland was planned and set on foot by the Jesuits :
certain it is that it has received their active sympathy.

This is a long list of troubles, commotions, and civil conflicts, in a period so short. But if the Church of Rome
has been found to be so ceaseless an intriguer against the
independence of nations, and so perpetual a disturber of
their peace in Catholic countries, she will be tenfold more
so in Great Britain, where a measure of liberty unknown in

despotic kingdoms is allowed to all parties. Yet here she has set up her government, legislative and executive, and now she claims the right to carry out her canon law under the plea of toleration. In fact, Rome has transplanted her seat from the banks of the Tiber to the banks of the Thames.

How dearly do nations buy their knowledge, and how unwilling are they to see those great truths which the Bible has plainly revealed! Not till disappointment, disaster, and suffering, prolonged, it may be, through many centuries, has taught them how true the Bible is, do they own the soundness of its maxims and the force of its warnings. The Reformation would have abolished by peaceable means the idolatrous faith and tyrannical government which have so long had their seat at Rome. The reformers warned Europe what the issue would be,—bloody wars and terrible uprisings. The warning was derided. No, said the kings of Europe; the Papacy shall not be abolished. The majority of the nations of the Continent said the same thing; and they continued to wear its yoke, never dreaming that a day would come when that yoke, which then crushed only religious men, would overwhelm themselves. Some millions of lives were sacrificed that the Papacy might be preserved; and what is the reward which the kings and nations of Europe have received from her whom they preserved at so vast a cost? Has she enriched their kingdoms? Has she consolidated their power? Has she diffused knowledge and loyalty among their subjects? Has she given quiet and peace to the world? Has she not wrought the very evils which the reformers said she would inevitably work, only on a scale immensely more stupendous than even they dared to anticipate? Has not the Popish faith ruined the intelligence, blighted the industry, annihilated the commerce, destroyed the loyalty, of every nation in which it has been retained? Has it not extinguished the light of art and science, and shrouded the Papal Europe of the

nineteenth century in the barbarism of the thirteenth ? Has
it not dug a mine below every throne, and suspended a sword
above every dwelling ?   And now, its oppressions rising to a
pitch which makes them no longer endurable, it has hung the
nations of Europe on "the perilous edge of battle,"—a battle
which, if one may judge from the unprecedented scale of the
preparations, will be such as the world has never before seen.
Have not the kings and nations of Europe been expending
their treasures and sacrificing their best subjects to preserve
their own destroyer,—the great Moloch of Europe ?

Would it not have been better to have listened to the reformers three centuries ago ?   Even ten years ago, would
it not have been better to have left the Papacy to the fate
to which the Revolution appeared to have consigned it ?   Instead of this, Louis Napoleon employed his armies to restore
it to its old seat and prestige at Rome.   A British Ministry
looked quietly on ; Lord Palmerston defended the step ; and
now both the Emperor of the French and the statesmen of
Britain confess that what they then did was a great blunder ;
that the Government they restored at such expense of life
and money has misgoverned and oppressed its subjects,—is,
in short, a thing so dangerous to the public peace, and so
scandalous to modern ideas, that what they went to war to
restore, they must now go to war to abolish.   Such is the
plain English of all that they are now saying and doing.
Could there be testimony more triumphant to the essential
wisdom and beneficent spirit of Protestantism ? or could confession be plainer that a mighty error was committed when
the Reformation was rejected, and that the long succession
of revolutions and wars which has since passed over Europe,
and of which as yet she sees not the close, is but the penalty
of her great transgression of three centuries ago ?

But if our statesmen really believe what they say, how
comes it that they have been striving, by a lavish expendi-

ture of the public money, to foster in Britain that very influence which they tell us has destroyed Italy ? This is an
anomaly which we beg they would explain to us. They either
believe or they do not believe the charge they prefer when
they lay at the door of the Papacy the fearful disorganization
and misery that reign in the Roman States, and the fatal
embroilment into which the Continent has now come. If
they do not believe it, they are maligners of the Pontifical Government. If they do believe it, they are conspirators against
Britain. They can choose whichever horn of the dilemma
they please on which to do penance.

If there is a Government in the world which might confidently reckon on being left undisturbed by the plottings of
Rome, surely it is the Government of France. Louis Napoleon keeps the Vatican for the Pope, and the city of Rome
for the Papacy, despite the wishes of the Italians and the
protestations of the rest of Europe. He has lately undertaken, at the instigation of the Jesuits, the conquest of Mexico,
and there restored the dominancy of the priests. All over
the East, French diplomacy and Jesuit missions are advancing
hand-in-hand : in fact, it is a grand Papal aggression which
is being prosecuted at this hour under the banners of the
Empire. These are substantial services. Yet this very Government, which is doing its utmost to serve them, the priests
are embroiling by their intrigues for pontifical absolutism.
Their object is to deal the *coup de grace* to the Gallican Liberties, by the introduction into France of the Roman liturgy.
The old liturgies of France are the expression, more or less,
of Gallicanism ; but the Roman liturgy, which Pius IX. and
Cardinal de Bonald insist on introducing into that country,
contains the Hildebrandine doctrine of *the Pope's right to
depose emperors and kings.* The matter, after long smouldering in secret, has now come to open war. The Pope has
published at Rome a brief, empowering the use of the Ro-

man liturgy in the churches of the diocese of Lyons; and
the Emperor, by a decree in the *Moniteur Officiel*, has forbidden the publication of the brief. Despite the opposition
of the Government, the priests have adopted the obnoxious
liturgy in other parts of France. And in this way does the
Pope repay Louis Napoleon for his great services. This dis-
pute teaches great lessons on the head of national independence. The kingdom that allows appeals to Rome, or freely
admits the briefs of the Pope, loses self-government. That
very power which the Emperor awes in its own capital is
nevertheless seen to be, through the machinery of appeals
and bulls, the real ruler of France. Louis Napoleon holds
Rome by his soldiers; but Pius IX. holds France through
the Jesuits.

Place the Church of Rome at the top or at the bottom of
society, in either position she is alike dangerous to the peace
of kingdoms. Is she low?—she becomes a base sycophant,
a hypocritical pretender to opinions she abhors, and a vile
panderer to the worst passions of the mob. Does she possess
restricted political rights?—she is a restless intriguer, ever
using her liberty to undermine liberty. Does she stand at
the summit of society?—she is a merciless tyrant. Through
these several grades has that Church passed since the memorable year 1848. In that year she was a Democrat in
one country, a Constitutionalist in another, and a Socialist
in a third. The sanguinary Dominic, which for ages she had
worshipped with bloody *autos da fe*, she professed to have
forsworn; and now the more grateful task had become hers
of sprinkling trees of liberty with holy water, and saying mass
for new Constitutions. But well she knew all the while what
she was about. Under cover of her new-born love of liberalism, she was maturing her plans; and before the trees she
had blessed had withered, these plans were ripened, and, the
signal being given from the Vatican, she and her vassal kings

commenced an armed re-action throughout Europe, which issued in the indiscriminate proscription of all rights, political and personal. For ten years the nations lay groaning in chains ten times heavier than those which the Revolution of 1848 had broken.

DEVELOPMENT OF JESUITISM.

THE Church of Rome has in our day undergone a remarkable change. The spread of ultramontanism has more thoroughly compacted and knit together that Church than she ever was before. It has given her a unity of a higher type than she possessed even during the palmy days of her Gregories and her Innocents. In those ages, she had, as it were, a double head,—the Pope and a Council,—who contested between them the dazzling prize of the spiritual sovereignty. This war is now at an end. The Council has been vanquished, and the Pope remains master of the field. There is now but one authority in the Roman body,—the chair of Peter,—whose superhuman prerogatives have extinguished all other pretence of authority and power. This prodigious centralization enables the Pope at any moment, and for any purpose, to call into action the whole resources of the Roman Church. He has but to speak, and the whole body is in motion to earth's extremities. All councils, all bishops, all priests, recognise in him their one and only chief. This is ultramontanism : it is the highest possible development of the Roman organization : it is the last refinement of the Roman policy.

Nor can it be said that there are any longer national Churches within the pale of Roman Catholicism. The Church of Rome in former days was to some extent a congeries of Churches, bound together by a common relation to and a common dependence upon the mother Church. Each en-

joyed a certain measure of liberty ; and the French Church,
as all know, was permitted a tolerable share of independence : but now this state of things is at an end. All geographical boundaries have been blotted out.   There is no longer
a French world, or a Spanish world : there is but a Roman
world.   The various national ecclesiasticisms, with their national synods, have been absorbed into the one colossal eccle-
siasticism of Rome.   It has come to be *ecclesiastically*, as
aforetime, when the empire had culminated, it was *politically*,
urbs et orbis. All centres in the Vatican. And the behests
given forth from that divine seat of sole authority, although
uttered by the feeble Pio Nono, find a more universal and
unhesitating response than they did when spoken by the
astute Hildebrand.

If, then, the Papacy has dropped, or professes to have
dropped, its temporal pretensions, it has vastly strengthened
its spiritual power.   The change is wise ; for, as the times
go, it will more thoroughly compass its political ends by using
only the spiritual sword. In other days it sometimes happened that the Pontiff, when carrying matters with a high
hand as regarded kings, had to submit to opposition and defeat from his own bishops.   This was especially true of the
French clergy.   From a comparatively remote period we can
trace two parties and two opinions in the Gallican Church ;
but since the days of Pascal and Bossuet this division has
been public and palpable.   The national clergy always struggled against the absorption with which they were ever threatened by the centralizing despotism of Rome.   Hence the
"Gallican Liberties," which were a struggle not more for
reform in doctrine than for national independence.   It may
be questioned how far such "liberties" as the "Gallican" are
possible under the Papacy : certain it is, their maintenance
is inconsistent with the fundamental principles of its rule.
The common saying, that Rome is the "mother and mistress

of all Churches," seems to put self-government, or independent rights, out of the question,—all the more so when it is remembered that Rome is an infallible mother. Such claims on the part of individual Churches have been simply tolerated, not sanctioned, by Rome. She has ever viewed them in the light of schisms or rebellions; and the steady aim of her policy has been to annihilate all such pretensions, and to reduce all Churches on the face of the earth, not more to unquestioning submission to her creed, than to slavish obedience to her sway; and in so far as the Papacy has come short of this in any particular country, it has to the same extent come short of a full and perfect development of itself. And so, after a long and glorious struggle, which forms the brightest page in the history of France, that which records the Huguenot struggle excepted, the Jansenists were vanquished. Gallicanism, with its Augustinian doctrine of grace, has completely disappeared. The energetic spirit of Bossuet, the mild benevolence of Fenelon, the noble patriotism and daring genius of Pascal, have left the French clergy. The forty thousand priests of France who share amongst them upwards of forty millions of francs of State money are almost to a man ultramontane and Jesuit. Neither the French nor any other Church is now anything: the See of Rome is everything. Ultramontanism is just the logical development of the Romish system. Towards that issue has it been steadily tending ever since the Council of Trent; and, having now reached it, the Church of Rome possesses a homogeneity of nature, a oneness of aim, a unity of policy, and a power of prompt and combined action, of which she could boast in no former age.

Another phase has passed upon the Popery of our day,— a consequence of the greater ultramontanism of the body,— even the rapid and portentous growth of societies, more or less secret, all under the direction of Jesuitism. The membership of these confraternities is counted in millions: they cover both hemispheres; their object being the aggrandisement of their Church,—an end which they are at liberty to pursue in any way that seems good to them. Although the name of these societies is already legion, not a year passes that does not see others added to their number, which, like their predecessors, proceed to enroll members by hundreds of thousands. They are all sworn to unconditional obedience; and, though they bear various names, they are in reality but one host, whose wing is stretched from the Orient to the Occident. They are a Church within a Church. For, in truth, we have now two Churches and two Popes. The one Church makes itself palpable to the world in its orders, councils, and canon law: the other, though everywhere present, is nowhere visible. It records its decrees in a book which no man can read; it utters its behests in a voice which no man can hear; yet it wields a power quick, irresistible, and illimitible. It speaks, and it is done. These two Churches have each their Pope. On the Seven Hills sits the one Pontiff, the golden head of that great colossus which comprehends the purple cardinal and the barefooted Carmelite, with all between. In night and darkness dwells the other and mightier Pontiff,—the General of the Jesuits,—the Appolyon of the Papal pandemonium. Popery is the last development of idolatry; and Jesuitism is the last development of Popery. It is not only the most wicked society that ever existed upon the earth: it is the most wicked society that ever *can* exist upon it. It is pure abstract vice embodied in a concrete organization. It is the incarnation of the "Wicked One." It is the veritable establishment of hell itself upon our earth.

Jesuitism has an ubiquitous body and an omniscient head. To that head there is nothing *thought* and nothing *done* under the sun that is not known. He hears the words which the monarch speaks in his bed-chamber, and the whisperings

which the conspirator breathes in his den. The secrets of
the Tuileries and of the Escurial, the musings of the Tartar
on his steppes, and the resolves of the Bedouin amid his sands,
are to him all alike open. The secrets of all the sons of men
are naked before him. There is not a shape the Jesuits cannot put on ; and consequently there is not a place into which
they cannot penetrate. They can sit unseen in Synod and
General Assembly ; they can enter unheard the monarch's
closet and statesman's cabinet ; they can assemble unsuspected
around the Council Board. They ply every trade, and speak
every tongue. In the pedlar, in the artizan, in the littera-
teur, in the tutor, in my lady's lady, in my lord's valet, we
find an affiliated member of the society. They dwell in all
the lands of earth, and they profess all the creeds of earth.
They are found sitting beneath the palm-trees of the tropics,
and wandering amid the snows of the pole. They pray to
Confucius in China ; they venerate the cow in India ; they
wash in the Ganges with the Brahman ; they adore the fire
with the Parsee ; they swear by the Prophet with the Mus-
sulman, whirl in the dance with the Dervish, and abominate
swine's flesh with the Jew. They have in past times exe-
crated the Pope with the Lutheran, and sworn the Solemn
League and Covenant with the Covenanter. Their organization is wonderful. While controlling the greatest matters,
the smallest are not overlooked by them. With equal ease
they put forth their power in crushing an obscure individual,
or in hurling a statesman from power, and burying a monarch
beneath the ruins of his throne and kingdom.

While in these respects the Church of Rome is more concentrated than she was aforetime, she is, as regards her operations, more diffusive in our day than she ever before was.
Of late years she has been conducting missions on a truly
colossal scale. She watches with sleepless eye, and follows
with untiring foot, the Protestant missionary, it matters not

to how distant a region or to how benighted a tribe. Nay,
sometimes she anticipates him; and before he has had time
to plant the banner of the Cross in some dark land, she takes
possession of the soil by unfurling over it her own black flag.
To what region, availing herself of the arms of France, and
the colonizing enterprise of Britain, has she not gone? In the
cities and fields of Syria, trodden of old by apostolic feet, and
by One greater than apostles, she is multiplying her monasteries, stationing bands of Jesuit missionaries, inflaming the
antipathies of race, and creating political embroglios, not for
the purpose of dispelling the darkness of the Moslem night,
but to prevent the return to these renowned lands of the
Truth which first went forth from them, and which is now,
after a long absence, beginning again to gladden them.
Among the mountains of the Nestorians she is striving to
engraft her own idolatry upon the feeble traces of an early
Christianity, which has come down to our day. On the banks
of the ancient streams of the Tigris and the Euphrates, and
all over the great plains which these rivers water, we find
that Church busy at work, laying her foundations around the
ruins of the earliest edifices of man. We meet her priests
in the cities of China and Japan, where French policy pro-
tects their operations and cherishes their intrigues. They
cross the missionary's path, and not unfrequently undo his
work, in the islands of the South Pacific. In short, that
Church is alike busy amid the blaze of British civilization and
the darkness of old Fetishism. Not that we deem her con-
versions of much worth; but she is sowing in those regions the seeds of the same political complications and religious troubles which meet us so plentifully at home, and
which, we may be certain, will be found on a future day to
present formidable obstacles to the spread of religion and
liberty over the earth.

Another striking feature of the Popery of our day is, that

it combines with great diffusiveness of action, great unity of plot. Operating over a hundred lands, and through hundreds of thousands of agents, Rome makes all her efforts, with unrivalled skill, to concentrate upon one country, and that country our own. Every year that passes makes it only the more apparent that the world is to be influenced and moulded from Britain, and that whatever form of government and religion may ultimately prevail in our country will prevail over all the earth. Of this truth none are more fully aware than Rome; and therefore, as a short road to the conversion of the world, she strives, by labours that never cease, and by ways that are infinite, to compass the conversion of Britain. Were she mistress of the political power, the commercial wealth, and the moral prestige of our country, she would stand at the head of the world once more ; and although these possessions, so coveted by her, would in no long time wither in her hands, seeing they are the fruits of a liberty which she would make it her first care to extinguish, they would serve her turn in the meantime, by lifting her to domination. Nothing, therefore, is done on her remotest field of action which has not been calculated with reference to its bearing on this great anticipated victory at home.

To conclude, there are two, and only two, paramount principles in the political and ecclesiastical world of Britain,—the Protestant and the Popish. Since the Reformation these two principles have been in ceaseless conflict ; and the history of our country is simply a record of this great struggle. There have been alternate cycles of repose and of outburst in this war. The latter cycle—that of open hostilities, to wit— came round in the days of the first Charles. The Protestant or Puritanic principle, after a period of steady ascendency under Elizabeth, and of as steady decadence under James, as related with so much candour and eloquence in Marsden's " Early Puritans," succumbed in the reign of

Charles to the Popish principle, which now revived under the form of Laudean Prelacy. The conflict, as all such conflicts have ever done in the past, and will ever do in the future, speedily passed into the civil region. It divided first the Parliament, and next the country; and, after a period of fierce civil war, it ultimately brought the King to the scaffold. After a pause of two centuries, the cycle of conflict has returned. The Popish principle has revived under the form of "Anglo-Catholicism," which attests its identity with the Popery of Laud, and with the Popery of a yet earlier day, by its doating fondness for ceremonies and vestments, by its exclusive and intolerant claims to apostolicity, and, above all, by its unqualified devotion to the principle of sacramental regeneration. Our times bear the very image of those of Charles I. The same principles and the same parties are again struggling together in the Church and nation of England, as they did before the era of the Commonwealth; while in Scotland we think we can see the spirit of the Solemn League, with its earnest evangelism and its growing union, springing up as of old.

In two points do our times differ from those of Charles; and these are noways in favour of Protestantism. The political Liberalism of the seventeenth century was in opposition to the Popish and despotic party; in our day political Liberalism has taken the Popish party under its special patronage. Moreover, a powerful infidelity is now rising in the Church and nation of England, sure to be found, when the struggle comes, on the side of Romanism. Events in our day travel fast. How long, we are compelled to ask, can the same Church hold in one body an aggressive Popery, a vigorous Infidelity, and a reviving Evangelism? But if the Church of England shall part in twain, the nation will inevitably, now as aforetime, part in twain; and the army also will be parted in twain. Of our soldiers, the one half, according to some,—the third, we shall say,—are Irish Romanists, with the majority of whom it will be found that the principle of ecclesiastical authority is stronger than the instinct of military obedience. It is important, too, in estimating the consequences of such division, to bear in mind that one at least of the existing parties in the nation openly holds that the Revolution of 1688, which placed the House of Hanover upon the throne, was rebellion ; and, of course, that the title of the reigning family, so long at least as it remains Protestant, is more than questionable. Let the nation be divided, and the point of conflict would immediately be the principle of the Protestant succession,—that principle which, according to Hume, has done more than any other to fix the Constitution of the country. This is now almost the only barrier in the way of the complete triumph of the Papal aggression ; and to remove it at once and for ever would become the combined object of the Romanist, the Puseyite, and the Rationalist. This is the conflict that lies before us, and from which nothing but God's merciful interposition can save us. It may come in a day ; but come it *must*, unless the national policy shall be instantly reversed. The same principles and parties will inevitably lead, nay, have already led, to the same actual divisions, though not as yet to the same open hostilities, as in the days of Charles and Laud ; and (may God avert the inauspicious omen !) these divisions will find, as they found in those unhappy times, their final arbitrament on the same red fields and black scaffolds.

THE END.

EDINBURGH : PRINTED BY FAIRLY, LYALL, & CO.

WORKS BY THE REV. DR WYLIE.

I.

THE PAPACY; its History, Dogmas, Genius, and Prospects. Being the Evangelical Alliance Prize Essay on Popery. Demy 8vo, cloth, price 8s. 6d.

[*Third Thousand.*

In the Press, a Cheap Edition, price 3s. 6d.

Opinions of the Press.

"The book of the age on the question."—*Rev. Mr Brocklehurst, in Corn Exchange, Manchester.*

"It would be difficult to determine which to admire most,—the breadth and comprehensiveness of the plan, the method of the argument, the clearness and copiousness of the details, the vividness and tact of the grouping, the fine healthy air of its high Christian philosophy, or the vigorous eloquence, rich imagery, and moral earnestness of its style."—*Glasgow Constitutional.*

"Dr Wylie's volume is learned, philosophical, and eloquent."—*British Quarterly Review.*

"This able and finished production combines at once the rare qualities of clear statement, vigorous logic, and eloquent style. Its tone and spirit are worthy of an Evangelical Alliance."—*Baptist Magazine.*

II.

PILGRIMAGE FROM THE ALPS TO THE TIBER; or, The Influence of Romanism on Trade, Justice, and Knowledge. Post 8vo, price 7s. 6d.

[*Second Thousand.*

CONTENTS.

1. The Introduction. 2. The Passage of the Alps. 3. Rise and Progress of Constitutionalism in Piedmont. 4. Structure and Charac-

teristics of the Vaudois Valleys. 5. State and Prospects of the Vaudois Church. 6. From Turin to Novara—Plain of Lombardy. 7. From Novara to Milan—Dogana—Chain of the Alps. 8. City and People of Milan. 9. Arco della Pace—St Ambrose. 10. The Duomo of Milan. 11. Milan to Brescia—The Reformers. 12. The Present the Image of the Past. 13. Scenery of Lake Garda—Peschiera—Verona. 14. From Verona to Venice—The Tyrolese Alps. 15. Venice—Death of Nations. 16. Padua—St Anthony—The Po —Arrest. 17. Ferrara—Renee and Olympia Moreta. 18. Bologna and the Apennines. 19. Florence and its Young Evangelism. 20. From Leghorn to Rome—Civita Vecchia. 21. Modern Rome. 22. Ancient Rome—The Seven Hills. 23. Sights in Rome—Catacombs —Pilate's Stairs—Pio Nono, &c. 24. Influence of Romanism on Trade. 25. Influence of Romanism on Trade—(continued). 26. Justice and Liberty in the Papal States. 27. Education and Knowledge in the Papal States. 28. Mental State of the Priesthood in Italy. 29. Social and Domestic Customs of the Romans. 30. The Argument from the whole; or, Rome her own Witness.

Opinions of the Press.

" Dr Wylie's sketches of Austrian and Papal Italy are replete with interest."—*Athenæum.*

" We are presented with the gist of the Popish controversy, freshened by new and very striking examples, and lightened by amusing incident and graphic description."—*Hugh Miller.*

"The Pilgrimage, both in matter and expression, is by far the most finished performance of the sort that has ever issued from the pen of an English traveller. I was unspeakably interested in its perusal, and in the sublime and awful delineations which it gives of the effect of the doctrines of Antichrist in the very centre of the Papal dominions."— *Rev. Dr Campbell of London.*

" It is no exaggeration to say, that many of these sketches are surpassed by no similar descriptions in the English language. The social workings of Romanism are here exhibited in the shape of undeniable, terrible facts."—*Londonderry Standard.*

III.

THE GREAT EXODUS; or, "The Time of the End."
Price 6s. 6d.   [*Second Thousand.*

CONTENTS.

PART I.—THE BONDAGE.

1. The Study of Prophecy: its Use and Abuse. 2. Study of Prophecy

Reformation and German Schools.	3. The Typology of Providence.
4. Divine Method of Revelation and Government.	5. Figuration
of the World's Day and the Church's Night.	6. The Four Mo-
narchies ; or, the Church's Oppressor.	7. The Four Beasts.	8.
The Dragon ; or, the Church's Real Oppressor.	9. The Commence-
ment of the Bondage ; or, the "Seven Times."	10. Length of the
"Seven Times."	11. Harmony of Prophetic Cycles.	12. Vision
of Cleansing, or Second Chronological Line.	13. The Three Times
and a Half, or Third Chronological Line.	14. Length of the Judg-
ment Day.

PART II.—THE EXODUS.

1. The Crisis of the Church and of the World.	2. The Son of Man ; or,
the Antithesis.	3. The Apocalypse, or Unveiling.	4. The Type
and the Antitype ; or, the First and Second Egypts.	5. The Coming
of the Ancient of Days.	6. The Opening of the Temple to the Na-
tions.	7. The First Vial.	8. The Second Vial ; or, the Sea of
Blood.	9. The Third Vial ; or, the Rivers and Fountains of Blood.
10. The Fourth Vial ; or, the Sun of Fire.	11. The Fifth Vial ;
or, the Darkness.	12. The Sixth Vial ; or, the Preparation.	13.
"It is Done."	14. The New Heavens and the New Earth.

Opinions of the Press.

"Dr Wylie does not follow the ordinary beaten path so commonly
trodden by the feet of 'students of prophecy.' He is neither literalist,
spiritualist, nor futurist. He thinks out of his own method, and follows
his own course, and is rather, if we might coin a word, a typologist. His
scheme of interpretation is worked out with great skill, precision, and
clearness."—*London Record.*

"This work is not only one of great ability, but it is in many respects
a remarkable production : it is so with regard to the amount of research
which is everywhere visible in its pages: it is, too, a remarkable work
viewed in relation to the hypothesis, if we may use the word, which the
volume develops, and which is so ably supported. In many respects Dr
Wylie differs on important points connected with prophecy, and with the
past history of the Church, from most, if not all, of our most popular
writers on prophetic questions. . . . The style of the work is indeed,
from the beginning to the end, characterized by great affluence. It is
one of the most interesting and valuable which has appeared for a long
time past on the subject of prophecy, and is destined to occupy a permanent place in the category of our Protestant theology."—*London
Morning Advertiser.*

"The charm not only of the style, but also of the matter, is irresistible.
You are hurried along, page after page, till, on reaching the last, you

are surprised to discover that you have read some four hundred pages without one feeling approaching to weariness ; nay, with a sincere wish that the book had been longer. In point of style and tone, of liberality of sentiment, and of painstaking research, combined with no ordinary scholarship, the volume is all that we could desire. The importance of the subject, and the skill with which it is treated, cannot fail in securing for the work a large circulation among all classes of reading and thinking men."— *Reformed Presbyterian Magazine.*

" The plan of the work is not less profound than it is simple and easily understood : not less philosophical than it is Scriptural."— *Glasgow Courier.*

" We never remember reading a work so much calculated to give an impulse to the study of prophecy."— *Original Secession Magazine.*

London : JAMES NISBET & Co., Berners Street.
Edinburgh : A. ELLIOT, 15, Princes Street.

IV.

ROME AND CIVIL LIBERTY; OR, THE PAPAL AGGRESSION IN ITS RELATION TO THE SOVEREIGNTY OF THE QUEEN AND THE INDEPENDENCE OF THE NATION.   Price 2s. 6d.

[*Eighth Thousand.*

Opinions of the Press.

" The author's charge is not that our statesmen have tolerated the religion of the Pope, but that they have sanctioned the religion of the Pope : not that they have permitted the spread of another faith, but that they have permitted the erection of another government. This is a serious charge ; but the most serious part of the matter is that it is here substantiated, not by a process of reasoning, but by a statement of facts. None can rise from a perusal of these facts without a profound apprehension of the dangers that threaten our liberties. To all who would see how Popery is playing its master-trick of shrouding the stiletto, meant for the heart of British freedom, under the garb of religion, we earnestly recommend the study of this eloquent volume."— *British and Foreign Evangelical Review.*

" As an able and eloquent expositor of the principles and working of the Papacy, Dr Wylie has earned for himself a reputation second to none of our living authorities. . . . . This volume is necessarily somewhat miscellaneous ; but it has the unity of principle as a display of Romanism in one of its leading peculiarities,—this, namely, that it is not properly a religion, but rather a system that knows nothing of the separation of things political, civil, temporal, from things spiritual. It goes fully into the whole matter of the rise, growth, and gradual evolution of the Papal Aggression, and shows its true bearing on all questions affecting both civil and religious liberty. If anything could open the eyes of our statesmen to the madness of the course they are pursuing with so eager speed, surely the facts so eloquently expounded by Dr Wylie might do so."—*London Record.*

"'The Papal Aggression.' Herein we find the clearest, most concise, and most logical account of that remarkable movement of old Rome towards the re-conquest of Britain, temporal and spiritual, which we have ever met with. . . . . The logic of its arguments, the honesty and fearlessness of its purpose, the healthiness of its Christianity, and the abundance of its facts, make this volume the text-book of those who would be armed with weapons to destroy the cobwebs of Jesuit sophistry and design."—*London Morning Advertiser.*

"No man has a better title to be attentively heard than our author. His work is embued with great principles, with large views both of civil and ecclesiastical history, and abounds in interesting facts illustrative of the present aims and machinations of Popery. All is marked by a noble enthusiasm for truth and liberty."—*Edinburgh Daily Review.*

"Dr Wylie's 'Papal Aggression' is written altogether in a beautifully eloquent style. Open the book where you will, and some cleverly wrought illustration catches your eye, and fixes your attention; and when we consider that so many people think all writing about Popery a "great bore," it is well to have such a brilliant writer as Dr Wylie to attract the attention of the multitude towards a subject which, though so important, is so much neglected. Each chapter in the work is an essay in itself; but the finest, in our opinion, is that of 'The Revolution—its Policy Reversed.' We cordially recommend this book to our readers."—*Liverpool Courier.*

London : HAMILTON, ADAMS, & Co.

Edinburgh : A. ELLIOT, 15, Prince's Street.

V.

THE SEVENTH VIAL; BEING AN EXPOSITION OF THE APOCALYPSE. [*Third Thousand.*

VI.

WANDERINGS AND MUSINGS IN THE VALLEYS OF THE WALDENSES. Cloth, crown 8vo, price 5s. 6d. [*Second Thousand.*

London : JAMES NISBET & Co.

VII.

THE MODERN JUDEA COMPARED WITH AN-
CIENT PROPHECY : WITH NOTES ILLUSTRATIVE OF
BIBLICAL SUBJECTS.   In cloth, lettered, with ten steel en-
gravings, 7s. 6d.; Cheap Series, 2s. 6d.

[*Tenth Thousand.*

Glasgow and London : WILLIAM COLLINS.

VIII.

SCENES FROM THE BIBLE.   Cloth, lettered, ten steel
engravings, 7s. 6d. ; Cheap Series, 2s. 6d.

[*Twelfth Thousand.*

Glasgow and London : WILLIAM COLLINS.

IX.

RUINS OF BIBLE LANDS : A JOURNEY OVER THE RE-
GION OF FULFILLED PROPHECY.   Price 3s. 6d.

[*Fifth Thousand.*

Glasgow : W. R. M'PHUN.

X.

THE GOSPEL MINISTRY : DUTY AND PRIVILEGE OF SUP-
PORTING IT.   First Prize Essay.   Price 1s. 6d. ; People's
Edition, 4d.   [*Seventh Thousand.*

London : JAMES NISBET & Co.